Thinking Beyond Code: A Human's Guide to Artificial Intelligence

Anshuman Mishra

Published by Anshuman Mishra, 2025.

THINKING BEYOND CODE: A HUMAN'S GUIDE TO ARTIFICIAL INTELLIGENCE

PREFACE V-IX

PART 1: THE BIG PICTURE OF ARTIFICIAL INTELLIGENCE

PART 2: UNDERSTANDING THE HUMAN-AI RELATIONSHIP

 Preface

Why This Book?

Artificial Intelligence (AI) is no longer a distant dream confined to science fiction novels or futuristic laboratories. It is here — woven into the fabric of our daily lives, often so seamlessly that we barely notice its presence. From smartphones that recognize our faces, to virtual assistants that schedule our meetings, to recommendation engines that suggest what music we should listen to, what movies to watch, and even what careers to pursue — AI has silently become a trusted advisor, a constant companion, and a powerful influencer.

Yet despite its growing influence, the conversation surrounding AI often feels inaccessible to many.
The dominant narratives are filled with technical jargon, complex equations, and programming details that alienate the everyday thinker — the artist, the teacher, the entrepreneur, the policymaker, the curious citizen.
The result? A technology that is deeply shaping society is often misunderstood, feared, or accepted blindly without reflection.

This book was born out of the urgent need to change that.
Thinking Beyond Code is not a manual on how to build AI systems, nor is it a textbook buried in algorithms and codes.
Instead, it is an invitation:

- An invitation to explore AI from a human-centered lens — asking not just *what* AI can do, but *how* it affects us as individuals and societies.
- An invitation to examine the ethical dilemmas, the philosophical questions, and the creative opportunities that AI presents.
- An invitation to understand the intelligence behind machines without getting lost in technical complexity — prioritizing **understanding** over **coding**, **insight** over **implementation**, and **reflection** over **blind acceptance**.

This book is for thinkers, not just technologists.
It is for those who wish to **question**, **imagine**, **challenge**, and **co-create** a future where AI serves humanity's deepest values rather than merely advancing technological prowess.

At its heart, **Thinking Beyond Code** seeks to bridge the widening gap between the **rapid advancements of AI** and our **human responsibility** to guide it wisely.
It explores the profound impact of AI not just on jobs and economies, but on our creativity, our emotional lives, our moral frameworks, and ultimately, on our evolving understanding of what it means to be human in an increasingly automated world.

This book is a **call to action**:

- To think critically, not passively consume.
- To engage creatively, not merely adapt.
- To act responsibly, not surrender the future to technology alone.

As we stand at the crossroads of human and machine intelligence, **the future is not written yet**. It will be shaped not just by engineers and corporations, but by all of us — thinking humans who dare to imagine a world where AI amplifies, rather than diminishes, the best of what we are.

Welcome to the journey of **Thinking Beyond Code**.
Let's explore, question, and shape the future — together.

Who Should Read This Book?

Artificial Intelligence is no longer a niche topic reserved for engineers, data scientists, or tech enthusiasts. It is a transformative force touching every sector, every profession, and every aspect of our lives.
Thinking Beyond Code is written for *anyone* who senses the seismic shift happening and wants to understand it from a human, ethical, and creative perspective — without needing to write a single line of code.

This book is crafted for a wide, diverse audience, including:

Curious Thinkers

For individuals who constantly wonder *"How is AI really changing our world?"* but feel overwhelmed by the technical jargon.
If you seek to grasp AI's essence without getting lost in algorithms and programming languages, this book is your guide — offering clear, thoughtful, and relatable explanations that fuel your curiosity rather than intimidate it.

Students and Lifelong Learners

Whether you're a student of computer science, humanities, social sciences, philosophy, business, or arts — or simply a lifelong learner passionate about understanding the future — this book provides a **broad, accessible, interdisciplinary entry point** into the world of AI.
You'll discover how AI connects to your studies, your passions, and your aspirations, no matter your field.

Professionals Across Industries

From **managers navigating AI-driven workplaces**, to **educators shaping the next generation**, to **healthcare professionals leveraging AI in diagnosis and treatment**, to **policymakers crafting regulations**

in an AI world —
this book is for every professional who needs to grasp AI's growing influence without having to become a data scientist or a programmer.
Understanding AI is no longer optional; it's a crucial part of leadership, decision-making, and responsible innovation in every field.

Ethicists, Philosophers, and Creatives

If you are fascinated by questions like:
"Can machines be moral?"
"Can AI create true art?"
"Will AI ever have consciousness?" —
then this book is written for you.
It explores the **deep ethical dilemmas**, the **philosophical challenges**, and the **creative frontiers** that AI introduces — offering you rich ground to think, debate, and imagine.

Skeptics and Dreamers Alike

Whether you view AI with suspicion, fearing a dystopian takeover, or whether you dream of a utopia where humans and machines co-evolve harmoniously, this guide welcomes you.
It is designed to challenge assumptions, open up new perspectives, and foster a more nuanced, balanced understanding — beyond the hype, beyond the fear.

You do not need a computer science degree to read this book.

What you need is a **curious mind**, an **open heart**, and a **willingness to explore** how technology and humanity are becoming increasingly intertwined.

In an age when AI is shaping decisions in politics, healthcare, education, entertainment, and even personal relationships, **every thinking human** has a role to play.
This book empowers you not just to understand AI passively, but to engage with it **actively, responsibly, and creatively** — helping shape a future that honors human dignity, wisdom, and imagination.

How to Use This Guide?

This book is not a dense textbook, nor a technical manual filled with code snippets and mathematical proofs.
Instead, **Thinking Beyond Code** is designed to be **flexible**, **inviting**, and **self-paced** — respecting the unique curiosity, background, and goals each reader brings to the journey.

Here's how you can make the most out of it:

1. Sequential Reading: A Journey from Foundations to Futures

If you enjoy structured learning, you can read this book **cover to cover**, as each part builds naturally upon the last.
We start by laying down the **fundamentals of AI** — what it is (and what it isn't), where it comes from, and how it works — before moving on to its **ethical implications**, its **real-world applications**, and its **future possibilities**.
This method will give you a **solid, layered understanding** — from basic concepts to big philosophical questions.

Think of it like building a house:
First the foundation (Part 1), then the walls and rooms (Part 2 and 3), and finally, the windows into the world beyond (Part 4 and 5).

2. Jump Around: Follow Your Curiosity

Prefer exploring based on your interests?
Each chapter is **self-contained enough** that you can jump directly to the topics that excite you most without feeling lost.

- Curious about **AI and creativity**? Start with **Part 4**.
- Worried about **ethical dilemmas and AI rights**? Dive into **Part 2**.
- Interested in **how deep learning actually works**? Head to **Part 3**.

This is *your* exploration. Follow the trails that spark your imagination.

3. Reflection and Discussion: Pause, Think, Converse

At the end of many chapters, you'll find **reflection questions**, **thought experiments**, and **discussion prompts**.
These are designed to encourage you to:

- **Pause and think** critically about what you've read.
- **Apply concepts** to real-world scenarios.
- **Engage in group discussions** or **debates** if you are reading this book in a classroom, book club, or team setting.

If you are a **teacher, leader, or facilitator**, you can even use these prompts as **ready-made discussion starters** to fuel meaningful conversations around AI.

4. Beyond the Book: Resources to Deepen Your Journey

Curiosity doesn't stop with the last page.

In the **Appendices**, you'll find **curated lists** of:

- Recommended **books**, **podcasts**, **videos**, and **documentaries**,
- **Projects** you can explore,
- **Organizations and communities** you can join if you wish to dive deeper.

Whether you want to specialize further, advocate for ethical AI, or simply stay informed, these resources will extend your learning journey well beyond this guide.

5. No Coding Required: Focus on Thinking, Not Programming

This is not a "learn to program AI" book — and intentionally so.

While we'll conceptually explore how machine learning, deep learning, and neural networks operate, there's **no expectation** that you:

- Write code,
- Solve mathematical formulas, or
- Possess prior technical expertise.

Instead, the focus is on **thinking critically about AI** — understanding its promises, its limitations, and its impact on humanity.
Reflection over replication. Understanding over engineering. Curiosity over credentials.

✹ Our True Goal

Above all, this book invites you to:

- **Think about AI thoughtfully,**
- **Question AI critically,**
- **Imagine AI creatively,** and
- **Engage with AI responsibly.**

Artificial Intelligence is shaping our future — but the future remains a **human story**.
And you, as a thinking human, are an essential part of that story.

ABOUT THE AUTHOR:

ANSHUMAN KUMAR MISHRA IS A SEASONED EDUCATOR AND PROLIFIC AUTHOR WITH OVER 20 YEARS OF EXPERIENCE IN THE TEACHING FIELD. HE HAS A DEEP PASSION FOR TECHNOLOGY AND A STRONG COMMITMENT TO MAKING COMPLEX CONCEPTS ACCESSIBLE TO STUDENTS AT ALL LEVELS. WITH AN M.TECH IN COMPUTER SCIENCE FROM BIT MESRA, HE BRINGS BOTH ACADEMIC EXPERTISE AND PRACTICAL EXPERIENCE TO HIS WORK.

CURRENTLY SERVING AS AN ASSISTANT PROFESSOR AT DORANDA COLLEGE, ANSHUMAN HAS BEEN A GUIDING FORCE FOR MANY ASPIRING COMPUTER SCIENTISTS AND ENGINEERS, NURTURING THEIR SKILLS IN VARIOUS PROGRAMMING LANGUAGES AND TECHNOLOGIES. HIS TEACHING STYLE IS FOCUSED ON CLARITY, HANDS-ON LEARNING, AND MAKING STUDENTS COMFORTABLE WITH BOTH THEORETICAL AND PRACTICAL ASPECTS OF COMPUTER SCIENCE.

THROUGHOUT HIS CAREER, ANSHUMAN KUMAR MISHRA HAS AUTHORED OVER 25 BOOKS ON A WIDE RANGE OF TOPICS INCLUDING PYTHON, JAVA, C, C++, DATA SCIENCE, ARTIFICIAL INTELLIGENCE, SQL, .NET, WEB PROGRAMMING, DATA STRUCTURES, AND MORE. HIS BOOKS HAVE BEEN WELL-RECEIVED BY STUDENTS, PROFESSIONALS, AND INSTITUTIONS ALIKE FOR THEIR STRAIGHTFORWARD EXPLANATIONS, PRACTICAL EXERCISES, AND DEEP INSIGHTS INTO THE SUBJECTS.

ANSHUMAN'S APPROACH TO TEACHING AND WRITING IS ROOTED IN HIS BELIEF THAT LEARNING SHOULD BE ENGAGING, INTUITIVE, AND HIGHLY APPLICABLE TO REAL-WORLD SCENARIOS. HIS EXPERIENCE IN BOTH ACADEMIA AND INDUSTRY HAS GIVEN HIM A UNIQUE PERSPECTIVE ON HOW TO BEST PREPARE STUDENTS FOR THE EVOLVING WORLD OF TECHNOLOGY.

IN HIS BOOKS, ANSHUMAN AIMS NOT ONLY TO IMPART KNOWLEDGE BUT ALSO TO INSPIRE A LIFELONG LOVE FOR LEARNING AND EXPLORATION IN THE WORLD OF COMPUTER SCIENCE AND PROGRAMMING.

Copyright Page

Title: THINKING BEYOND CODE: A HUMAN'S GUIDE TO ARTIFICIAL INTELLIGENCE

Author: Anshuman Kumar Mishra
Copyright © 2025 by Anshuman Kumar Mishra

CHAPTER 1: INTRODUCTION TO ARTIFICIAL INTELLIGENCE

What is AI, Really?

Artificial Intelligence (AI) is a term that has captured the imagination of the world, often appearing in science fiction movies and fueling discussions about the future of technology. But what does it truly mean?

The provided text offers a great starting point: "At its core, AI is the science and engineering of creating machines that can perform tasks that typically require human intelligence." Let's break this down step-by-step.

1. The Foundation: Science and Engineering

AI is not magic. It's built upon a foundation of scientific research and engineering principles.

- **Science:** AI draws from various scientific disciplines, including:
  - **Computer Science:** Provides the algorithms, data structures, and computational methods.
  - **Mathematics:** Underpins the statistical models, optimization techniques, and logical frameworks.
  - **Cognitive Science:** Studies how humans think, learn, and solve problems, providing insights for designing intelligent machines.
  - **Neuroscience:** Explores the structure and function of the brain, inspiring the development of artificial neural networks.
- **Engineering:** AI involves the practical application of these scientific principles to build actual systems and machines. This includes:
  - **Software Engineering:** Developing the software that implements AI algorithms.
  - **Hardware Engineering:** Designing specialized hardware (like GPUs and TPUs) to accelerate AI computations.
  - **Robotics:** Integrating AI into physical machines to enable them to interact with the real world.

2. The Goal: Mimicking Human Intelligence

The central goal of AI is to create machines that can perform tasks that, historically, have required human intelligence. The text highlights several examples:

- **Recognizing speech:** Converting spoken language into text, as seen in voice assistants like Siri, Google Assistant, and Alexa.
- **Understanding language:** Processing and interpreting the meaning of text, enabling tasks like machine translation, sentiment analysis, and question answering.
- **Playing chess:** Developing strategies, evaluating positions, and making decisions in a complex game, as demonstrated by AI programs like Deep Blue and AlphaZero.
- **Driving a car:** Perceiving the environment, navigating roads, and making real-time decisions, as seen in self-driving cars.

- **Diagnosing diseases:** Analyzing medical images, patient records, and other data to identify illnesses, often with accuracy comparable to or exceeding human experts.

3. The Essence: Cognitive Functions

The text further clarifies that if a machine can mimic cognitive functions that we associate with the human mind, it falls under the broad umbrella of AI. These functions include:

- **Learning:** Acquiring knowledge and skills from experience, as seen in machines that can improve their performance on a task over time.
- **Reasoning:** Drawing logical inferences, making deductions, and solving problems based on available information.
- **Problem-solving:** Identifying, analyzing, and finding solutions to complex challenges.
- **Perception:** Interpreting sensory information, such as recognizing objects in images, understanding speech, or processing touch.
- **Planning:** Setting goals, developing strategies, and sequencing actions to achieve those goals.
- **Creativity:** Generating novel and valuable ideas, as seen in AI systems that can compose music, write poetry, or create art.

4. Important Clarifications:

The provided text also emphasizes what AI is *not*:

- **Not "alive" or "conscious" (yet):** Current AI systems, even the most advanced ones, do not possess sentience, self-awareness, or consciousness in the way that humans do. They operate based on algorithms and data, not on subjective experience. This is a very important distinction.
- **Not robots that want to take over the world:** The idea of malevolent AI robots is a common trope in science fiction, but it's not a realistic portrayal of the current state of AI. AI is a tool, and its impact depends on how humans choose to develop and use it.
- **Machines that analyze, decide, and act on data:** This is a crucial point. AI systems are designed to process information, identify patterns, and take actions based on that information. They can often do this faster and more accurately than humans, especially when dealing with large amounts of data.

5. Examples in Action:

The text provides two excellent examples of AI in everyday life:

- **Face ID:** When you unlock your phone with Face ID, the phone's AI system:
    - Captures an image of your face.
    - Analyzes the image to identify key facial features (e.g., the distance between your eyes, the shape of your nose).
    - Creates a digital representation of your face.
    - Compares this representation to the stored representation of your face.

- If there's a close enough match, the phone unlocks. This process happens almost instantly.
- **Netflix Recommendations:** When Netflix suggests a movie, its AI algorithms:
  - Collect data about your past viewing habits (e.g., the movies and shows you've watched, rated, or searched for).
  - Analyze this data to identify your preferences (e.g., genres you like, actors you prefer).
  - Compare your preferences to those of other users and to the characteristics of different movies.
  - Predict which movies you are most likely to enjoy.
  - Present you with a personalized list of recommendations.

In essence, AI is about creating machines that can automate tasks, augment human capabilities, and solve complex problems by mimicking intelligent behavior. It's a rapidly evolving field with the potential to transform many aspects of our lives.

Evolution of AI: From Dreams to Reality

The journey of Artificial Intelligence is a long and winding one, stretching from ancient myths to the cutting-edge technologies of today. As the provided text notes, "The story of AI didn't start in Silicon Valley. It began in ancient dreams, long before computers even existed."

Step 1: Ancient Aspirations

- **The Dream of Artificial Beings:** The desire to create artificial beings is deeply rooted in human history. Long before the advent of computers, people imagined and told stories about creating artificial life.
- **Greek Mythology:** The text mentions Hephaestus, the Greek god of blacksmiths and craftsmen. Hephaestus was said to have created mechanical servants, beings of metal that could perform tasks. This reflects an early human fascination with the idea of creating artificial helpers.
- **Jewish Folklore:** The Golem, a creature from Jewish folklore, is another example. The Golem was a clay figure that was magically brought to life, often to serve or protect its creator. This story explores the idea of imbuing inanimate matter with life and purpose.
- **Da Vinci's Designs:** Leonardo da Vinci, the renowned Renaissance artist and inventor, sketched designs for mechanical knights. These designs, though never fully realized in his time, demonstrate a vision of creating automated machines capable of complex actions.
- **The Underlying Desire:** These ancient stories and designs, as the text points out, reflect a "deep desire: Could humans create life from non-life?" This is a fundamental question that has driven much of the thinking and research in AI. It's about the desire to understand the essence of life and intelligence and to replicate it in a synthetic form.

Step 2: The Birth of Modern AI (1950s)

- **The Mid-20th Century:** The mid-20th century marked a crucial turning point, as the development of computers provided the necessary tools to begin seriously exploring the creation of artificial intelligence.
- **Alan Turing's Question:** Alan Turing, a brilliant British mathematician, played a pivotal role. In 1950, he posed a groundbreaking question: "Can machines think?" This question shifted the focus from simply creating artificial beings to exploring the very nature of intelligence itself.
- **The Turing Test:** To address this question, Turing proposed the Turing Test. This test, as described in the text, suggests that if a machine can engage in a conversation with a human in such a way that the human cannot reliably distinguish the machine from another human, then the machine could be said to "think" or to possess intelligence. The Turing Test provided a concrete way to evaluate machine intelligence.
- **The Dartmouth Workshop:** In 1956, a landmark event took place: the Dartmouth Workshop. At this conference, the term "Artificial Intelligence" was officially coined by John McCarthy. This workshop brought together leading researchers and is widely considered the birthplace of AI as a formal field of study.
- **Early Optimism:** The researchers at the Dartmouth Workshop, including John McCarthy, were filled with optimism. They envisioned a future where machines could:
  - **Learn:** Acquire knowledge and skills from experience.
  - **Reason:** Draw logical inferences and make deductions.
  - **Solve problems:** Find solutions to complex challenges.
  - **Improve themselves:** Learn from their mistakes and become more capable over time.
- **Ambitious Predictions:** There was a strong belief that achieving human-level AI was just around the corner, perhaps within a few decades. This early enthusiasm, though ultimately proven to be premature, fueled significant initial research and development.

Step 3: AI Winters and Slow Progress

- **The Hard Reality:** The initial optimism of the 1950s soon encountered significant challenges. The task of creating truly intelligent machines turned out to be far more complex than initially anticipated.
- **Limitations of Early Computers:** Early computers were slow and expensive. They lacked the computational power and memory needed to handle the complex algorithms and vast amounts of data required for advanced AI.
- **Toy Problems:** Early AI programs were often limited to solving "toy problems," simplified versions of real-world challenges. These programs could perform well in highly constrained environments but struggled to generalize to the complexities of the real world.
- **AI Winters:** The limitations of early AI led to periods of reduced funding and diminished interest in the field. These periods, known as "AI Winters," occurred in the 1970s and the late 1980s. During these winters, research funding dried up, and progress slowed significantly.
- **The Lesson Learned:** The AI Winters taught researchers a valuable lesson: creating human-like intelligence is an incredibly difficult challenge. It requires not only powerful

hardware and sophisticated algorithms but also a deep understanding of how intelligence works.

Step 4: The Rise of Modern AI (2000s–Today)

- **A Resurgence:** Starting around the 2000s, AI experienced a dramatic resurgence, leading to the rapid advancements we see today. Several key factors contributed to this resurgence:
- **Data Explosion:** The internet and the proliferation of smartphones generated massive amounts of data. This "data explosion" provided the raw material needed to train more sophisticated AI models, particularly those based on machine learning.
- **Better Algorithms:** Researchers developed new and more powerful algorithms, most notably deep learning. Deep learning, inspired by the structure of the human brain, enabled machines to learn from data in more complex and nuanced ways.
- **Faster Computers:** The development of GPUs (Graphics Processing Units) and the rise of cloud computing provided the necessary "brain power" for AI. GPUs, originally designed for graphics processing, proved to be highly efficient at performing the matrix operations that underlie many AI algorithms. Cloud computing provided access to vast computing resources on demand, making it possible to train and deploy large-scale AI models.
- **AI Today:** Today, AI is no longer a futuristic dream but a rapidly evolving reality. The text highlights several examples of AI in action:
  - **Voice assistants:** Siri and Alexa, powered by natural language processing, allow us to interact with devices using our voices.
  - **Self-driving cars:** Tesla and other companies are developing self-driving cars that use AI to perceive the environment and navigate roads.
  - **Medical diagnosis systems:** AI is being used to analyze medical images and patient data, assisting doctors in diagnosing diseases with increasing accuracy.
  - **Recommendation engines:** AI powers the recommendation systems used by shopping websites, streaming services, and social media platforms, personalizing our online experiences.
- **A Realistic Perspective:** While AI has made remarkable progress, it's important to maintain a realistic perspective. As the text notes, "We still don't have machines that 'think' like humans." General Artificial Intelligence (AGI), which would possess human-level cognitive abilities across a wide range of tasks, remains a long-term goal.
- **Narrow AI:** However, AI is incredibly effective at performing "narrow tasks." These are specific, well-defined problems, such as image recognition, speech recognition, or playing a particular game. In these narrow domains, AI can often outperform humans.

Myths vs. Reality

As the text aptly states, "With great technological power comes great misunderstanding!" AI, with its increasing capabilities, has also become a source of several myths and misconceptions.

It's crucial to separate fact from fiction to have a clear understanding of what AI is and what it is not.

Here's a breakdown of some of the biggest myths around AI, along with the realities:

Myth 1: AI is Conscious.

- **The Myth:** This myth suggests that AI systems possess awareness, feelings, and subjective experiences, similar to human consciousness.
- **Reality:** The text firmly states, "AI does not 'feel' or 'think' the way humans do." Even the most advanced AI systems, whether they are sophisticated language models or impressive robot dogs, lack genuine consciousness, emotions, and desires.
- **Explanation:**
    - AI systems operate based on algorithms and data processing. They are designed to perform specific tasks by analyzing information and identifying patterns.
    - They do not have a sense of self, subjective experiences, or an understanding of the world in the same way that humans do.
    - While AI can mimic certain aspects of human behavior, such as generating creative content or engaging in conversations, these are based on learned patterns and computational processes, not on genuine feelings or thoughts.
- **Example:**
    - The text provides a compelling example: "When an AI art generator creates a beautiful painting, it doesn't 'feel' joy or pride."
    - The AI system analyzes a vast dataset of existing artwork, learns the patterns and styles, and then uses this knowledge to generate a new image.
    - The resulting artwork may be aesthetically pleasing and even appear creative, but it is the product of algorithmic computation, not of artistic inspiration or emotional expression.

Myth 2: AI Will Soon Take Over the World.

- **The Myth:** This myth, often fueled by science fiction, portrays AI as a looming threat that will surpass human intelligence and ultimately control or replace humanity.
- **Reality:** The text clarifies that while AI can excel in specific tasks, it lacks the general and flexible intelligence that humans possess.
- **Explanation:**
    - AI systems are typically designed to perform narrow tasks within well-defined domains. They can achieve superhuman performance in these specific areas, such as playing chess, diagnosing diseases, or analyzing financial data.
    - However, they struggle with tasks that require common sense, adaptability, and the ability to transfer knowledge from one domain to another.
    - Building an AI system with general intelligence (AGI) – one that can understand the world with the breadth and depth of a human child – remains a significant and distant challenge.
- **Example:**

- o The text provides a vivid illustration: "An AI might beat the world champion at Go, a complex board game, but it cannot tie its shoelaces, make a sandwich, or hold a meaningful conversation about philosophy."
- o This example highlights the difference between narrow AI, which excels in specific domains, and general AI, which would possess human-level cognitive abilities across a wide range of tasks.

Myth 3: AI is Objective and Fair.

- **The Myth:** This myth suggests that AI systems are inherently objective and unbiased, making decisions based on pure logic and data, free from human prejudices.
- **Reality:** The text points out that AI systems can inherit and even amplify biases present in the data they are trained on.
- **Explanation:**
  - o AI models learn from data, and if that data reflects existing societal biases, the model will inevitably reflect those biases as well.
  - o Data can be biased in various ways, including:
    - **Historical bias:** Data from the past may reflect discriminatory practices or societal inequalities.
    - **Representation bias:** Certain groups may be underrepresented or overrepresented in the data.
    - **Measurement bias:** The way data is collected or measured may introduce biases.
  - o When an AI model is trained on biased data, it learns to associate certain patterns or characteristics with specific outcomes, perpetuating and potentially amplifying the original biases.
- **Example:**
  - o The text gives a concerning example: "If a hiring AI is trained on past resumes that favored men over women, it might continue discriminating – even though it 'believes' it's being objective."
  - o The AI system, trained on biased data, learns to associate male names or experiences with successful candidates, leading to discriminatory hiring practices.

Myth 4: AI Will Solve All Our Problems.

- **The Myth:** This myth portrays AI as a panacea, a magical solution that can effortlessly solve all of humanity's problems.
- **Reality:** The text offers a more nuanced perspective, emphasizing that "AI is a tool, not magic."
- **Explanation:**
  - o AI has the potential to be a powerful tool for addressing a wide range of complex issues, from healthcare and climate change to education and poverty.
  - o However, AI is not a self-sufficient solution. Its effectiveness depends on how it is developed, deployed, and used by humans.
  - o Without careful consideration of ethical implications, societal values, and human oversight, AI can also create new problems and exacerbate existing ones.

- **Example:**
  - The text highlights some of the potential downsides: "Without human wisdom, values, and oversight, it can also create new problems – like misinformation, surveillance, or inequality."
  - AI can be used to generate and spread misinformation, erode privacy through mass surveillance, or exacerbate economic inequality by automating jobs and concentrating wealth.

In conclusion, it's essential to approach AI with a balanced perspective, recognizing its immense potential while remaining aware of its limitations and potential risks. By dispelling these myths and understanding the true nature of AI, we can harness its power responsibly and ethically for the benefit of humanity.

Key Takeaway for Chapter 1

Artificial Intelligence is neither a miracle nor a monster.
It is a human-made technology, shaped by our intentions, limited by our understanding, and full of potential for both good and harm.

✓ **At the end of this chapter**, readers will have a realistic, balanced understanding of:

- What AI is and isn't,
- How it evolved over time, and
- What myths we must leave behind to think clearly about its future.

MCQs: Chapter 1 - Artificial Intelligence

Part A: What is AI, Really?

1. **Which of the following best defines Artificial Intelligence?**
   A) Machines that work faster than humans
   B) Machines that exhibit human-like cognitive skills
   C) Robots that look like humans
   D) Computer programming for websites
   → ☐ **Answer: B**

2. **AI mainly involves which of the following tasks?**
   A) Solving mathematical puzzles
   B) Mimicking human intelligence
   C) Building mechanical parts
   D) Repairing broken computers
   → Answer: **B**
3. **Which is an example of AI in everyday life?**
   A) Microwave oven
   B) Washing machine
   C) Voice assistant like Siri
   D) Refrigerator
   → Answer: **C**
4. **AI systems primarily operate based on:**
   A) Human emotions
   B) Natural instincts
   C) Data and algorithms
   D) Luck
   → Answer: **C**
5. **A self-driving car uses AI to:**
   A) Clean itself
   B) Understand road conditions and make driving decisions
   C) Play music
   D) Refuel automatically
   → Answer: **B**
6. **Facial recognition on smartphones is an example of:**
   A) Data compression
   B) Machine learning
   C) Graphic design
   D) Sound engineering
   → Answer: **B**
7. **The primary goal of AI is to:**
   A) Replace all human workers
   B) Make machines mimic intelligent behavior
   C) Create robots that look human
   D) Build faster computers
   → Answer: **B**
8. **Which of the following is NOT a feature of AI?**
   A) Learning
   B) Reasoning
   C) Sleeping
   D) Problem-solving
   → Answer: **C**
9. **AI can best be thought of as:**
   A) A single technology
   B) A collection of techniques and ideas

C) A type of hardware

D) A fantasy idea

➡️ **Answer: B**

10. **Which branch is most closely related to AI?**
    A) Astrology
    B) Cognitive science
    C) Architecture
    D) Painting
    ➡️ **Answer: B**

Part B: Evolution of AI: From Dreams to Reality

11. **Which ancient civilization spoke of mechanical beings like the Golem?**
    A) Greek
    B) Egyptian
    C) Jewish
    D) Chinese
    ➡️ **Answer: C**

12. **Which mythological figure created mechanical servants in Greek mythology?**
    A) Zeus
    B) Hephaestus
    C) Apollo
    D) Hermes
    ➡️ **Answer: B**

13. **Who proposed the question "Can machines think?"**
    A) Isaac Newton
    B) Alan Turing
    C) Albert Einstein
    D) John McCarthy
    ➡️ **Answer: B**

14. **The "Turing Test" checks if a machine can:**
    A) Solve math problems faster
    B) Fool a human into thinking it's another human
    C) Build its own hardware
    D) Become conscious
    ➡️ **Answer: B**

15. **The term "Artificial Intelligence" was coined by:**
    A) Marvin Minsky
    B) John McCarthy
    C) Alan Turing
    D) Geoffrey Hinton
    ➡️ **Answer: B**

16. **In which year was the term "Artificial Intelligence" first coined?**
    A) 1956
    B) 1965
    C) 1943
    D) 1972
    ➙ **Answer: A**

17. **The Dartmouth Conference is famous for:**
    A) Launching the first robot
    B) Introducing the term "AI"
    C) Inventing the internet
    D) Developing smartphones
    ➙ **Answer: B**

18. **Early AI researchers believed human-level AI would be achieved in:**
    A) A few months
    B) A few years
    C) A few decades
    D) Centuries
    ➙ **Answer: C**

19. **What slowed down AI progress in the 1970s and 1980s?**
    A) Lack of data
    B) High costs and technical limitations
    C) No public interest
    D) Too many robots
    ➙ **Answer: B**

20. **"AI Winter" refers to:**
    A) A time when robots froze
    B) A period of reduced AI funding and interest
    C) Cold storage of AI servers
    D) AI taking control during winter
    ➙ **Answer: B**

21. **Modern AI growth is fueled by:**
    A) Decrease in electricity prices
    B) Data explosion and faster computers
    C) Magic spells
    D) Newer viruses
    ➙ **Answer: B**

22. **Which of the following is NOT a driver of modern AI success?**
    A) Big Data
    B) Deep Learning
    C) Supercomputers
    D) Paper-based filing
    ➙ **Answer: D**

23. **Which AI method is inspired by the human brain?**
    A) Blockchain
    B) Neural Networks

C) Relational databases

D) CPU pipelines

➡️ **Answer: B**

24. **Deep Learning mainly uses:**

A) Decision trees

B) Neural networks with multiple layers

C) Spreadsheets

D) Search engines

➡️ **Answer: B**

25. **Self-driving technology heavily relies on:**

A) Radio frequencies

B) Manual programming

C) AI algorithms and sensors

D) Random guessing

➡️ **Answer: C**

Part C: Myths vs. Reality

26. **Which of the following is a myth about AI?**

A) AI can be biased

B) AI systems are conscious

C) AI helps recommend movies

D) AI assists doctors

➡️ **Answer: B**

27. **True AI consciousness means:**

A) Understanding and feeling emotions

B) Solving puzzles faster

C) Having a large database

D) Writing codes automatically

➡️ **Answer: A**

28. **Which of these is NOT true about current AI?**

A) It can learn from data

B) It feels pride when it wins

C) It can detect faces

D) It can play complex games

➡️ **Answer: B**

29. **The idea that AI will take over the world soon is:**

A) An agreed scientific fact

B) A myth

C) An urgent reality

D) Already happening

➡️ **Answer: B**

30. **Bias in AI arises mainly because:**
   A) AI chooses to be unfair
   B) Data used to train AI is biased
   C) AI has political opinions
   D) Machines have free will
   ➡️ **Answer: B**

31. **An AI system trained only on Western faces might struggle with:**
   A) Speed tests
   B) Recognizing diverse ethnicities
   C) Counting numbers
   D) Reading poetry
   ➡️ **Answer: B**

32. **A major risk with AI decision-making is:**
   A) It will always be perfect
   B) It will build robots
   C) It may inherit human biases
   D) It will stop working in winter
   ➡️ **Answer: C**

33. **AI today is best described as:**
   A) General intelligence
   B) Narrow and specialized intelligence
   C) Conscious being
   D) Ethical decision-maker
   ➡️ **Answer: B**

34. **Which industry does NOT use AI today?**
   A) Healthcare
   B) Agriculture
   C) Movie making
   D) Ancient history research (without technology)
   ➡️ **Answer: D**

35. **One of the dangers of misunderstanding AI is:**
   A) Ignoring its ethical impacts
   B) Building better smartphones
   C) Reducing internet speed
   D) Slowing down coding
   ➡️ **Answer: A**

36. **AI cannot currently:**
   A) Translate languages
   B) Understand emotions like humans
   C) Recommend products
   D) Play music
   ➡️ **Answer: B**

37. **Myths about AI are often fueled by:**
   A) Movies and popular culture
   B) University textbooks

C) Scientific conferences

D) Research journals

➡️ **Answer: A**

38. **The Turing Test measures:**

A) Machine speed

B) Machine-human indistinguishability

C) Algorithm length

D) Software price

➡️ **Answer: B**

39. **Current AI cannot:**

A) Beat humans in chess

B) Feel sadness after losing a game

C) Predict trends

D) Suggest friends on social media

➡️ **Answer: B**

40. **One main limitation of AI today is:**

A) Lack of speed

B) Lack of electricity

C) Lack of common sense reasoning

D) Too much data access

➡️ **Answer: C**

Bonus Conceptual MCQs

41. **AI's greatest strength today is its ability to:**

A) Solve a wide range of open-ended problems

B) Specialize in narrow tasks

C) Build its own rules

D) Program itself freely

➡️ **Answer: B**

42. **The fear that AI will "replace" all human jobs is:**

A) Fully justified

B) A complex issue requiring deeper analysis

C) Already happening at large scale

D) Ignored by researchers

➡️ **Answer: B**

43. **One way to make AI more ethical is:**

A) Give it more data

B) Include diverse human perspectives in its design

C) Remove all coding

D) Allow it to vote

➡️ **Answer: B**

44. **The intelligence of AI today is mostly:**
   A) Creative
   B) Emotional
   C) Statistical and logical
   D) Random
   ➡️ **Answer: C**

45. **Self-driving cars face challenges mainly in:**
   A) Perfect weather
   B) Recognizing complex real-world situations
   C) Running faster processors
   D) Singing songs
   ➡️ **Answer: B**

46. **A real-world example of AI in healthcare is:**
   A) Automatic plant watering
   B) Medical image diagnosis
   C) Keeping hospital floors clean
   D) Designing hospital uniforms
   ➡️ **Answer: B**

47. **Deep Learning became practical because of:**
   A) Slower computers
   B) Lack of storage
   C) Faster hardware like GPUs
   D) Smaller datasets
   ➡️ **Answer: C**

48. **If AI behaves unfairly, the primary blame often lies with:**
   A) Technology itself
   B) Human design choices
   C) Weather
   D) Random luck
   ➡️ **Answer: B**

49. **AI systems are most successful when:**
   A) No humans supervise them
   B) They are carefully designed and monitored
   C) They run without data
   D) They replace all human workers
   ➡️ **Answer: B**

50. **In short, AI is:**
   A) Conscious human-like machine
   B) A human-created tool with great potential and limits
   C) A supernatural force
   D) A hidden conspiracy
   ➡️ **Answer: B**

CHAPTER 2: THE CORE COMPONENTS OF AI

Artificial Intelligence (AI) is not a monolithic concept; rather, it is composed of several essential components that work together to enable machines to perform tasks that typically require human intelligence. The principal components that form the foundation of AI include **Machine Learning**, **Deep Learning**, **Neural Networks**, **Natural Language Processing (NLP)**, and **Computer Vision**.

Each of these components has distinct roles, methods, and applications, yet they are interconnected and often function synergistically.

Let us understand each core component step-by-step.

2.1 Machine Learning (ML)

The provided text offers a concise and accurate definition of Machine Learning: "Machine Learning is a subset of AI that enables computers to learn patterns from data and make decisions or predictions without being explicitly programmed for each task." Let's delve deeper into this concept.

Definition: Learning from Data

- **A Subset of AI:** Machine Learning is a specific branch within the broader field of Artificial Intelligence. While AI encompasses various techniques for creating intelligent machines, ML focuses specifically on enabling machines to learn from data.
- **Learning Patterns:** The core idea behind ML is that instead of writing explicit instructions for a computer to follow, we provide it with a large amount of data and allow it to discover the underlying patterns and relationships within that data.
- **Making Decisions or Predictions:** Once an ML algorithm has learned these patterns, it can use them to make predictions or decisions on new, unseen data. This could involve classifying data points into categories, predicting numerical values, or performing other types of tasks.
- **Without Explicit Programming:** This is a key distinction. Traditional programming requires developers to write detailed, step-by-step instructions for every possible scenario. In contrast, ML algorithms learn from data, allowing them to adapt to new situations and make predictions even when they haven't been explicitly programmed for those specific cases.

Key Concept: Statistical Techniques

The text highlights that "Instead of being programmed with specific rules, ML algorithms use statistical techniques to find patterns in data." This is a crucial point.

- **Statistical Foundation:** ML algorithms are built upon statistical principles. They use statistical methods to:
  - Identify correlations and dependencies between different variables in the data.
  - Estimate the probability of certain outcomes.
  - Generalize from the observed data to make predictions on unseen data.
- **Examples of Statistical Techniques:**
  - **Regression:** Used to predict numerical values (e.g., predicting house prices).
  - **Classification:** Used to categorize data points (e.g., classifying emails as spam or not spam).
  - **Clustering:** Used to group similar data points together (e.g., segmenting customers based on their behavior).
  - **Probability distributions:** Used to model the likelihood of different events (e.g., predicting the probability of a user clicking on an ad).

Step-by-Step Explanation of the ML Process:

The text outlines a general step-by-step process for building and deploying an ML system. Let's expand on each step with more details and examples:

1. **Input Data Collection:**
   - **What it involves:** The first step is to gather the data that will be used to train the ML model. This data should be relevant to the problem you're trying to solve and should be of sufficient quality and quantity.
   - **Data sources:** Data can come from various sources, including databases, log files, sensors, APIs, and web scraping.
   - **Example:** As the text suggests, "Collect thousands of labeled images of cats and dogs."
     - In this case, the data consists of images, and each image is labeled with the correct category ("cat" or "dog"). This labeled data is essential for training a model to distinguish between the two types of images.
2. **Feature Extraction:**
   - **What it involves:** Raw data is often in a format that's not directly suitable for ML algorithms. Feature extraction involves transforming the raw data into a set of numerical features that the model can understand.
   - **Features:** Features are the input variables that the model uses to make predictions. They should be informative and relevant to the task at hand.
   - **Example:** "Identify characteristics like shape, color, fur pattern, etc."
     - For the cat and dog image classification problem, we need to extract features from the images that will help the model differentiate between cats and dogs. These features could include:
       - **Shape:** The shape of the ears, face, and body.
       - **Color:** The dominant colors in the image.
       - **Fur pattern:** The texture and pattern of the fur.
       - **Edges:** The presence of edges in specific orientations.
       - These features can be extracted using image processing techniques.
3. **Model Selection:**

- o **What it involves:** Choosing the appropriate ML algorithm for the task. Different algorithms have different strengths and weaknesses, and the best choice depends on the type of data, the problem you're trying to solve, and the desired performance.
- o **Algorithm examples:** The text mentions several common ML algorithms:
  - **Decision Tree:** A tree-like structure that splits the data based on feature values.
  - **Support Vector Machine (SVM):** Finds the optimal boundary to separate data points of different classes.
  - **k-Nearest Neighbor (k-NN):** Classifies a data point based on the majority class of its k nearest neighbors.
  - Other algorithms include:
    - **Linear Regression:** For predicting numerical values.
    - **Logistic Regression:** For binary classification.
    - **Neural Networks:** For complex tasks like image and speech recognition.
- o **Example:** For the cat and dog image classification problem, you might consider using a Convolutional Neural Network (CNN), which is well-suited for image data.

4. **Training the Model:**
   - o **What it involves:** The training process involves feeding the labeled data (input features and corresponding labels) to the selected ML algorithm. The algorithm uses this data to learn the relationship between the features and the labels.
   - o **Learning patterns:** During training, the model adjusts its internal parameters to minimize the difference between its predictions and the actual labels.
   - o **Example:** "Feed the labeled data to the model to help it learn the patterns."
     - The CNN is fed the labeled images of cats and dogs. During training, the CNN learns to identify the features that are most discriminative between the two classes (e.g., cats have pointy ears, dogs have floppy ears).

5. **Testing and Validation:**
   - o **What it involves:** After the model is trained, it's essential to evaluate its performance. This involves testing the model on a separate set of data that it hasn't seen before (unseen data).
   - o **Evaluating performance:** This step measures how well the model generalizes to new data and how accurately it can make predictions.
   - o **Metrics:** Various metrics can be used to evaluate performance, depending on the task. For example:
     - **Accuracy:** The percentage of correct predictions (for classification).
     - **Precision and Recall:** Measures of how well the model identifies positive cases (for classification).
     - **Mean Squared Error:** The average difference between predicted and actual values (for regression).
   - o **Example:** "Test the model on unseen data to evaluate performance."
     - After training the CNN on a set of cat and dog images, you would test it on a separate set of images that the model has never seen before. You

would then measure the model's accuracy in correctly classifying these new images.

6. **Deployment:**
   - **What it involves:** If the model performs well during testing, it can be deployed to make predictions on real-world data.
   - **Real-world predictions:** Deployment involves integrating the trained model into a production system or application.
   - **Example:** "Deploy the trained model to make real-world predictions."
     - The trained CNN can be deployed as part of a mobile app or website that can automatically classify images as containing a cat or a dog.

Example: Predicting House Prices

The text provides a common example of an ML application: "Predicting house prices based on features like size, location, and number of bedrooms." Let's elaborate on this example:

- **Input Data Collection:** Collect data on past house sales, including the selling price and relevant features like:
  - Size (square footage)
  - Location (e.g., zip code, neighborhood)
  - Number of bedrooms
  - Number of bathrooms
  - Age of the house
  - Lot size
- **Feature Extraction:** The features listed above are already in a numerical format, but some may require further processing. For example:
  - Location (zip code) might be one-hot encoded.
- **Model Selection:** Choose a regression algorithm, such as:
  - Linear Regression
  - Decision Tree Regression
  - Random Forest Regression
  - Gradient Boosting Regression
- **Training the Model:** Feed the house sales data to the chosen regression algorithm to learn the relationship between the features and the selling price.
- **Testing and Validation:** Evaluate the model's performance on a separate set of house sales data using metrics like:
  - Mean Squared Error (MSE)
  - R-squared
- **Deployment:** Deploy the trained model as part of a website or app that allows users to input the features of a house and get an estimated price.

2.2 Deep Learning (DL)

The provided text offers a clear and concise definition: "Deep Learning is a specialized subfield of Machine Learning that uses artificial neural networks with many layers (hence 'deep') to model complex patterns in large amounts of data." Let's break this down further.

Definition: Deep Neural Networks

- **A Subfield of Machine Learning:** Deep Learning is a specific approach within the broader field of Machine Learning. It's a technique for achieving machine learning.
- **Artificial Neural Networks:** Deep Learning is based on the concept of artificial neural networks, which are computational models inspired by the structure and function of the human brain.
- **Many Layers:** The key characteristic of Deep Learning that distinguishes it from traditional neural networks is the use of "many layers." These layers are stacked on top of each other, allowing the network to learn increasingly complex and abstract representations of the data. The "deep" in Deep Learning refers to this depth of layers.
- **Complex Patterns:** Deep Learning models are particularly well-suited for learning intricate and hierarchical patterns in data that are difficult for traditional machine learning algorithms to capture.
- **Large Amounts of Data:** Deep Learning models typically require very large datasets to train effectively. The more data they have, the better they can learn and generalize.

Key Concept: Automated Feature Extraction

The text highlights a crucial advantage of Deep Learning: "Deep learning automates feature extraction and works exceptionally well with unstructured data like images, audio, and text."

- **Feature Extraction in Traditional ML:** In traditional machine learning, feature extraction is often a manual and time-consuming process. Data scientists need to carefully design and engineer features that are relevant to the task at hand.
- **Automated Feature Extraction in DL:** Deep Learning models, particularly Convolutional Neural Networks (CNNs) for images and Recurrent Neural Networks (RNNs) or Transformers for text, can automatically learn relevant features from the raw data. The multiple layers of the network progressively learn more abstract representations, eliminating the need for manual feature engineering.
- **Unstructured Data:** Deep Learning excels at handling unstructured data, which includes data that doesn't fit neatly into tables or databases. Examples include:
  - **Images:** Pixels representing visual information.
  - **Audio:** Sound waves representing auditory information.
  - **Text:** Sequences of words representing linguistic information.

Step-by-Step Explanation of the Deep Learning Process:

The text outlines a general step-by-step process for training a Deep Learning model. Let's expand on each step with more details and examples:

1. **Data Collection:**

- **What it involves:** The first step is to gather a large dataset that is relevant to the problem you're trying to solve. The size and quality of the dataset are crucial for training effective Deep Learning models.
- **Example:** "Gather a large dataset (e.g., 1 million images of handwritten digits)."
  - For training a model to recognize handwritten digits (like in the MNIST dataset), you would collect a large number of images, each showing a single digit (0-9). Each image is labeled with the corresponding digit.

2. **Design a Neural Network:**
   - **What it involves:** Designing the architecture of the neural network, which involves specifying the number of layers, the types of layers, and how they are connected.
   - **Neural Network Architecture:**
     - **Input Layer:** The first layer, which receives the raw data.
     - **Hidden Layers:** The intermediate layers, which perform complex computations on the input data to extract relevant features. Deep Learning models have multiple hidden layers.
     - **Output Layer:** The final layer, which produces the model's output (e.g., the predicted digit).
   - **Example:** "A network with multiple layers—input, hidden, and output layers."
     - For the handwritten digit recognition task, you might design a Convolutional Neural Network (CNN) with:
       - An input layer to receive the image pixels.
       - Several convolutional layers to extract features like edges and shapes.
       - Pooling layers to reduce the dimensionality of the feature maps.
       - Fully connected layers to combine the extracted features and produce the final digit classification.
       - An output layer with 10 neurons, one for each digit (0-9).

3. **Feedforward Propagation:**
   - **What it involves:** The process of passing the input data through the neural network, layer by layer, to produce an output.
   - **Layer-by-Layer Processing:** Each neuron in a layer receives input from the neurons in the previous layer, performs a calculation (typically a weighted sum followed by an activation function), and passes its output to the neurons in the next layer.
   - **Example:** The image of a handwritten digit is fed into the input layer of the CNN. The information flows through the convolutional and pooling layers, where features are extracted. Finally, the fully connected layers combine these features to produce a probability distribution over the 10 digits.

4. **Loss Calculation:**
   - **What it involves:** Comparing the network's output with the actual (true) result to measure how well the network is performing. This difference is quantified as a "loss" or "error."
   - **Loss Function:** A loss function is used to calculate the error. The choice of loss function depends on the task.
     - For classification: Cross-entropy loss

- For regression: Mean squared error
  - o **Example:** "Compare the network's output with the actual result to compute an error (loss)."
    - If the network predicts that the image is a "3" with a probability of 0.8, but the actual digit is "3," the loss would be small. If the network predicts "8" with a probability of 0.8, the loss would be large.
5. **Backpropagation:**
   - o **What it involves:** The process of adjusting the weights of the connections between neurons in the network to minimize the loss.
   - o **Gradient Descent:** Backpropagation uses an optimization algorithm, typically gradient descent, to calculate how much each weight contributed to the overall loss.
   - o **Weight Adjustment:** The weights are then adjusted in the opposite direction of the gradient, effectively "pushing" the network towards a state where it makes more accurate predictions.
   - o **Example:** "Adjust the weights of the network to minimize the loss."
     - The error signal is propagated backward through the network, layer by layer. The weights in each layer are updated proportionally to their contribution to the error, making the network more likely to correctly classify the digit in the future.
6. **Training Iterations (Epochs):**
   - o **What it involves:** Repeating the feedforward propagation and backpropagation steps multiple times to train the network.
   - o **Epochs:** One complete pass through the entire training dataset is called an epoch.
   - o **Convergence:** The training process continues for a sufficient number of epochs until the network's performance on the training data (and ideally, on a separate validation set) reaches a satisfactory level.
   - o **Example:** "Repeat feedforward and backpropagation many times."
     - The CNN is trained for hundreds or thousands of epochs, repeatedly processing the handwritten digit images and adjusting its weights. Over time, the network learns to accurately recognize the digits.

Example: Automatic Translation

The text provides an example of Deep Learning in action: "Automatic translation of text from English to French using deep learning models like Transformer Networks." Let's elaborate:

- **Data Collection:** Collect a large dataset of paired English and French sentences (parallel corpus).
- **Design a Neural Network:** Use a Transformer network, a powerful Deep Learning architecture for sequence-to-sequence tasks.
  - o The Transformer consists of encoder and decoder components, both built from self-attention mechanisms.
- **Feedforward Propagation:** The English sentence is fed into the encoder, which transforms it into a sequence of numerical representations. The decoder then uses these representations to generate the French translation, word by word.

- **Loss Calculation:** Compare the generated French translation with the actual French translation from the dataset using a loss function like cross-entropy.
- **Backpropagation:** Adjust the weights of the Transformer network to minimize the translation error.
- **Training Iterations (Epochs):** Train the Transformer on the parallel corpus for many epochs until it can accurately translate English sentences into French.

2.3 Neural Networks

The text provides a concise and accurate definition: "Neural Networks are computational models inspired by the human brain's interconnected neuron structure, designed to recognize patterns and solve complex problems." Let's break this down further.

Definition: Inspired by the Brain

- **Computational Models:** Neural networks are mathematical models implemented as computer programs. They are not physical replicas of the brain, but rather abstract representations.
- **Inspired by the Human Brain:** The structure of neural networks is loosely based on the way neurons (nerve cells) are interconnected in the brain. Neurons in the brain form complex networks that process and transmit information.
- **Interconnected Neuron Structure:** The key idea is that, like the brain, neural networks consist of interconnected processing units (analogous to neurons) that work together to solve problems.
- **Designed to Recognize Patterns:** Neural networks are particularly well-suited for tasks that involve recognizing patterns in data. This includes tasks like image recognition, speech recognition, and natural language processing.
- **Solve Complex Problems:** By learning to recognize complex patterns, neural networks can be used to solve problems that are difficult or impossible to solve with traditional computer programs.

Key Concept: Simple Computation, Intricate Relationships

The text highlights a fundamental principle: "Each 'neuron' (node) performs a simple computation. A network of such neurons can model intricate relationships."

- **Neuron (Node):** In a neural network, the basic processing unit is called a neuron or a node. Each neuron receives input, performs a simple calculation, and produces an output.
- **Simple Computation:** The computation performed by a neuron typically involves:
  - Multiplying each input by a weight.
  - Summing the weighted inputs.
  - Adding a bias.
  - Applying an activation function (more on this later).

- **Network of Neurons:** A neural network consists of many neurons organized into layers. These layers are interconnected, allowing information to flow from one layer to the next.
- **Intricate Relationships:** By combining the simple computations of many interconnected neurons, neural networks can learn to model very complex and non-linear relationships in data. This is what makes them so powerful for solving challenging problems.

Step-by-Step Explanation of a Neural Network:

The text outlines the basic structure and operation of a neural network. Let's expand on each step with more details and examples:

1. **Input Layer:**
   - **What it does:** The input layer is the first layer of the neural network. It receives the raw input data that you want the network to process.
   - **Raw Input:** The format of the raw input depends on the problem. It could be numerical data, pixel values from an image, audio samples, or text.
   - **Example:** "Pixel values of an image."
     - If you're using a neural network to classify images, the input layer would receive the pixel values of each image. For example, if you have a 28x28 pixel grayscale image, the input layer would have 784 neurons, each representing the intensity of one pixel.
2. **Hidden Layers:**
   - **What they do:** Hidden layers are the intermediate layers between the input layer and the output layer. They perform the bulk of the computation in the network, transforming the input features into a more abstract representation.
   - **Multiple Layers:** A neural network can have one or more hidden layers. The more hidden layers a network has, the "deeper" it is, and the more complex patterns it can learn (this is the basis of "Deep Learning").
   - **Activation Function:** Each neuron in a hidden layer applies an activation function to its input. The activation function introduces non-linearity, which is essential for the network to learn complex relationships.
     - **ReLU (Rectified Linear Unit):** A popular activation function that outputs the input directly if it is positive, and zero otherwise.
     - **Sigmoid:** An activation function that squashes the input to a range between 0 and 1.
     - **Tanh (Hyperbolic Tangent):** An activation function that squashes the input to a range between -1 and 1.
   - **Example:** In a neural network for image classification, the first hidden layers might learn to detect edges and simple shapes, while deeper layers might learn to recognize more complex objects like eyes, ears, or entire faces.
3. **Output Layer:**
   - **What it does:** The output layer is the final layer of the neural network. It produces the network's final result or prediction.
   - **Output Format:** The format of the output depends on the problem.

- For classification: The output layer might have one neuron for each class, with the neuron's output representing the probability of the input belonging to that class.
- For regression: The output layer might have a single neuron that outputs a numerical value (the prediction).
  - **Example:** "Classify an image as 'dog' or 'cat.'"
    - In a neural network designed to classify images as either "dog" or "cat," the output layer would have two neurons: one for "dog" and one for "cat." The output of each neuron would represent the probability that the image belongs to that class. The neuron with the highest probability would determine the network's prediction.

4. **Weights and Biases:**
   - **Weights:** "Neurons are connected via weights." Weights are numerical values that determine the strength of the connection between two neurons. They control how much influence the output of one neuron has on the input of another neuron.
   - **Biases:** "Each has a bias to adjust outputs." A bias is a numerical value associated with each neuron. It allows the neuron to shift its activation function, giving it more flexibility in modeling the data.
   - **Role of Weights and Biases:** Weights and biases are the parameters of the neural network that are learned during the training process. By adjusting these parameters, the network can learn to map inputs to desired outputs.

5. **Training:**
   - **What it is:** "Using algorithms like backpropagation to adjust weights and biases." Training a neural network involves adjusting its weights and biases to minimize the difference between its predictions and the actual (true) values.
   - **Backpropagation:** Backpropagation is the most common algorithm used to train neural networks. It involves:
     - Calculating the error (or loss) between the network's output and the true output.
     - Propagating this error backward through the network, layer by layer.
     - Calculating the gradient of the error with respect to each weight and bias.
     - Updating the weights and biases in the direction that reduces the error (using an optimization algorithm like gradient descent).
   - **Optimization:** The goal of training is to find the set of weights and biases that minimizes the loss function, resulting in a network that makes accurate predictions.

Example: Speech Recognition

The text provides a common example of neural networks in action: "Speech recognition systems use neural networks to convert spoken language into text." Let's elaborate:

- **Input Layer:** The input layer receives the raw audio data, typically in the form of a spectrogram (a visual representation of the audio signal's frequencies over time).

- **Hidden Layers:** The hidden layers, often using Recurrent Neural Networks (RNNs) or Transformer networks, process the audio data to extract features like phonemes (basic units of sound), words, and sentence structure.
- **Output Layer:** The output layer produces a sequence of characters or words, representing the transcribed text.
- **Weights and Biases:** The weights and biases in the network are adjusted during training to learn the complex relationships between audio signals and corresponding text.
- **Training:** The neural network is trained on a large dataset of spoken audio and corresponding transcriptions using backpropagation. The network learns to map audio patterns to the correct sequence of words.

2.4 Natural Language Processing (NLP)

The text provides a clear and concise definition: "Natural Language Processing is the branch of AI that focuses on the interaction between computers and human (natural) languages." Let's delve deeper into this.

Definition: Bridging the Gap

- **Branch of AI:** NLP is a specialized field within Artificial Intelligence. It's the area of AI dedicated to enabling computers to understand and process human language.
- **Interaction with Human Languages:** NLP aims to make it possible for computers to communicate with humans in their own languages (like English, Spanish, Mandarin), rather than requiring humans to learn specialized computer languages.
- **Natural Languages:** The term "natural languages" refers to the languages that humans use to communicate with each other, as opposed to artificial languages like programming languages.

Key Concept: Reading, Understanding, and Deriving Meaning

The text highlights a crucial aspect of NLP: "NLP allows machines to read, understand, and derive meaning from human languages."

- **Reading:** This involves the ability of a computer to take in text or speech as input.
- **Understanding:** This is the more challenging part, where the computer attempts to parse the structure of the language (grammar, syntax) and grasp the meaning of the words and sentences.
- **Deriving Meaning:** This goes beyond simply understanding the literal meaning of words. It involves the ability to infer context, identify sentiment, and understand the intent behind the language.

Step-by-Step Explanation of the NLP Process:

The text outlines a general step-by-step process for NLP. Let's expand on each step with more details and examples:

1. **Text Preprocessing:**
   - **What it involves:** Raw text data is often messy and unstructured. Text preprocessing involves cleaning and transforming the text into a format that is more suitable for NLP models.
   - **Tokenization:** "Breaking text into words or phrases."
     - This is the process of splitting a text string into individual units called tokens. Tokens can be words, sub-word units (like "un-" or "-ing"), or punctuation marks.
     - Example: The sentence "The quick brown fox jumps over the lazy dog." would be tokenized into: ["The", "quick", "brown", "fox", "jumps", "over", "the", "lazy", "dog", "."]
   - **Stopword Removal:** "Removing common words like 'is,' 'the,' etc."
     - Stopwords are words that occur very frequently in a language but typically don't carry much meaning (e.g., "a", "an", "the", "is", "are", "of", "and"). Removing them can help to focus on the more important words.
     - Example: After stopword removal, the sentence above might become: ["quick", "brown", "fox", "jumps", "over", "lazy", "dog"]
   - **Stemming/Lemmatization:** "Reducing words to their base forms."
     - These are techniques for reducing words to their root form.
     - Stemming: A simpler approach that chops off the ends of words using heuristics (rules). It can sometimes result in non-words.
       - Example: "running" -> "run", "jumps" -> "jump", "easily" -> "easi"
     - Lemmatization: A more sophisticated approach that uses a dictionary and morphological analysis to find the base form of a word (the lemma). It always produces a valid word.
       - Example: "running" -> "run", "jumps" -> "jump", "easily" -> "easily"
     - Lemmatization is generally preferred because it produces more meaningful root forms.
2. **Feature Extraction:**
   - **What it involves:** Converting the preprocessed text into a numerical representation that can be understood by machine learning models.
   - **Example:** "Bag of Words, TF-IDF (Term Frequency-Inverse Document Frequency)."
     - **Bag of Words (BoW):** A simple representation that counts the occurrences of each word in a document. It ignores the order of the words.
       - Example: For the sentence "The quick brown fox jumps over the lazy dog", the BoW representation might be a vector where each element corresponds to a word in the vocabulary, and the value is the count of that word in the sentence.

- **TF-IDF (Term Frequency-Inverse Document Frequency):** A more sophisticated representation that weighs words based on their importance in a document and across the entire corpus.
  - Term Frequency (TF): How often a word appears in a document.
  - Inverse Document Frequency (IDF): How rare a word is across all documents.
  - TF-IDF gives higher weights to words that are frequent in a specific document but rare in general.
- Other feature extraction techniques include:
  - **Word embeddings:** (e.g., Word2Vec, GloVe, BERT embeddings) Represent words as dense numerical vectors that capture semantic relationships.

3. **Model Building:**
   - **What it involves:** Choosing and training a machine learning model to perform a specific NLP task.
   - **NLP Tasks:**
     - **Sentiment analysis:** Determining the emotional tone of a text (positive, negative, neutral).
     - **Text classification:** Categorizing text into predefined categories (e.g., spam detection, topic classification).
     - **Machine translation:** Converting text from one language to another.
     - **Named entity recognition (NER):** Identifying and classifying named entities in text (e.g., people, organizations, locations).
     - **Question answering:** Answering questions based on a given text.
     - **Text summarization:** Generating a concise summary of a longer text.
   - **Model Examples:** "Train a model (e.g., Naive Bayes, Transformer models) to perform tasks like sentiment analysis."
     - **Naive Bayes:** A simple probabilistic model often used for text classification.
     - **Transformer models:** (e.g., BERT, GPT) Powerful neural network architectures that have revolutionized many NLP tasks, particularly those involving sequential data.
     - Other models include:
       - **Recurrent Neural Networks (RNNs):** For processing sequential data like text.
       - **Convolutional Neural Networks (CNNs):** Can be used for some NLP tasks, especially those involving short texts.

4. **Evaluation:**
   - **What it involves:** Measuring the performance of the trained NLP model.
   - **Metrics:** "Measure accuracy, precision, recall, and F1-score."
     - **Accuracy:** The percentage of correct predictions (for classification).
     - **Precision:** The proportion of positive predictions that were actually correct.
     - **Recall:** The proportion of actual positive cases that were correctly identified.

- **F1-score:** The harmonic mean of precision and recall, providing a balanced measure of performance.
- Other metrics include:
  - **BLEU (Bilingual Evaluation Understudy):** For machine translation.
  - **ROUGE (Recall-Oriented Understudy for Gisting Evaluation):** For text summarization.

Example: Chatbots

The text provides a common example of NLP in action: "Chatbots like Siri and Alexa understanding and responding to user queries." Let's elaborate:

- **Text Preprocessing:** When a user speaks to Siri or Alexa, the speech is converted into text, and then that text is preprocessed (tokenization, stopword removal, etc.).
- **Feature Extraction:** The preprocessed text is converted into a numerical representation (e.g., using word embeddings).
- **Model Building:** A sophisticated NLP model (often a Transformer-based model) is used to:
  - Understand the user's intent (e.g., "set an alarm," "play music," "get the weather").
  - Generate an appropriate response.
- **Evaluation:** The chatbot's performance is evaluated based on its ability to:
  - Accurately understand user queries.
  - Provide relevant and helpful responses.
  - Maintain a coherent and natural conversation.

2.5 Computer Vision

Definition:

Computer Vision, at its core, is an interdisciplinary field within Artificial Intelligence that endeavors to equip computers with the capability to "see" and interpret the visual world in a manner akin to human vision. It involves the development of theoretical and algorithmic foundations that enable machines to extract meaningful information from digital images, videos, and other visual inputs, thereby facilitating understanding and automated action based on this visual perception.

Key Concept:

The central tenet of computer vision lies in leveraging digital imagery obtained from various sources, such as cameras and video streams, and employing sophisticated computational models, particularly deep learning architectures, to enable machines to perform tasks that traditionally require human visual intelligence. This includes the precise identification, localization, and categorization of objects within a visual scene, ultimately allowing the system to react intelligently to the perceived environment.

Step-by-Step Explanation:

The process of enabling a computer to "see" involves a sequence of carefully orchestrated steps, transforming raw visual data into actionable insights. Let's delve into each stage with detailed explanations and illustrative examples:

1. Image Acquisition:

- **Explanation:** This initial phase involves the capture of visual data from the real world. This can be achieved through various imaging devices, including digital cameras (still or video), specialized sensors (like infrared or depth cameras), or even through accessing existing digital image or video datasets. The quality and characteristics of the acquired image (e.g., resolution, lighting conditions, noise levels) significantly impact the subsequent stages of the computer vision pipeline.
- "The genesis of the computer vision process lies in the acquisition of visual stimuli, typically in the form of discrete pixel arrays representing light intensity and color information, captured by an imaging sensor. The fidelity and modality of this initial data capture form the bedrock upon which subsequent analytical processes are built."
- **Example:** Imagine a security camera monitoring a hallway. The image acquisition step involves the camera's sensor capturing a series of still frames (for image processing) or a continuous stream of frames (for video processing) of the hallway environment over time. Each frame is essentially a grid of pixel values representing the visual information at that particular moment.

2. Preprocessing:

- **Explanation:** Raw images acquired from sensors often contain imperfections or may not be in an optimal format for direct analysis. Preprocessing techniques aim to enhance the image quality, reduce unwanted noise, and standardize the data to improve the performance of subsequent feature extraction and model training stages. Common preprocessing operations include:
    - **Noise Reduction:** Techniques like Gaussian blur or median filtering are applied to smooth out random variations in pixel intensities, which can obscure meaningful details.
    - **Image Resizing:** Images may be scaled up or down to a consistent size required by the processing pipeline or the machine learning model.
    - **Normalization:** Pixel intensity values are often scaled to a specific range (e.g., 0 to 1 or -1 to 1) to ensure numerical stability and faster convergence during model training.
    - **Contrast Enhancement:** Techniques like histogram equalization can improve the visibility of details in images with poor contrast.

- o **Color Space Conversion:** Images might be converted from one color space (e.g., RGB) to another (e.g., grayscale, HSV) depending on the specific task and the features being extracted.
- "Subsequent to image acquisition, a crucial phase of preprocessing ensues, wherein the raw visual data undergoes a series of transformations aimed at mitigating sensor-induced artifacts and standardizing the input format. These operations serve to enhance the signal-to-noise ratio and optimize the data for downstream analytical procedures."
- **Example:** Consider a medical image, like an X-ray, which might have some grainy noise. A preprocessing step could involve applying a median filter to reduce this noise, making the underlying anatomical structures clearer for subsequent analysis by a computer vision system designed to detect anomalies. Similarly, if the X-ray image is very large, it might be resized to a smaller, standardized dimension before being fed into a diagnostic model.

3. Feature Extraction:

- **Explanation:** This stage involves identifying and extracting salient information or "features" from the preprocessed image that are crucial for distinguishing between different objects or patterns. These features are essentially numerical representations of important visual characteristics. Early computer vision approaches relied on hand-engineered features, such as:
  - o **Edges:** Boundaries between regions of different pixel intensities, often indicative of object contours. Algorithms like Canny or Sobel are used for edge detection.
  - o **Corners:** Points in an image where edges intersect, providing important local information. The Harris corner detector is a classic example.
  - o **Shapes:** Representing the overall form of an object, often using techniques like Hough transforms to detect lines, circles, or other geometric shapes.
  - o **Textures:** Describing the surface properties of regions in an image, using methods like Local Binary Patterns (LBP) or Gabor filters.
  - o **Scale-Invariant Feature Transform (SIFT) and Speeded Up Robust Features (SURF):** These are more sophisticated algorithms that detect distinctive keypoints in an image that are invariant to changes in scale, rotation, and illumination.
- "The subsequent analytical stage involves the extraction of salient visual primitives, termed 'features,' which serve as compact and informative descriptors of the image content. These features, whether handcrafted based on domain-specific knowledge or learned through data-driven approaches, aim to capture the essential discriminatory attributes present within the visual data."
- **Example:** Imagine a computer vision system trying to identify different types of fruits in an image. Feature extraction might involve identifying the round shape and the smooth texture as characteristic features of an apple, while a longer, curved shape and a bumpy texture might be features associated with a banana. Algorithms like SIFT could detect unique keypoints on the fruit that remain consistent even if the fruit is rotated or partially obscured.

4. Model Training:

- **Explanation:** With the advent of deep learning, the paradigm of feature extraction has largely shifted towards learning these features directly from the data. Convolutional Neural Networks (CNNs) have become the dominant architecture for computer vision tasks. The model training process involves feeding a CNN with a large dataset of labeled images (e.g., images of cats labeled as "cat," images of dogs labeled as "dog"). During training, the CNN learns hierarchical representations of visual features through its convolutional layers, pooling layers, and fully connected layers. The network adjusts its internal parameters (weights and biases) iteratively based on the difference between its predictions and the ground truth labels, aiming to minimize a loss function.
- "The paradigm of modern computer vision heavily leverages data-driven learning methodologies, particularly Convolutional Neural Networks (CNNs). The training phase entails exposing these network architectures to vast quantities of annotated visual data, enabling them to autonomously learn hierarchical representations of image features. Through iterative optimization of network parameters based on a defined loss function, the model progressively refines its ability to map visual input to corresponding semantic labels or predictions."
- **Example:** To train a CNN to recognize cats and dogs, a massive dataset of images containing cats and dogs, with their respective labels, is used. The CNN processes these images, learns to identify distinctive features (e.g., pointy ears, whiskers for cats; floppy ears, snout for dogs), and adjusts its internal connections until it can accurately classify new, unseen images of cats and dogs.

5. Object Detection/Classification:

- **Explanation:** Once a model is trained, it can be used to perform various computer vision tasks on new, unseen images or video frames.
  - **Image Classification:** This task involves assigning a single label to an entire image, indicating the primary object or scene present (e.g., classifying an image as containing a "cat" or a "dog").
  - **Object Detection:** This is a more complex task that involves not only identifying the presence of specific objects in an image but also localizing them by drawing bounding boxes around each detected object. The output typically includes the class label for each detected object and its spatial coordinates within the image.
  - **Instance Segmentation:** This goes a step further than object detection by not only detecting and localizing objects but also delineating the precise pixel-level boundaries of each individual object instance in the image.
- "Upon successful completion of the training regimen, the learned model can be deployed to perform inferential tasks on novel visual data. This encompasses a spectrum of applications, ranging from holistic image categorization to the precise localization and identification of multiple object instances within a scene. Advanced methodologies extend to pixel-level segmentation, delineating the exact spatial extent of each detected entity."
- **Example (Classification):** Given a new photograph, an image classification model trained on animal datasets might output a prediction like "This image contains a cat" with a certain confidence score.

- **Example (Object Detection):** A self-driving car's computer vision system might process a camera frame and detect multiple objects, such as "pedestrian" with a bounding box around a person crossing the street, "car" with bounding boxes around other vehicles, and "traffic light" with a bounding box around the signal.
- **Example (Instance Segmentation):** In a medical imaging application, a segmentation model might not only detect the presence of multiple tumor cells but also precisely outline the boundaries of each individual tumor at the pixel level.

6. Post-processing:

- **Explanation:** The raw output from object detection or segmentation models can sometimes contain redundant or overlapping detections, or the predictions might need further refinement. Post-processing techniques are applied to enhance the model's decision and produce more coherent and accurate results. A common technique is **Non-Maximum Suppression (NMS)**. In object detection, NMS helps to filter out redundant bounding boxes that are predicting the same object. It works by selecting the bounding box with the highest confidence score and then suppressing other overlapping boxes with lower scores. Other post-processing steps might involve filtering predictions based on confidence thresholds, refining segmentation masks, or tracking objects across consecutive video frames.
- "The final stage in the computer vision pipeline often involves post-processing of the model's raw output to refine the predictions and ensure coherence. Techniques such as Non-Maximum Suppression (NMS) are employed to eliminate redundant detections, while other methodologies may focus on enhancing the spatial accuracy of segmentation masks or establishing temporal consistency in video analysis."
- **Example:** In the self-driving car scenario, the object detection model might initially output several overlapping bounding boxes around the same pedestrian. NMS would then analyze these boxes and retain only the one with the highest confidence score, effectively eliminating the redundant detections and providing a single, accurate bounding box around the pedestrian.

Example: Self-Driving Cars

As highlighted in your initial description, self-driving cars are a prime example of the intricate application of computer vision. Their "eyes" are a suite of cameras and other sensors that continuously capture the surrounding environment (Image Acquisition). The raw images are then preprocessed to remove noise and adjust for lighting conditions (Preprocessing). Sophisticated deep learning models, trained on vast datasets of road scenes, perform feature extraction and object detection/classification to identify critical elements such as lane markings, pedestrians, other vehicles, traffic signals, and road signs. Post-processing algorithms ensure the robustness and accuracy of these detections, enabling the car's control systems to make informed decisions and navigate autonomously.

Summary Table

Component	Purpose	Example Application
Machine Learning	Learning patterns from data	Stock market prediction
Deep Learning	Handling large-scale, unstructured data	Voice assistants
Neural Networks	Mimicking human brain processing	Medical image diagnosis
Natural Language Processing	Understanding and generating human language	Email spam detection
Computer Vision	Interpreting visual information	Autonomous vehicles

50 MCQ Questions with Answers

Machine Learning (10 Questions)

1. What is the primary goal of Machine Learning?

A) To manually program computers

B) To allow machines to learn from data

C) To create hardware components

D) To build websites

Answer: B

2. In supervised learning, the training data contains:

A) Only input data

B) Only output data

C) Both input and corresponding output

D) No labels

Answer: C

3. Which algorithm is used for classification problems?

A) K-Means Clustering

B) Linear Regression

C) Decision Tree

D) Principal Component Analysis

Answer: C

4. Which of the following is an unsupervised learning method?

A) Support Vector Machine

B) Logistic Regression

C) K-Means Clustering

D) Linear Regression

Answer: C

5. Overfitting occurs when a model:

A) Learns too little

B) Performs poorly on training data

C) Memorizes the training data perfectly

D) Ignores the input data

Answer: C

6. Which technique helps prevent overfitting?

A) Increasing learning rate

B) Adding more layers

C) Regularization

D) Decreasing data size

Answer: C

7. What is the output of a regression problem?

A) Category

B) Discrete label

C) Continuous value

D) Cluster

Answer: C

8. In Machine Learning, "feature" refers to:

A) A program

B) An algorithm

C) An individual measurable property

D) A label

Answer: C

9. Which evaluation metric is used for classification?

A) Mean Squared Error

B) Accuracy

C) R-Squared

D) Root Mean Squared Error

Answer: B

10. In reinforcement learning, the agent learns by:

A) Being supervised

B) Receiving rewards or penalties

C) Clustering the data

D) Predicting continuous values

Answer: B

Deep Learning (10 Questions)

11. Deep Learning models are typically based on:

A) Decision Trees

B) Support Vector Machines

C) Neural Networks

D) Rule-based Systems

Answer: C

12. What is a key characteristic of Deep Learning?

A) Manual feature engineering

B) Shallow structures

C) Automatic feature extraction

D) Simple linear models

Answer: C

13. A very deep neural network is likely to suffer from:

A) Underfitting

B) Overfitting

C) Vanishing Gradient Problem

D) Data redundancy

Answer: C

14. Which Deep Learning model is commonly used for image data?

A) RNN

B) CNN

C) Naive Bayes

D) Random Forest

Answer: B

15. LSTM networks are mainly used for:

A) Image classification

B) Time-series data

C) Object detection

D) Clustering

Answer: B

16. Which optimizer is widely used in Deep Learning?

A) Newton's Method

B) Genetic Algorithm

C) Adam Optimizer

D) Hill Climbing

Answer: C

17. Dropout technique is used to:

A) Increase training time

B) Prevent overfitting

C) Speed up predictions

D) Store weights

Answer: B

18. ReLU activation function is mostly used because:

A) It's complex

B) It introduces non-linearity

C) It's linear

D) It normalizes data

Answer: B

19. In Deep Learning, the term "epoch" refers to:

A) One complete pass through all training samples

B) One forward pass only

C) Random sampling

D) Parameter tuning

Answer: A

20. Deep Learning requires:

A) Small datasets

B) Large amounts of labeled data

C) No data at all

D) Only numerical data

Answer: B

Neural Networks (10 Questions)

21. Neural Networks are inspired by:

A) Computer networks

B) Telephone networks

C) Biological neurons

D) Mathematical graphs

Answer: C

22. In an Artificial Neural Network, the function applied at each node is called:

A) Error function

B) Activation function

C) Cost function

D) Learning function

Answer: B

23. The simplest type of neural network is known as:

A) Convolutional Neural Network

B) Recurrent Neural Network

C) Perceptron

D) Multilayer Perceptron

Answer: C

24. Which architecture is suitable for sequence data?

A) CNN

B) RNN

C) GAN

D) DBN

Answer: B

25. A neuron in a neural network computes:

A) Sum of inputs only

B) Weighted sum followed by activation

C) Multiplication of inputs

D) Sorting of inputs

Answer: B

26. Backpropagation is used to:

A) Find clusters

B) Update weights in neural networks

C) Visualize data

D) Collect data

Answer: B

27. Which of the following is not an activation function?

A) Sigmoid

B) Tanh

C) ReLU

D) SVM

Answer: D

28. What is the typical range of outputs for a sigmoid activation function?

A) 0 to 1

B) -1 to 1

C) 0 to infinity

D) -infinity to +infinity

Answer: A

29. Which activation function is best suited to output probabilities?

A) ReLU

B) Softmax

C) Tanh

D) Sigmoid

Answer: B

30. Gradient Descent algorithm minimizes:

A) Activation

B) Loss function

C) Accuracy

D) Output layer

Answer: B

Natural Language Processing (NLP) (10 Questions)

31. NLP stands for:

A) Natural Light Processing

B) Neural Learning Processing

C) Natural Language Processing

D) Neural Logic Prediction

Answer: C

32. Which task is NOT part of NLP?

A) Speech Recognition

B) Text Summarization

C) Image Classification

D) Sentiment Analysis

Answer: C

33. Tokenization is the process of:

A) Combining words

B) Splitting text into smaller units

C) Translating text

D) Encrypting text

Answer: B

34. POS tagging stands for:

A) Probability of Speech

B) Part of Speech tagging

C) Part of Sentiment tagging

D) Programming of Syntax

Answer: B

35. Word Embeddings are used to:

A) Sort documents alphabetically

B) Reduce vocabulary size

C) Represent words as vectors

D) Encrypt the text

Answer: C

36. Which of the following is an example of a word embedding model?

A) KNN

B) Word2Vec

C) CNN

D) RNN

Answer: B

37. Named Entity Recognition (NER) identifies:

A) Random words

B) Parts of speech

C) Specific names and places

D) Grammar mistakes

Answer: C

38. TF-IDF is used for:

A) Text encoding

B) Image compression

C) Feature extraction from text

D) Data encryption

Answer: C

39. Which model architecture powers Google Translate?

A) Convolutional Networks

B) Recurrent Neural Networks

C) Transformer Networks

D) Decision Trees

Answer: C

40. In NLP, Stopwords are:

A) Important keywords

B) Common words filtered out

C) Technical terms

D) Sentiment words

Answer: B

Computer Vision (10 Questions)

41. Computer Vision enables machines to:

A) Hear sounds

B) Understand text

C) See and interpret images

D) Make phone calls

Answer: C

42. A popular deep learning model for image tasks is:

A) CNN

B) RNN

C) SVM

D) LDA

Answer: A

43. Object detection identifies:

A) Sentences in a paragraph

B) Specific objects and their locations in an image

C) Grammar mistakes

D) Voice commands

Answer: B

44. Image classification assigns:

A) A numeric value to each image

B) A class label to an image

C) A sound to an image

D) A text to an image

Answer: B

45. Face recognition is an application of:

A) NLP

B) Reinforcement Learning

C) Computer Vision

D) Genetic Algorithms

Answer: C

46. Which technique is used to reduce image dimensions?

A) Feature Scaling

B) Principal Component Analysis (PCA)

C) Linear Regression

D) K-Means

Answer: B

47. Edge detection is useful for:

A) Finding sharp changes in images

B) Smoothing images

C) Compressing images

D) De-noising images

Answer: A

48. The convolution operation in CNNs mainly does:

A) Activation

B) Feature extraction

C) Weight adjustment

D) Normalization

Answer: B

49. Pooling layers are used in CNN to:

A) Increase image size

B) Decrease computational complexity

C) Create new images

D) Perform clustering

Answer: B

50. Image segmentation divides an image into:

A) Different shapes

B) Different languages

C) Different regions/objects

D) Different sounds

Answer: C

CHAPTER 3: HOW AI "THINKS"

In this chapter, we will explore how Artificial Intelligence (AI) "thinks" — its core mechanisms, algorithms, decision-making processes, and learning strategies. We will discuss the essential methods AI uses to analyze data, make decisions, and improve its performance. Additionally, we'll uncover the challenges AI faces, such as biases in AI systems.

Algorithms and Decision-Making in Artificial Intelligence

What is an Algorithm?

At its fundamental level, an **algorithm** represents a well-defined, finite sequence of unambiguous instructions meticulously designed to solve a specific problem or accomplish a particular task. In the realm of Artificial Intelligence, algorithms serve as the computational engines that empower machines to process vast quantities of data, derive meaningful insights, make informed decisions, and exhibit learning behaviors over time. Essentially, an algorithm provides the AI system with a structured and logical framework for "thinking" and acting.

"An algorithm, within the context of computational systems and particularly in Artificial Intelligence, constitutes a precise and deterministic set of procedural steps that, when executed, transform a given input into a desired output or achieve a specified computational goal. It embodies the logical blueprint that guides the AI's cognitive processes, enabling it to reason, learn, and interact with its environment in a purposeful manner."

Types of Algorithms in AI:

The field of AI employs a diverse array of algorithmic approaches, each tailored to address specific types of problems and computational demands. Here, we delve deeper into some common categories:

1. Search Algorithms:

- **Explanation:** Search algorithms are instrumental in navigating through a defined "problem space" – a set of all possible states or solutions – to locate a specific target state or an optimal solution. These algorithms systematically explore the problem space based on predefined rules and strategies.
  - **Breadth-First Search (BFS):**
    - **Explanation:** BFS is a graph traversal algorithm that explores all the neighbor nodes at the present depth level before moving on to the nodes at the next depth level. It systematically expands the search frontier layer by layer. This ensures that the algorithm finds the shortest path (in terms of the number of steps) from the starting node to the goal node in an unweighted graph.
    - "Breadth-First Search operates by exhaustively examining all nodes at a given depth within the search space prior to proceeding to nodes at the

subsequent depth. This level-by-level exploration guarantees the discovery of the shortest path in terms of edge count from the initial state to the target state."

- **Example:** Consider an AI tasked with finding the shortest route between two cities on a map. Using BFS, the AI would first explore all cities directly connected to the starting city, then all cities connected to those neighbors, and so on, expanding outwards in concentric circles until the destination city is reached. This ensures the route with the fewest intermediate stops is found.

- **Depth-First Search (DFS):**
  - **Explanation:** DFS is another graph traversal algorithm that explores as far as possible along each branch before backtracking. It delves deep into one path until it reaches a dead end or the goal is found, and then it backtracks to explore other branches. DFS can be implemented recursively or iteratively using a stack.
  - "Depth-First Search employs a strategy of exhaustive exploration along a single path within the search space until a terminal state or a predefined depth limit is encountered. Upon reaching such a point, the algorithm backtracks to the most recent unvisited node and continues its exploration along an alternative path."
  - **Example:** Imagine an AI solving a maze. Using DFS, the AI might choose a direction and follow it until it hits a wall. Then, it would backtrack to the last intersection and try a different path. This approach can quickly find a solution if one exists along a particular deep path, but it might not necessarily find the shortest path.

2. Optimization Algorithms:

- **Explanation:** Optimization algorithms are designed to find the best possible solution from a set of feasible solutions, often by maximizing or minimizing an objective function that quantifies the quality of a solution. These algorithms are crucial in machine learning for tuning model parameters and in various AI applications for decision-making under constraints.
  - **Gradient Descent:**
    - **Explanation:** Gradient Descent is a foundational optimization algorithm widely used in training machine learning models, particularly neural networks. Its primary goal is to minimize a cost or loss function, which measures the discrepancy between the model's predictions and the actual values in the training data. The algorithm iteratively adjusts the model's parameters (e.g., weights and biases) in the direction of the negative gradient of the loss function. The gradient indicates the direction of the steepest increase in the loss, so moving in the opposite direction leads towards a minimum. The "learning rate" controls the size of the steps taken during each iteration.
    - "Gradient Descent is an iterative optimization technique that seeks to minimize a differentiable objective function by repeatedly moving in the

direction of the negative gradient. In the context of machine learning, this algorithm is instrumental in adjusting model parameters to reduce the discrepancy between predicted and actual outputs, with the step size governed by a parameter known as the learning rate."

- **Example:** Consider training a linear regression model to predict house prices based on their size. The loss function might measure the average squared difference between the predicted prices and the actual prices in the training data. Gradient descent would iteratively adjust the slope and intercept of the regression line by calculating the gradient of the loss function with respect to these parameters and moving in the opposite direction until a minimum loss (i.e., the best-fitting line) is found.

3. Decision Trees:

- **Explanation:** Decision Trees are supervised learning algorithms that model decisions and their potential consequences in a hierarchical, tree-like structure. Each internal node in the tree represents a test on an attribute (a feature of the data), each branch represents the outcome of that test, and each leaf node represents a class label or a predicted value. Decision trees [1] partition the data based on a series of sequential decisions, ultimately leading to a classification or regression outcome.

- "Decision Trees are hierarchical classification or regression models that partition the input space into rectangular regions. Each internal node corresponds to a test on an attribute, with branches representing the possible outcomes of the test. The leaf nodes of the tree contain the predicted class label or value for instances that fall into the corresponding region."

- **Example:** An AI system designed to decide whether to approve a loan application might use a decision tree. The root node could test the applicant's credit score. If the score is above 700, the tree might branch to a node testing their income level. If the income is above a certain threshold, the tree might lead to a leaf node predicting "Approve Loan." Conversely, if the credit score is below 700, the tree might branch to a node testing their debt-to-income ratio, and based on that, lead to either "Approve Loan with Conditions" or "Reject Loan." The path taken through the tree for a specific loan application determines the final decision.

How AI Makes Decisions:

AI systems make decisions by employing algorithms to evaluate various available options based on the data they have been trained on or the rules they have been programmed with. The decision-making process can range from simple rule-based systems to complex evaluations performed by sophisticated machine learning models.

- **Simple Decision-Making (Rule-Based Systems):** In basic AI systems, decisions might be made using a set of predefined rules, often expressed as "if-then-else" statements. The AI evaluates the current situation against these rules and takes the action associated with the first rule that matches.

- **Complex Decision-Making (Machine Learning Models):** More advanced AI systems, particularly those based on machine learning, make decisions by evaluating patterns learned from large datasets. For instance, a neural network, after being trained, takes an input, processes it through its layers of interconnected nodes, and produces an output that represents a decision or a prediction. The "evaluation" here involves complex mathematical computations based on the learned weights and biases within the network.

"The decision-making process in AI systems hinges on the algorithmic evaluation of available choices in light of the system's knowledge base or learned representations. This evaluation can manifest as the application of explicit rule sets or the complex inferential computations performed by trained machine learning models, ultimately leading to the selection of the option deemed most optimal according to the system's objectives."

Example: E-commerce Product Recommendations:

Consider an AI system powering product recommendations on an e-commerce website. This AI might employ a combination of algorithms and decision-making processes:

1. **Data Collection:** The AI gathers data on customer behavior, including purchase history, browsing patterns, items added to wishlists, and demographic information.
2. **Feature Engineering:** Algorithms are used to extract relevant features from this data, such as frequently co-purchased items, categories of interest, and customer segments with similar preferences.
3. **Recommendation Algorithm (e.g., Collaborative Filtering, Content-Based Filtering, or a hybrid approach):**
   - **Collaborative Filtering:** This algorithm identifies users with similar purchase histories and recommends items that those similar users have liked or purchased. The decision of which items to recommend is based on the preferences of a "neighborhood" of similar users.
   - **Content-Based Filtering:** This algorithm recommends items that are similar to those the user has previously interacted with. The decision is based on the features of the items the user has shown interest in.
   - **Hybrid Approach:** This combines the strengths of both methods to provide more robust and personalized recommendations.
4. **Decision Tree (as a post-processing step):** After the recommendation algorithm generates a list of potential products, a decision tree might be used to further refine the recommendations based on factors like:
   - **Inventory Levels:** If a recommended item is out of stock, the decision tree might branch to suggest a similar alternative that is currently available.
   - **Promotions:** If a recommended item is part of a current promotion, the decision tree might prioritize its display to encourage sales.
   - **User Context:** Factors like the time of day or whether the user is a new or returning customer might influence the final recommendations based on rules embedded in the decision tree.

In this example, the AI uses sophisticated algorithms to analyze user data and predict relevant products. The final decision of which products to display is then influenced by additional rules and considerations, potentially implemented through a decision tree, to optimize the user experience and business goals.

By understanding the principles of algorithms and decision-making, we gain crucial insights into how AI systems operate, learn, and interact with the world around them. The choice and design of these algorithms are fundamental to the capabilities and effectiveness of any AI application.

Learning from Data in Artificial Intelligence: Supervised, Unsupervised, and Reinforcement

Artificial Intelligence systems acquire knowledge and refine their capabilities through the process of learning from data. This fundamental aspect of AI is primarily categorized into three distinct paradigms: supervised learning, unsupervised learning, and reinforcement learning, each with its unique approach to data utilization and learning objectives. Let's delve into each of these methodologies in detail.

Supervised Learning:

- **Explanation:** Supervised learning is a learning paradigm where an AI model is trained on a dataset that is meticulously **labeled**. This implies that for each input data point (comprising various features or attributes), the corresponding correct output or target variable (the "label") is provided. The core objective of supervised learning is for the AI to discern the underlying relationship or mapping function between the input features and their respective output labels. Once this relationship is learned during the training phase, the model can then generalize this knowledge to predict the correct output for new, unseen input data.
- "Supervised learning constitutes a paradigm of machine learning wherein an algorithm is presented with a training dataset comprising instances that are explicitly associated with their corresponding target outputs or labels. The learning objective is to induce a functional mapping from the input feature space to the output space, enabling the model to accurately predict the labels of novel, unobserved data points based on the learned relationships."
- **Steps:**
  1. **Data Collection:** The initial step involves the meticulous collection of a comprehensive dataset. Each data instance within this dataset consists of a set of input features (the independent variables) and their corresponding known output label (the dependent variable). The quality and representativeness of this labeled data are paramount to the success of the supervised learning process.
     - **Example:** In a medical diagnosis scenario, the dataset might include patient records with features like age, blood pressure, symptoms, and the

corresponding label indicating whether the patient has a particular disease or not.

2. **Model Training:** During the training phase, a chosen supervised learning algorithm (e.g., linear regression, logistic regression, support vector machines, decision trees, neural networks) is fed the labeled training data. The algorithm iteratively adjusts its internal parameters to minimize the error between its predictions and the true labels provided in the training data. This process aims to learn the intricate patterns and relationships that link the input features to the output labels.

   - **Example:** For the email spam detection task, a logistic regression model would be trained on a dataset of emails labeled as "spam" or "not spam." The model would learn the weights associated with different words and features in the email text that are indicative of spam or legitimate emails.

3. **Prediction:** Once the training process is complete and the model has learned the underlying mapping, it can be deployed to make predictions on new, unseen data points for which the true labels are unknown. The model takes the input features of the new data and, based on the learned relationship, outputs a predicted label.

   - **Example:** When a new, unclassified email arrives, the trained spam detection model analyzes its text and features, and based on the patterns it learned during training, predicts whether the email is "spam" or "not spam."

- **Example:** A classic illustration of supervised learning is **image classification**. An AI is trained on a vast dataset of images where each image is labeled with the object it contains (e.g., "cat," "dog," "car"). The AI learns to identify visual features (e.g., shapes, textures, colors) associated with each label. Once trained, the model can take a new, unlabeled image and predict the object present in it.

Unsupervised Learning:

- **Explanation:** In contrast to supervised learning, unsupervised learning deals with datasets that lack explicit labels. The primary objective here is for the AI to autonomously discover inherent patterns, structures, or relationships within the unlabeled data. This type of learning is particularly useful when we do not have prior knowledge about the data's underlying categories or when the goal is to gain insights into the data's natural organization.

- "Unsupervised learning encompasses a class of machine learning techniques applied to datasets devoid of explicit output labels. The central aim is to uncover latent structures, groupings, or associations within the data distribution, enabling the identification of inherent patterns and the extraction of meaningful insights without prior specification of target variables."

- **Steps:**
   1. **Data Collection:** The initial step involves gathering a dataset that contains input features but no corresponding output labels. The focus is on the inherent characteristics and distributions of the data points themselves.

- **Example:** A dataset for customer segmentation might include information about customers' purchase history, browsing behavior, demographics, but without any pre-assigned customer segments.

2. **Clustering or Association:** The AI employs unsupervised learning algorithms to analyze the unlabeled data. Common tasks include:
   - **Clustering:** Grouping similar data points together based on their intrinsic characteristics. Algorithms like K-means, DBSCAN, and hierarchical clustering are used to identify clusters.
   - **Association Rule Mining:** Discovering interesting relationships or associations between different variables in the dataset. The Apriori algorithm is a well-known technique for this.
   - **Dimensionality Reduction:** Reducing the number of variables in the dataset while preserving its essential structure. Techniques like Principal Component Analysis (PCA) and t-SNE fall under this category and can aid in visualization and pattern discovery.
   - **Example (Clustering):** Applying a K-means clustering algorithm to the customer purchase data might reveal distinct groups of customers who exhibit similar buying patterns (e.g., those who frequently buy electronics, those who primarily purchase clothing, etc.).
   - **Example (Association):** Using association rule mining on a market basket analysis dataset might reveal that customers who buy bread and butter frequently also buy milk.

3. **Insight Extraction:** The final step involves interpreting the patterns or structures discovered by the AI. This might involve understanding the characteristics of the identified clusters, the nature of the associations between data points, or the key underlying dimensions of the data.
   - **Example:** In the market segmentation scenario, the identified customer clusters can provide valuable insights for targeted marketing campaigns and product recommendations tailored to each segment's preferences.

- **Example: Anomaly detection** is a significant application of unsupervised learning. An AI is trained on a dataset of normal system behavior (e.g., network traffic patterns). Without explicit labels for anomalies, the AI learns the typical patterns. When new data arrives, the AI can identify data points that deviate significantly from the learned normal behavior, flagging them as potential anomalies (e.g., network intrusions, fraudulent transactions).

Reinforcement Learning:

- **Explanation:** Reinforcement learning is a paradigm where an AI agent learns to make decisions by interacting with its environment. The agent takes actions within the environment and receives feedback in the form of rewards (positive signals for desirable actions) or penalties (negative signals for undesirable actions). The agent's goal is to learn an optimal policy – a strategy that dictates which action to take in each state of the environment – to maximize its cumulative reward over time. This learning process often involves a balance between exploration (trying out new actions) and exploitation (leveraging actions that have yielded high rewards in the past).

- "Reinforcement learning is a goal-oriented learning paradigm wherein an autonomous agent learns to behave optimally in a dynamic environment through iterative interaction. The agent performs actions and receives scalar feedback signals, termed rewards or penalties, which serve to guide the learning process towards maximizing the cumulative reward over a sequence of interactions. This paradigm necessitates a balance between exploring the state-action space and exploiting learned policies."
- **Steps:**
  1. **Exploration:** The AI agent begins by exploring the environment, trying out different actions in various states. Initially, its actions might be random or based on a predefined exploration strategy.
     - **Example:** In a video game, an AI agent might randomly try different joystick movements and button presses to see what happens.
  2. **Reward:** After each action, the environment provides feedback to the agent in the form of a reward or a penalty. The reward signal indicates how good the action was in relation to the agent's goal.
     - **Example:** In the video game, the agent might receive a positive reward for collecting a power-up or defeating an enemy, and a negative reward (penalty) for losing health or dying.
  3. **Optimization:** Based on the received rewards and penalties, the AI agent adjusts its strategy (policy) to learn which actions are most likely to lead to higher cumulative rewards in the long run. This often involves using algorithms like Q-learning or policy gradients to update the agent's understanding of the value of different states and actions.
     - **Example:** Over time, the video game-playing agent learns that certain sequences of actions (e.g., jumping and shooting at a specific time) consistently lead to higher scores and level completion, and it starts to favor these actions.
- **Example:** Training an AI to control a **robotic arm** to perform a specific task, such as picking up an object. The robot explores different movements of its joints (exploration). If the arm gets closer to the object, it receives a small positive reward. If it drops the object or moves away, it receives a negative reward (penalty). Through repeated trials and feedback, the AI learns the optimal sequence of movements to successfully grasp the object (optimization).

Biases in AI Systems

What is Bias in AI?

Bias in Artificial Intelligence refers to systematic and unfair tendencies within AI systems that result in skewed predictions, discriminatory decisions, or inequitable outcomes for certain individuals or groups. These biases can originate from various sources, including prejudiced data used for training, inherent limitations or flaws in the algorithms themselves, or biased human interactions with the AI system. The presence of bias in AI is a critical concern, particularly as these systems are increasingly deployed in high-stakes domains such as hiring processes, law enforcement, financial services, and healthcare, where unfair outcomes can have profound societal consequences.

"Bias in the context of Artificial Intelligence denotes a systematic deviation from fairness or accuracy in an AI system's outputs or behaviors, leading to differential and often detrimental effects on specific demographic groups or individuals. This phenomenon can manifest as a result of skewed training data, inherent limitations within the algorithmic design, or prejudiced human input, thereby undermining the principles of equity and justice in AI applications."

Types of Bias in AI:

The emergence of bias in AI systems can be attributed to several key sources:

1. Data Bias:

- **Explanation:** AI algorithms are fundamentally data-driven; they learn patterns and relationships from the historical data they are trained on. Consequently, if this training data reflects existing societal biases, historical inequalities, or underrepresentation of certain demographic groups, the AI system will inevitably learn and perpetuate these biases in its predictions and decisions. This is a particularly prevalent issue in domains where historical data captures past discriminatory practices. A well-cited example is the reduced accuracy of early facial recognition systems for individuals with darker skin tones, a direct consequence of training datasets that predominantly featured images of lighter-skinned individuals. Studies have shown significantly higher error rates for darker-skinned individuals compared to lighter-skinned individuals in certain facial recognition technologies due to this data imbalance.
- "Data bias arises when the training dataset utilized to develop an AI model inadequately or unfairly represents the diversity of the real-world population or phenomenon it is intended to model. This skewed representation leads the AI to learn and amplify existing societal prejudices or historical disparities, resulting in outputs that disproportionately disadvantage underrepresented groups."
- **Example:** Consider a hiring AI system trained on a decade of hiring data from a company where the workforce in technical roles was historically predominantly male. If the training data lacks sufficient representation of qualified female applicants who were either not hired due to past biases or did not apply due to systemic barriers, the AI might learn to associate maleness with success in these roles. Consequently, when presented with applications from equally qualified male and female candidates, the AI might unfairly favor male applicants, not based on their actual skills or qualifications, but due to the patterns it learned from the biased historical data.

2. Algorithmic Bias:

- **Explanation:** Even in scenarios where the training data is seemingly balanced and representative, biases can still be introduced or amplified by the design and implementation of the algorithm itself. This can occur when the algorithm inherently prioritizes certain features or attributes over others in a way that leads to unfair outcomes for specific groups. The choice of model architecture, the objective function used during training, or specific constraints imposed on the model can unintentionally encode biases. For instance, an algorithm might be designed to optimize for a specific metric that correlates with a protected attribute (like zip code correlating with race or socioeconomic status), leading to discriminatory outcomes even without explicitly using the protected attribute as a feature.

- "Algorithmic bias refers to the introduction of systematic errors or unfairness into an AI system's outputs as a consequence of the inherent design, assumptions, or optimization objectives of the algorithm itself. This can manifest even when the training data is ostensibly unbiased, as the algorithmic structure may inadvertently prioritize certain features or decision boundaries that lead to disparate impacts across different groups."

- **Example:** Imagine a loan approval algorithm that, while not directly using race as a feature, heavily weighs the applicant's zip code as an indicator of creditworthiness. If historical redlining practices have resulted in lower-income neighborhoods (which may disproportionately consist of certain racial or ethnic groups) having lower average credit scores, the algorithm might unfairly deny loans to creditworthy individuals residing in these zip codes, effectively perpetuating historical discriminatory patterns through an ostensibly neutral feature.

3. Interaction Bias:

- **Explanation:** Interaction bias arises from the way humans interact with and influence AI systems throughout their lifecycle, from data labeling and annotation to deployment and feedback. If human annotators hold conscious or unconscious biases when labeling data, these biases will be learned by the AI. Similarly, if user feedback mechanisms are skewed or if the AI is deployed in an environment where human biases influence its inputs or interpretations, this can lead to biased outcomes. For example, if law enforcement officers disproportionately flag individuals from certain racial groups in a crime database used to train a risk assessment AI, this human bias in labeling will directly impact the fairness of the AI's risk predictions.

- "Interaction bias emerges from the influence of human actions, beliefs, or prejudices on the development and deployment of AI systems. This can occur during data annotation, where human labelers may introduce their own biases, or through skewed feedback loops and usage patterns that reinforce or amplify existing societal biases within the AI's behavior."

- **Example:** Consider an AI system used in a criminal justice system to assess the risk of recidivism (the likelihood of re-offending). If human operators, consciously or unconsciously, label individuals from certain racial or ethnic groups as higher risk based on prejudiced criteria rather than objective evidence, the AI trained on this labeled data will learn to associate these demographic factors with higher risk. Consequently, the AI will likely produce biased risk assessments, potentially leading to harsher sentencing or denial of parole for individuals from these groups, irrespective of their actual risk level.

Mitigating Bias in AI:

Addressing and mitigating bias in AI systems is a multifaceted and ongoing challenge that requires a combination of technical, ethical, and societal approaches. Key strategies include:

- **Diverse Data:** Ensuring that the training data used to develop AI models is representative of the real-world population and includes a broad and diverse range of demographics, characteristics, and scenarios. Actively seeking out and incorporating underrepresented data is crucial.
- **Bias Detection:** Implementing rigorous testing and auditing procedures to proactively identify and quantify potential biases in AI models throughout their development and deployment lifecycle. This involves using fairness metrics to assess whether the model's predictions or decisions disproportionately affect certain groups.
- **Transparency and Fairness:** Striving for greater transparency in the AI decision-making process, making it more explainable and understandable. Additionally, explicitly incorporating fairness constraints and ethical considerations into the design and training of AI algorithms to ensure they adhere to principles of equity and non-discrimination.
- **Example:** To mitigate gender bias in hiring systems, companies might focus on:
  - **Data Augmentation:** Actively seeking and including more data on successful female candidates in historically male-dominated roles.
  - **Blinding Data:** Removing demographic information like gender, race, and age from resumes and applications during the initial screening process to prevent the AI from learning biased associations.
  - **Fairness Metrics:** Evaluating the AI's performance using fairness metrics that assess whether male and female candidates with similar qualifications receive similar scores or advancement opportunities.
  - **Algorithmic Auditing:** Regularly auditing the hiring algorithm to identify and address any unintentional biases in how it weighs different features and makes recommendations.

By diligently addressing these sources of bias and implementing robust mitigation strategies, we can strive to develop AI systems that are more equitable, just, and beneficial for all members of society. The ongoing research and development in the field of fair and ethical AI are crucial for realizing the positive potential of this technology while minimizing its risks.

40 multiple-choice questions (MCQs) on the topics of **Algorithms and Decision-Making**, **Learning from Data (Supervised, Unsupervised, and Reinforcement Learning)**, and **Biases in AI Systems**, along with their answers:

Algorithms and Decision-Making

1. **What is an algorithm in AI?**
   - a) A set of instructions to solve a problem
   - b) A type of data storage
   - c) A method for calculating data
   - d) A machine learning model
   - **Answer:** a) A set of instructions to solve a problem
2. **Which of the following is NOT a type of search algorithm in AI?**

- a) Breadth-First Search
- b) Depth-First Search
- c) Binary Search
- d) Naive Bayes Algorithm
- **Answer:** d) Naive Bayes Algorithm

3. **What is the primary function of optimization algorithms in AI?**
   - a) To make decisions based on input data
   - b) To find the best solution from a set of possible solutions
   - c) To classify data into categories
   - d) To segment data into groups
   - **Answer:** b) To find the best solution from a set of possible solutions

4. **Which of the following decision-making models is used to make decisions based on a series of if-else conditions?**
   - a) Neural Networks
   - b) Decision Trees
   - c) Genetic Algorithms
   - d) Linear Regression
   - **Answer:** b) Decision Trees

5. **In the context of AI, what is a decision tree used for?**
   - a) To cluster data into different groups
   - b) To make predictions based on input features
   - c) To optimize the solution of an equation
   - d) To visualize data distributions
   - **Answer:** b) To make predictions based on input features

6. **Which of the following is a key characteristic of algorithms in AI decision-making?**
   - a) They always lead to optimal solutions
   - b) They are deterministic and provide the same result for the same input
   - c) They can only be used for classification problems
   - d) They ignore feedback and environmental changes
   - **Answer:** b) They are deterministic and provide the same result for the same input

7. **Which algorithm is commonly used to minimize the error in machine learning models?**
   - a) K-means clustering
   - b) Gradient Descent
   - c) K-nearest neighbors
   - d) Random Forest
   - **Answer:** b) Gradient Descent

8. **What is the main purpose of AI algorithms in decision-making?**
   - a) To predict the future without input data
   - b) To process large amounts of data and find patterns
   - c) To analyze data without any decision-making process
   - d) To execute decision-making without human intervention
   - **Answer:** b) To process large amounts of data and find patterns

9. **Which search algorithm expands all nodes at the present depth level before moving on to the next level?**
   - a) Depth-First Search
   - b) A* Algorithm
   - c) Breadth-First Search
   - d) Binary Search

- o **Answer:** c) Breadth-First Search
10. **Which is an example of a greedy algorithm?**
    - o a) Decision Tree
    - o b) A* Algorithm
    - o c) Knapsack Problem
    - o d) Depth-First Search
    - o **Answer:** c) Knapsack Problem

Learning from Data: Supervised, Unsupervised, and Reinforcement Learning

11. **In supervised learning, what type of data is used for training?**
    - o a) Labeled data
    - o b) Unlabeled data
    - o c) Reinforcement data
    - o d) Data with noise
    - o **Answer:** a) Labeled data
12. **Which of the following is an example of supervised learning?**
    - o a) Image recognition
    - o b) Customer segmentation
    - o c) Market basket analysis
    - o d) Fraud detection
    - o **Answer:** a) Image recognition
13. **In unsupervised learning, the AI is trained on:**
    - o a) Labeled data
    - o b) Unlabeled data
    - o c) Supervised data
    - o d) Reinforcement data
    - o **Answer:** b) Unlabeled data
14. **Which technique is commonly used for unsupervised learning?**
    - o a) K-means clustering
    - o b) Linear Regression
    - o c) Decision Trees
    - o d) Support Vector Machines
    - o **Answer:** a) K-means clustering
15. **Which of the following is an example of unsupervised learning?**
    - o a) Predicting house prices
    - o b) Classifying emails as spam or not spam
    - o c) Market segmentation
    - o d) Identifying diseases from medical images
    - o **Answer:** c) Market segmentation
16. **What is the primary goal of reinforcement learning?**
    - o a) To predict outputs from labeled data
    - o b) To find hidden patterns in data
    - o c) To maximize rewards through trial and error
    - o d) To classify data into predefined categories
    - o **Answer:** c) To maximize rewards through trial and error

17. **In reinforcement learning, what does the "agent" do?**
    - o a) Interacts with the environment
    - o b) Labels data
    - o c) Detects anomalies
    - o d) Classifies data into groups
    - o **Answer:** a) Interacts with the environment
18. **What is the purpose of the "reward" in reinforcement learning?**
    - o a) To provide feedback to the agent about its actions
    - o b) To label the data for classification
    - o c) To optimize the machine learning model
    - o d) To clean the input data
    - o **Answer:** a) To provide feedback to the agent about its actions
19. **Which of the following is a key difference between supervised and unsupervised learning?**
    - o a) Supervised learning uses labeled data, while unsupervised learning uses unlabeled data
    - o b) Unsupervised learning uses labeled data, while supervised learning uses unlabeled data
    - o c) Unsupervised learning requires more computational power
    - o d) Supervised learning is slower than unsupervised learning
    - o **Answer:** a) Supervised learning uses labeled data, while unsupervised learning uses unlabeled data
20. **Which learning technique is best suited for game-playing AI (e.g., chess or Go)?**
    - o a) Supervised Learning
    - o b) Unsupervised Learning
    - o c) Reinforcement Learning
    - o d) Deep Learning
    - o **Answer:** c) Reinforcement Learning

Biases in AI Systems

21. **What is bias in AI systems?**
    - o a) The AI system's ability to make decisions without human intervention
    - o b) Systematic errors or unfair outcomes caused by prejudiced data or algorithms
    - o c) The system's ability to recognize patterns in data
    - o d) The failure of AI to learn from data
    - o **Answer:** b) Systematic errors or unfair outcomes caused by prejudiced data or algorithms
22. **Which of the following is a type of bias that occurs due to prejudiced or unrepresentative data?**
    - o a) Algorithmic Bias
    - o b) Data Bias
    - o c) Interaction Bias
    - o d) Statistical Bias
    - o **Answer:** b) Data Bias
23. **What is one example of data bias in AI?**
    - o a) A facial recognition system that performs poorly on people with darker skin tones

- o b) A model that optimizes search results based on user preferences
- o c) A reinforcement learning agent learning the optimal path to a goal
- o d) A supervised learning model classifying emails as spam
- o **Answer:** a) A facial recognition system that performs poorly on people with darker skin tones

24. **How can algorithmic bias be reduced?**
- o a) By increasing the complexity of the algorithm
- o b) By using more data
- o c) By ensuring that the algorithm is transparent and auditable
- o d) By reducing the size of the dataset
- o **Answer:** c) By ensuring that the algorithm is transparent and auditable

25. **What is a potential consequence of bias in AI decision-making systems?**
- o a) Improved predictions and outcomes
- o b) More fairness and equality
- o c) Unfair, discriminatory decisions
- o d) Increased computational efficiency
- o **Answer:** c) Unfair, discriminatory decisions

26. **Which of the following is NOT a common form of bias in AI systems?**
- o a) Data Bias
- o b) Algorithmic Bias
- o c) Reinforcement Bias
- o d) Interaction Bias
- o **Answer:** c) Reinforcement Bias

27. **Which of the following is an example of interaction bias?**
- o a) Biased results caused by human labeling of data
- o b) Bias introduced by flawed training data
- o c) Discrimination due to model errors
- o d) Lack of diversity in the training dataset
- o **Answer:** a) Biased results caused by human labeling of data

28. **What type of bias occurs when a model's outcome is unfairly influenced by historical data?**
- o a) Algorithmic Bias
- o b) Statistical Bias
- o c) Historical Bias
- o d) Sampling Bias
- o **Answer:** c) Historical Bias

29. **Which method helps mitigate bias in AI systems?**
- o a) Using a diverse and representative dataset
- o b) Using more complex algorithms
- o c) Ignoring the ethical implications of AI
- o d) Reducing the training data
- o **Answer:** a) Using a diverse and representative dataset

30. **How can AI models be tested for bias?**
- o a) By reviewing their performance on various demographic groups
- o b) By increasing their complexity
- o c) By making them smarter
- o d) By reducing the amount of data used
- o **Answer:** a) By reviewing their performance on various demographic groups

31. **Which type of bias is most likely to occur in AI systems trained on historical data with inherent societal prejudices?**
    - ○ a) Algorithmic Bias
    - ○ b) Historical Bias
    - ○ c) Selection Bias
    - ○ d) Data Bias
    - ○ **Answer:** b) Historical Bias

32. **Which algorithmic model is known for its potential to introduce bias in decision-making?**
    - ○ a) Linear Regression
    - ○ b) Decision Trees
    - ○ c) Neural Networks
    - ○ d) Naive Bayes
    - ○ **Answer:** b) Decision Trees

33. **Which AI method relies on learning from feedback through rewards and penalties?**
    - ○ a) Supervised Learning
    - ○ b) Unsupervised Learning
    - ○ c) Reinforcement Learning
    - ○ d) Deep Learning
    - ○ **Answer:** c) Reinforcement Learning

34. **Bias in AI can arise due to:**
    - ○ a) Ethical programming
    - ○ b) Homogeneous data
    - ○ c) More training data
    - ○ d) Increased model complexity
    - ○ **Answer:** b) Homogeneous data

35. **Which bias is introduced when an algorithm favors individuals who are similar to the data on which it was trained?**
    - ○ a) Data Bias
    - ○ b) Sampling Bias
    - ○ c) Confirmation Bias
    - ○ d) Representational Bias
    - ○ **Answer:** d) Representational Bias

36. **How can reinforcement learning algorithms address bias?**
    - ○ a) By considering diverse feedback and rewards
    - ○ b) By reducing training data size
    - ○ c) By simplifying the decision-making process
    - ○ d) By using only historical data
    - ○ **Answer:** a) By considering diverse feedback and rewards

37. **Which type of learning involves the AI system making decisions by trial and error, receiving feedback through rewards or penalties?**
    - ○ a) Supervised Learning
    - ○ b) Unsupervised Learning
    - ○ c) Reinforcement Learning
    - ○ d) Semi-supervised Learning

- o **Answer:** c) Reinforcement Learning
38. **Which AI technique involves making predictions about unknown data based on labeled training data?**
    - o a) Clustering
    - o b) Supervised Learning
    - o c) Reinforcement Learning
    - o d) Association Rule Mining
    - o **Answer:** b) Supervised Learning
39. **Which of the following is an example of a reinforcement learning application?**
    - o a) Spam email filtering
    - o b) Autonomous vehicle navigation
    - o c) Market segmentation
    - o d) Handwriting recognition
    - o **Answer:** b) Autonomous vehicle navigation
40. **Which of the following can help reduce biases in AI systems?**
    - o a) Avoiding all use of historical data
    - o b) Increasing model complexity
    - o c) Continuous monitoring and auditing of AI models
    - o d) Reducing feedback loops
    - o **Answer:** c) Continuous monitoring and auditing of AI models

CHAPTER 4: HUMANS VS. MACHINES: WHAT'S DIFFERENT?

In this chapter, we explore the differences between human intelligence and machine intelligence. Understanding these differences is critical to how we perceive AI's role in society and its potential future impact.

Biological vs. Artificial Intelligence

The quest to understand and replicate intelligence has led to the development of Artificial Intelligence (AI), a field that seeks to imbue machines with cognitive capabilities akin to those exhibited by humans. While both biological intelligence (inherent in living organisms, particularly humans) and artificial intelligence aim to process information and solve problems, they arise from fundamentally different substrates and exhibit distinct characteristics.

1. Biological vs. Artificial Intelligence:

- **Explanation:** Human intelligence is an emergent property of complex biological systems, primarily the brain. This intricate organ, composed of approximately 86 billion neurons interconnected through a vast network of synapses, processes information using a combination of electrochemical signals. This biological architecture allows for remarkable adaptability, flexibility, and the capacity to perform a diverse array of tasks, ranging from complex reasoning and problem-solving to nuanced social interactions and creative endeavors.

  In stark contrast, artificial intelligence is an artifact of human engineering. It is realized through machine learning algorithms, sophisticated data processing techniques, and computer hardware systems. AI systems are designed to replicate specific cognitive tasks that are traditionally associated with human intellect. These tasks can include pattern recognition, learning from data, decision-making, and problem-solving. However, the underlying mechanisms are computational rather than biological.

- "Biological intelligence, exemplified by the human brain, is an evolved phenomenon arising from intricate biochemical and electrical processes within a highly complex neural network. Its hallmarks include plasticity, versatility, and a broad spectrum of cognitive abilities. Conversely, artificial intelligence represents a synthetic construct, instantiated through computational algorithms and engineered hardware, aimed at emulating specific aspects of human cognition through data manipulation and pattern recognition."

- **Example:**
  - **Human Brain:** When confronted with a novel puzzle, a human brain engages in a flexible and often creative process of exploration and hypothesis testing. Drawing upon prior knowledge, intuition, and the ability to recognize abstract relationships, an individual can manipulate the puzzle pieces, try different configurations, and adapt their approach based on visual and spatial feedback, even without prior experience with that specific type of puzzle.

- **Machine:** A machine learning model designed to solve puzzles, on the other hand, operates based on patterns it has learned from extensive datasets of solved puzzles. During its training phase, the model identifies recurring structures and successful solution strategies. When presented with a new puzzle, it attempts to match its features to the patterns it has learned. However, if the new puzzle deviates significantly from the types of puzzles it was trained on, or requires a novel, intuitive leap not captured in the training data, the machine may struggle or fail to find a solution. Its problem-solving is constrained by the scope and characteristics of its training data.

2. Memory and Learning:

- **Explanation:** Human learning is a rich and multifaceted process deeply intertwined with experiences that are shaped by emotions, social interactions, and contextual understanding. Our memories are not merely repositories of factual information; they are also imbued with emotional valence, contextual details, and sensory impressions. A significant event from childhood, for instance, might be vividly recalled not just for the facts of what happened, but also for the feelings associated with it, the surrounding environment, and the people involved.

  Machines, in contrast, learn from data that is explicitly inputted into them. The efficacy of machine learning models often improves with the quantity and quality of the data they are exposed to. By analyzing large datasets, AI can identify statistical correlations and patterns that enable it to perform specific tasks with increasing accuracy. However, this learning process lacks the human-like emotional and experiential context. Machines store and process data as numerical representations, without the subjective understanding or emotional resonance that characterizes human memory.

- "Human memory and learning are experience-driven, intricately woven with affective responses, interpersonal dynamics, and situational context. The retention of information is not solely factual but also encompasses emotional encodings, contextual nuances, and sensory modalities. In contradistinction, machine learning is a data-centric process, wherein knowledge acquisition is predicated on the ingestion and analysis of structured input. While the performance of AI systems can be enhanced through increased data exposure, they inherently lack the subjective, emotional, and experiential grounding that defines human cognition."
- **Example:**
  - **Human Memory:** An individual might vividly remember a specific childhood experience, such as a family trip to the mountains, not just for the factual details of the location and activities, but also for the overwhelming sense of joy and togetherness they felt. The memory is likely to be accompanied by sensory details like the smell of pine trees, the crispness of the air, and the sound of laughter, all contributing to a rich and emotionally charged recollection.
  - **Machine Memory:** An AI system tasked with processing data about the same family trip might store information such as geographical coordinates, dates, times, and perhaps even textual descriptions or images associated with the trip.

However, this data storage lacks any inherent emotional understanding or subjective experience. The machine can retrieve and process this information, but it cannot "feel" the happiness of the family or experience the sensory details in the same way a human does.

3. Problem-Solving Approaches:

- **Explanation:** Humans possess a remarkable capacity for creative and intuitive problem-solving. We can often draw upon knowledge and experiences from seemingly disparate fields, apply abstract reasoning, and make insightful leaps that lead to novel solutions. Our problem-solving is often guided by intuition, a form of subconscious reasoning based on accumulated experience and pattern recognition. Furthermore, humans excel at handling ill-defined problems that lack clear parameters or complete information, leveraging context, emotional intelligence, and adaptability to navigate ambiguity.

  Machines, on the other hand, typically excel at solving problems that have well-defined parameters, clear objectives, and structured data that can be algorithmically processed. They can perform complex calculations and analyze vast amounts of data with speed and accuracy far exceeding human capabilities. However, they are generally less adept at handling tasks that demand creativity, emotional intelligence, common sense reasoning, or the ability to generalize knowledge across vastly different contexts without explicit training.

- "Human problem-solving is characterized by creativity, the capacity for interdisciplinary knowledge transfer, and the utilization of intuition as a cognitive tool. Humans exhibit proficiency in addressing ambiguous and ill-defined problems by leveraging contextual understanding and emotional intelligence. Conversely, machine problem-solving is typically optimized for well-structured tasks with clearly defined parameters and relies on algorithmic processing of structured data. While machines demonstrate superior computational speed and data analysis capabilities, they often lack the creative flexibility and contextual adaptability inherent in human cognition."

- **Example:**
  - **Human Problem-Solving:** If asked to conceive a new idea for a movie, a human screenwriter can draw upon a vast reservoir of personal experiences, emotional understanding, cultural knowledge, and narrative conventions. They can blend elements from different genres, explore complex human relationships, evoke specific emotions in the audience, and craft a compelling narrative that resonates on multiple levels. This process involves a high degree of creativity, empathy, and the ability to synthesize diverse and often abstract concepts.
  - **Machine Problem-Solving:** An AI system designed to generate movie ideas might analyze a large database of successful movie scripts, identifying patterns in plot structures, character archetypes, and thematic elements. Based on this analysis, it could generate new plot outlines or character suggestions. However, it lacks the deep emotional understanding, nuanced cultural awareness, and subjective experiences that a human screenwriter brings to the process. While the machine might produce statistically plausible ideas based on past successes, it is

unlikely to generate truly innovative or emotionally resonant narratives that stem from genuine human insight.

Consciousness and Intuition: Exploring the Human Edge in Intelligence

Consciousness and intuition represent intricate facets of human cognition that distinguish our intellectual landscape. Consciousness, the very fabric of our subjective experience, underpins our awareness of self and surroundings. Intuition, that enigmatic "gut feeling," allows us to grasp understanding without explicit logical deduction. While Artificial Intelligence strives to emulate human intellect, these two concepts remain predominantly within the realm of biological minds.

1. Consciousness in Humans:

- **Explanation:** Human consciousness is the profound state of being aware – aware of one's own thoughts, feelings, perceptions, and the external environment. It is the arena where our subjective experiences unfold, allowing us to reflect upon our internal states, deliberate on choices based on personal history and values, and intricately weave emotions into our reasoning processes. Consciousness grants us the unique capacity for *qualia* – the qualitative, subjective character of our experiences, the "what it's like" to feel happiness, sadness, or the warmth of sunlight. This internal, subjective world is deeply personal and shaped by our individual biographies and emotional landscapes.
- "Human consciousness embodies the subjective awareness of one's internal mental states and the external world, affording the capacity for introspection, value-driven decision-making, and the integration of affective responses into cognitive processes. It is characterized by phenomenal experience, the qualitative 'what-it-is-like' aspect of subjective states, uniquely shaped by individual history and emotional context."
- **Example:** When you listen to a familiar melody that evokes vivid memories of your childhood home, you are not merely processing auditory information. You are consciously aware of the music's notes and rhythm, and simultaneously experiencing a cascade of emotions – perhaps nostalgia, warmth, or a sense of longing. This subjective experience, the unique way that particular song "feels" to you, is deeply intertwined with your personal history, the emotional associations you've formed with that music and time, and your conscious awareness of these internal states as you listen.

2. Can Machines Be Conscious?

- **Explanation:** As of the current understanding in neuroscience and artificial intelligence, machines do not possess consciousness in the way that humans do. While AI systems can process vast amounts of data, recognize complex patterns, and even generate outputs that mimic conscious behavior (such as natural language generation or responding to emotional cues), they lack the fundamental substrate of biological neural networks that gives rise to subjective experience in humans. The operations of AI are based on programmed algorithms and mathematical computations. Even the most sophisticated AI that simulates conversation or performs intricate tasks does so without an internal "feeling" or awareness of itself or its actions. Their behavior is a result of complex pattern matching and rule-based responses, not genuine self-awareness or sentience.

- "Contemporary artificial intelligence systems, despite their advanced capabilities in data processing and behavioral simulation, do not exhibit consciousness as understood in human terms. While AI can emulate behaviors associated with awareness, these actions are rooted in algorithmic execution rather than genuine self-awareness, the capacity for subjective experience, or the presence of qualia. The computational substrate of current AI lacks the biological complexity believed to underlie human consciousness."

- **Example:** A sophisticated humanoid robot might be programmed to walk with fluid movements and engage in seemingly natural conversation. It might even respond appropriately to expressions of human emotion. However, these actions are the result of intricate algorithms controlling its motors and processing linguistic input. The robot is not aware of the act of walking, does not "feel" the ground beneath its feet, and does not experience emotions in response to the conversation in the same subjective way a human does. Its behavior, however convincing, remains a simulation driven by its programming, not by an internal state of awareness.

3. Intuition and Machines:

- **Explanation:** Human intuition is often described as a form of rapid, non-conscious cognition – the ability to "know" or understand something instinctively, without the need for explicit, step-by-step logical reasoning. This "gut feeling" or immediate insight is believed to be influenced by a complex interplay of emotions, accumulated past experiences (even those not consciously recalled), and the brain's unconscious processing of subtle patterns and cues. Intuition allows humans to make quick judgments and form hypotheses based on incomplete information or in situations requiring rapid responses.

  AI, in its current form, does not possess intuition in this human sense. While AI systems, particularly deep learning models, can make remarkably accurate predictions based on the vast amounts of data they are trained on, their "decisions" are fundamentally data-driven. They identify statistical correlations and patterns within the data and use these patterns to make inferences about new data. Although an AI might rapidly process information and arrive at a conclusion that appears "intuitive" to an observer, this process lacks the subjective, emotional context and the holistic, unconscious processing that characterize human intuition.

- "Human intuition represents a form of rapid, non-deliberative cognition, characterized by immediate understanding or judgment without explicit conscious reasoning. It is posited to arise from the integration of affective states, the residue of past experiences processed unconsciously, and the brain's capacity for implicit pattern recognition. In contrast, AI decision-making, while capable of high-speed data analysis and pattern-based prediction, lacks the subjective and emotional underpinnings that drive human intuitive insights."

- **Example:** If you meet someone for the first time and immediately form a strong positive or negative impression based on their facial expressions, body language, or tone of voice, this is an example of human intuition at play. You might not be able to articulate precisely why you feel a certain way, but your "gut feeling" guides your initial interaction. An AI system trained to recognize facial expressions might accurately classify the person's expression as "happy" or "angry" based on pixel patterns. However, it would not have the same immediate, holistic "feeling" or intuitive judgment about the person's overall character or trustworthiness that a human might experience. The AI's assessment is based on learned correlations between visual features and labeled emotions in its training data, devoid of the complex emotional and experiential context that shapes human intuition.

Creativity, Emotion, and Ethics: Exploring the Human Dimensions Beyond Artificial Intelligence

Creativity, emotion, and ethics are fundamental aspects of human intelligence that profoundly shape our thoughts, actions, and interactions. Creativity fuels innovation through the generation of novel and valuable ideas, often stemming from the unique synthesis of diverse concepts and experiences. Emotion imbues our experiences with meaning, influencing our decisions and judgments. Ethics provides the moral compass that guides our behavior and decision-making, often rooted in complex social and cultural contexts. While Artificial Intelligence strives to emulate human cognitive abilities, these three domains highlight significant distinctions.

1. Can Machines Be Creative?

- **Explanation:** AI systems have demonstrated the capacity to generate outputs that exhibit characteristics of creativity, such as producing artwork, composing music, or writing poetry. These feats are typically achieved through machine learning models trained on vast datasets of human-created content. By learning the underlying patterns, styles, and structures within this data, AI can recombine and synthesize elements in novel ways, resulting in outputs that can be aesthetically pleasing or intellectually stimulating. However, the "creativity" exhibited by AI is fundamentally constrained by the patterns it has learned. It lacks the subjective experience, emotional depth, and personal perspective that often serve as the wellspring of human creativity. Human creativity frequently arises from deeply personal insights, emotional responses to the world, and the ability to connect seemingly disparate concepts in ways that transcend learned patterns.
- "Artificial intelligence systems can simulate creative processes by learning from extensive corpora of human-generated artifacts, enabling them to produce novel combinations and variations of existing styles and structures. However, this generative capacity is inherently bounded by the statistical patterns extracted from the training data, lacking the intrinsic emotional resonance and idiosyncratic perspectives that underpin the originality of human creative endeavors."
- **Example:** AI-generated art can be visually striking, often exhibiting novel combinations of artistic styles and techniques learned from a vast dataset of paintings. However, the creation process is driven by the model's analysis of existing artworks, identifying and

recombining visual features. A human artist, on the other hand, might create a painting inspired by a profound personal experience, a deeply felt emotion, or a unique insight into the human condition. The artwork becomes an expression of this internal world, imbued with a personal perspective that transcends mere pattern replication. While the AI's output might be aesthetically interesting, it typically lacks this underlying emotional and experiential depth.

2. Emotional Intelligence in Machines:

- **Explanation:** Humans navigate the complexities of life not only through rational thought but also through a rich tapestry of emotions. Our emotions influence how we perceive and interpret situations, guide our interactions with others, and play a crucial role in our moral judgments, helping us discern right from wrong based on empathy and our understanding of human well-being. While AI has made strides in simulating aspects of emotional intelligence, such as sentiment analysis (identifying emotions in text or speech) and generating empathetic-sounding responses in applications like customer service chatbots, it does not possess genuine emotions. AI systems operate based on algorithms and data processing; they can recognize patterns associated with human emotions and respond in a way that mimics emotional understanding, but they do not "feel" these emotions themselves. Consequently, AI lacks the profound depth and nuanced understanding of human emotional experience.
- "Human emotional intelligence encompasses the capacity to perceive, understand, manage, and utilize emotions in oneself and others, profoundly influencing interpersonal interactions and ethical judgments. While artificial intelligence can achieve a semblance of emotional understanding through sentiment analysis and the generation of contextually appropriate responses, it lacks the intrinsic subjective experience of emotions that characterizes human affective states, thus limiting the depth of its 'emotional intelligence'."
- **Example:** An AI-powered customer support chatbot might be able to detect frustration in a user's text based on the language used and respond with pre-programmed empathetic phrases like "I understand your frustration." While this response can be helpful in de-escalating a situation, the AI does not genuinely "feel" empathy for the user's plight. Its response is based on pattern recognition and rule-based actions designed to simulate empathy and improve customer satisfaction. A human customer service agent, on the other hand, can truly empathize with the user, drawing upon their own experiences and emotional understanding to offer more nuanced and genuinely caring support.

3. Ethical Decision-Making:

- **Explanation:** Human ethical decision-making is a complex process informed by a multifaceted web of moral principles, cultural norms, emotional considerations, and personal values. We often grapple with ethical dilemmas by weighing competing values, considering the potential impact of our actions on ourselves and others, and drawing upon our sense of empathy and moral intuition. Machines, in contrast, make decisions based on the predefined rules, algorithms, and datasets they are programmed with. Ethical considerations in AI are typically translated into explicit rules or constraints embedded within the system's design. However, due to the lack of human-like experiences, emotions, and comprehensive cultural understanding, the ethical decisions made by AI may not always align with nuanced human values or be sensitive to the complexities of real-world ethical dilemmas.

- "Human ethical decision-making is a complex interplay of moral principles, cultural context, affective responses, and individual values, involving nuanced deliberation and consideration of consequences. Artificial intelligence systems, in their decision-making processes, rely on pre-programmed rules and data-driven algorithms, limiting their capacity for ethical reasoning to the explicit frameworks encoded within them and lacking the experiential and cultural understanding that informs human moral judgment."

- **Example:** Consider an autonomous vehicle facing an unavoidable accident scenario where it must choose between two harmful outcomes. The ethical decision programmed into its algorithms (e.g., prioritize the safety of the vehicle's occupants, minimize the total number of lives lost) will dictate its action. However, a human driver in the same situation might make a split-second decision influenced by a complex interplay of factors, including instinct, emotional responses, and a subjective assessment of the situation that goes beyond pre-defined rules. The AI, lacking human-like moral intuition and the ability to weigh the value of different lives in a nuanced, context-dependent way, operates solely based on its programmed ethical framework, which may not always align with human ethical sensibilities in all possible scenarios.

Can Machines "Think"? Exploring Cognition, Reasoning, and Understanding in Artificial Intelligence

The question of whether machines can truly "think" lies at the intersection of artificial intelligence, philosophy, and cognitive science. Traditional notions of thinking encompass awareness, reasoning, problem-solving, and a fundamental level of understanding. To approach this complex question, we must delve into how machines process information, the nature of their reasoning capabilities, and whether they can genuinely achieve understanding in a manner comparable to human cognition.

1. Cognition in Machines:

- **Explanation:** Artificial intelligence systems are undeniably capable of processing information and executing tasks that, to an external observer, might appear to be indicative of "thinking." For instance, a sophisticated chess-playing AI can analyze an astronomical number of potential moves, evaluate their strategic implications based on pre-programmed rules and learned patterns from countless games, and ultimately select a move deemed most likely to lead to victory. Similarly, AI can perform complex calculations, identify intricate patterns in data, and make predictions with remarkable accuracy. However, it is crucial to distinguish this information processing from human thinking. Current AI operates based on algorithms and statistical models. It lacks the subjective experience of being, the awareness of its own processes, and a genuine understanding of the information it manipulates.

- "Cognition in artificial intelligence refers to the capacity of machines to process information and perform tasks that simulate aspects of human intellectual function. While AI excels at computational analysis, pattern recognition, and strategic evaluation within defined domains, its operations are fundamentally rooted in algorithmic execution and statistical inference, devoid of the subjective awareness, phenomenal consciousness, and intrinsic understanding that characterize human cognitive processes."

- **Example:** A chess-playing computer, such as AlphaZero, can indeed defeat human grandmasters, demonstrating a mastery of the game that surpasses human capabilities in strategic depth and tactical calculation. However, this mastery stems from its ability to evaluate millions of board states and their potential outcomes based on learned patterns and game rules. The AI does not "understand" the rich history of chess, the psychological aspects of a tournament, or the aesthetic beauty that humans might find in a particular move. It operates purely on the statistical probability of winning based on its training data and algorithmic evaluation function. It doesn't experience the thrill of victory or the agony of defeat; it simply executes the move that its algorithms deem optimal.

2. Reasoning in Machines:

- **Explanation:** Reasoning, in the human context, involves the ability to draw logical conclusions from available information, make inferences, and apply knowledge to novel situations. AI systems can perform certain types of reasoning through the implementation of algorithms such as decision trees, rule-based systems, and neural networks. These algorithms can process data and derive outputs based on logical structures or learned associations. For example, an AI trained on image recognition can "reason" that an object with a round shape, red color, and a stem is likely an apple based on the features it has learned to associate with apples. However, this form of reasoning often lacks the depth and flexibility of human reasoning, which is underpinned by understanding, common sense, and the ability to apply knowledge across diverse and unforeseen contexts. Human reasoning can involve abstract thought, analogy, and the consideration of nuanced relationships that are difficult to explicitly program or learn from data alone.

- "Reasoning in artificial intelligence entails the algorithmic derivation of inferences and conclusions from given data or rules. While AI can implement logical structures and learn complex associations to perform reasoning tasks, it typically lacks the human capacity for abstract thought, analogical reasoning, and the flexible application of knowledge to genuinely novel and unscripted situations, which are hallmarks of human understanding."

- **Example:** An AI trained to identify fruits might correctly classify a red, round object as an apple based on its learned features. However, a human can reason about apples in a much more abstract way. We understand why we might prefer one apple over another based on its taste, texture, or even the memories associated with eating apples in a particular context (e.g., picking apples at an orchard). We can also reason about apples in metaphorical or symbolic ways, drawing connections to concepts like health, temptation, or even historical narratives. This level of abstract and context-dependent reasoning, grounded in human experience and understanding, is currently beyond the capabilities of AI.

3. Can Machines Achieve True Thinking?

- **Explanation:** Machines have undeniably demonstrated the ability to simulate certain aspects of human thought, particularly in well-defined domains such as problem-solving and decision-making within those domains. They can process information, identify patterns, and make choices based on their programming and learned data. However, the critical distinction lies in the absence of consciousness, emotional understanding, and subjective experience in current AI systems. True human thinking is deeply intertwined with our awareness of ourselves and the world around us, our capacity to feel and understand emotions, and the subjective nature of our experiences. Because machines lack these fundamental attributes, their information processing, however sophisticated, does not equate to "thinking" in the full human sense. They operate by following instructions and processing data, but they do not possess genuine awareness, insight, or the capacity for independent, consciousness-driven thought.
- "While artificial intelligence systems can effectively simulate certain cognitive functions, such as problem-solving and decision-making within specific parameters, they fall short of achieving true human-like thinking due to the absence of phenomenal consciousness, affective understanding, and subjective experience. Their operations, though complex, remain rooted in algorithmic execution and data manipulation, lacking the intrinsic awareness and insightful reasoning that characterize human thought processes."
- **Example:** An AI might be programmed to play a game of trivia and possess a vast database of factual information, allowing it to answer a wide range of questions correctly. However, it does not have a deep understanding of the cultural references, historical context, or the human significance behind the questions and answers. It merely retrieves and outputs information based on pattern matching and its programmed knowledge base. It doesn't experience the joy of recalling a forgotten fact or the frustration of not knowing an answer. Its performance is based on information retrieval, not on a genuine understanding or appreciation of the knowledge itself.

30 multiple-choice questions (MCQs) with answers on the topics of **Consciousness and Intuition, Creativity, Emotion, and Ethics**, and **Can Machines "Think"?**

Consciousness and Intuition

1. **What is consciousness?**
   - A) Awareness of one's surroundings
   - B) Awareness of one's thoughts and experiences
   - C) Ability to solve problems
   - D) Ability to recall information
   - **Answer: B) Awareness of one's thoughts and experiences**
2. **Which of the following is NOT a characteristic of human consciousness?**
   - A) Self-awareness

- B) Subjective experience
- C) Pattern recognition
- D) Lack of emotional influence
- **Answer: D) Lack of emotional influence**

3. **Intuition is best described as:**
   - A) Logical reasoning based on facts
   - B) Instinctive understanding without the need for reasoning
   - C) Memory recall from prior experiences
   - D) Conscious decision-making based on data
   - **Answer: B) Instinctive understanding without the need for reasoning**

4. **Which of the following is an example of human intuition?**
   - A) Solving an equation
   - B) Recognizing a friend in a crowd
   - C) Reciting a poem from memory
   - D) Using a calculator to compute a sum
   - **Answer: B) Recognizing a friend in a crowd**

5. **What is the primary difference between machine intelligence and human consciousness?**
   - A) Machines have self-awareness
   - B) Humans have emotional responses, but machines do not
   - C) Machines can experience subjectivity
   - D) Both have the same level of awareness
   - **Answer: B) Humans have emotional responses, but machines do not**

6. **Which of the following is a limitation of AI concerning intuition?**
   - A) AI processes data and follows predefined patterns
   - B) AI mimics emotional responses
   - C) AI makes creative decisions
   - D) AI develops emotional intelligence
   - **Answer: A) AI processes data and follows predefined patterns**

7. **Which of the following factors influence human intuition?**
   - A) Data processing
   - B) Past experiences and emotions
   - C) Logical reasoning only
   - D) Random chance
   - **Answer: B) Past experiences and emotions**

8. **Consciousness in humans allows for:**
   - A) Understanding emotions
   - B) Performing repetitive tasks without awareness
   - C) Executing predefined commands
   - D) Problem-solving without context
   - **Answer: A) Understanding emotions**

9. **Intuition is influenced by which of the following?**
   - A) Data input and output
   - B) Emotional and experiential contexts
   - C) Physical hardware limitations
   - D) Software algorithms
   - **Answer: B) Emotional and experiential contexts**

10. **Which of the following does NOT reflect human consciousness?**
    - A) Sensory perception

- o B) Subjective experiences
- o C) Ability to mimic behavior
- o D) Awareness of self
- o **Answer: C) Ability to mimic behavior**

Creativity, Emotion, and Ethics

11. **Can machines display creativity in the same way humans do?**
    - o A) Yes, machines are naturally creative
    - o B) No, machines can only mimic creativity
    - o C) Yes, but only through random chance
    - o D) No, machines are not capable of creativity
    - o **Answer: B) No, machines can only mimic creativity**
12. **What role does emotion play in human creativity?**
    - o A) It hinders creativity
    - o B) It is irrelevant to creativity
    - o C) It fuels and inspires creativity
    - o D) It only affects creative decisions in a negative way
    - o **Answer: C) It fuels and inspires creativity**
13. **Which of the following is a limitation of AI when it comes to creativity?**
    - o A) AI can think outside of defined rules
    - o B) AI can generate novel solutions
    - o C) AI lacks emotional depth and subjective experience
    - o D) AI can engage in artistic expression like humans
    - o **Answer: C) AI lacks emotional depth and subjective experience**
14. **What is ethical decision-making?**
    - o A) Making decisions based on data
    - o B) Making decisions based on emotional reactions
    - o C) Making decisions based on a set of moral principles
    - o D) Making decisions based on efficiency
    - o **Answer: C) Making decisions based on a set of moral principles**
15. **Which of the following is a challenge in AI ethics?**
    - o A) AI lacks the ability to make decisions based on ethics
    - o B) AI is free of human bias
    - o C) AI cannot understand moral complexities
    - o D) AI automatically follows ethical guidelines
    - o **Answer: C) AI cannot understand moral complexities**
16. **Which human characteristic is essential for creativity but missing in AI?**
    - o A) Memory
    - o B) Emotional experiences
    - o C) Problem-solving ability
    - o D) Logical reasoning
    - o **Answer: B) Emotional experiences**
17. **What does AI lack in terms of ethics?**
    - o A) Logical reasoning
    - o B) Decision-making speed

- C) Emotional awareness and moral judgment
- D) Computational power
- **Answer: C) Emotional awareness and moral judgment**

18. **Ethics in AI requires:**
    - A) Programming algorithms for decision-making
    - B) Limiting AI's potential to avoid harm
    - C) Limiting the scope of AI development
    - D) Understanding human emotions and moral complexities
    - **Answer: D) Understanding human emotions and moral complexities**

19. **Human creativity is often influenced by:**
    - A) Strict rules and patterns
    - B) A desire for efficiency and speed
    - C) Personal experiences, emotions, and imagination
    - D) Limited access to resources
    - **Answer: C) Personal experiences, emotions, and imagination**

20. **AI's lack of emotional depth means:**
    - A) It is incapable of making ethical decisions
    - B) It is more objective in decision-making
    - C) It can make moral judgments better than humans
    - D) It can generate creative ideas without bias
    - **Answer: B) It is more objective in decision-making**

Can Machines "Think"?

21. **What is the primary question when asking if machines can "think"?**
    - A) Can machines process data?
    - B) Can machines make decisions based on data alone?
    - C) Can machines simulate human thought and reasoning?
    - D) Can machines create new technologies?
    - **Answer: C) Can machines simulate human thought and reasoning?**

22. **Machines can perform tasks similar to human thought, but they lack:**
    - A) Programming instructions
    - B) Memory capacity
    - C) Emotional depth and awareness
    - D) Computational resources
    - **Answer: C) Emotional depth and awareness**

23. **Which of the following is NOT a function machines can perform?**
    - A) Problem-solving
    - B) Creative thinking
    - C) Pattern recognition
    - D) Mimicking human reasoning
    - **Answer: B) Creative thinking**

24. **What is required for a machine to "think" in a human-like way?**
    - A) Complex algorithms
    - B) Awareness and emotions
    - C) Unlimited computational resources

- o   D) Predefined tasks
- o   **Answer: B) Awareness and emotions**

25. **Which of the following best describes machine learning?**
    - o   A) A machine that learns from pre-programmed tasks
    - o   B) A machine that automatically learns from data and improves its performance
    - o   C) A machine that mimics human creativity
    - o   D) A machine that can think without any input
    - o   **Answer: B) A machine that automatically learns from data and improves its performance**

26. **What is the key difference between human thinking and machine processing?**
    - o   A) Humans rely on data alone, while machines use intuition
    - o   B) Humans think based on emotions and experiences, while machines process data
    - o   C) Humans use algorithms, while machines use emotions
    - o   D) Humans are faster than machines at processing information
    - o   **Answer: B) Humans think based on emotions and experiences, while machines process data**

27. **Can machines experience self-awareness?**
    - o   A) Yes, if programmed correctly
    - o   B) No, they only simulate awareness
    - o   C) Yes, through advanced programming
    - o   D) Yes, but only in limited tasks
    - o   **Answer: B) No, they only simulate awareness**

28. **Which of the following is NOT something that machines can currently do?**
    - o   A) Solve complex mathematical problems
    - o   B) Experience emotions like humans
    - o   C) Play strategic games like chess
    - o   D) Recognize patterns in data
    - o   **Answer: B) Experience emotions like humans**

29. **Can AI replicate human creativity?**
    - o   A) Yes, AI can replicate creativity by combining existing data
    - o   B) No, AI cannot generate original creative thoughts
    - o   C) Yes, AI can outperform human creativity
    - o   D) No, AI can only perform basic tasks
    - o   **Answer: A) Yes, AI can replicate creativity by combining existing data**

30. **Which of the following is true about AI and human cognition?**
    - o   A) AI uses emotional experiences to make decisions
    - o   B) AI processes vast amounts of data but lacks human-like reasoning
    - o   C) Human cognition is less complex than AI
    - o   D) AI can perfectly replicate human thinking and reasoning
    - o   **Answer: B) AI processes vast amounts of data but lacks human-like reasoning**

CHAPTER 5: ETHICAL AI: FRIEND OR FOE?

Artificial Intelligence (AI) has made tremendous strides in recent years, transforming industries, creating efficiencies, and solving problems that once seemed insurmountable. However, as its capabilities grow, so too does the responsibility to ensure that AI is developed and applied ethically. **Ethical AI** refers to the branch of artificial intelligence concerned with the moral implications of AI systems, their design, and their impact on society. This chapter delves into the critical aspects of **Ethical AI**, the **moral dilemmas** it poses, its intersection with **human rights**, and the vital question of **accountability**.

What is Ethical AI?

Ethical AI is a multidisciplinary field that strives to ensure that artificial intelligence systems are designed, developed, and deployed in a manner that aligns with human values, moral principles, and legal frameworks. The overarching objective of ethical AI is to mitigate the potential for AI to cause harm, perpetuate biases, infringe upon fundamental rights, or undermine societal well-being. It necessitates the establishment of guidelines, regulations, and best practices that steer the creation and application of AI technologies towards outcomes that uphold human dignity, fairness, transparency, accountability, privacy, and safety.

 "Ethical Artificial Intelligence represents a commitment to the principled design, development, and deployment of AI systems, guided by a framework of human values, moral imperatives, and legal statutes. Its central tenet is the proactive minimization of potential harms, biases, rights infringements, and societal detriments that may arise from AI applications, achieved through the formulation and adherence to comprehensive ethical guidelines encompassing fairness, transparency, accountability, privacy preservation, and safety assurance."

Key Aspects of Ethical AI:

The pursuit of ethical AI is multifaceted, encompassing several critical dimensions:

1. Fairness:

- **Explanation:** Fairness in AI mandates that AI systems should treat all individuals and groups equitably, without exhibiting discrimination based on protected characteristics such as race, gender, age, religion, sexual orientation, disability, or socioeconomic status. Achieving fairness requires careful consideration of potential biases in training data, algorithmic design, and deployment contexts. It involves striving for equitable outcomes and ensuring that AI systems do not disproportionately disadvantage or advantage specific groups. Various mathematical definitions of fairness are explored in the field, each addressing different aspects of non-discrimination.
- "Fairness in the context of Ethical AI necessitates the equitable treatment of all individuals and demographic groups by AI systems, precluding discriminatory outcomes based on protected attributes. Achieving fairness demands meticulous attention to potential sources of bias throughout the AI lifecycle, aiming for parity in benefits and burdens across diverse populations."

- **Example:** Consider a credit scoring AI used by a bank to determine loan eligibility. Ethical AI principles dictate that this system should not unfairly discriminate against applicants based on their race or gender. Even if the training data inadvertently contains historical lending biases, the AI should be designed and evaluated to ensure that individuals with similar financial profiles receive similar credit scores and loan decisions, regardless of their protected characteristics. This might involve techniques to detect and mitigate bias in the model's predictions and ensure that relevant fairness metrics are satisfied across different demographic groups.

2. Transparency:

- **Explanation:** Transparency in AI refers to the principle that the decision-making processes of AI systems should be understandable and accessible to humans. This is particularly crucial for high-stakes applications where AI decisions can significantly impact individuals' lives. Transparency can be achieved through various means, including providing explanations for AI outputs (explainable AI or XAI), documenting the system's architecture and training data, and ensuring that the logic behind its decisions can be traced and scrutinized. Understanding how AI systems arrive at their conclusions fosters trust, facilitates accountability, and allows for the identification and correction of potential errors or biases.
- "Transparency in Ethical AI underscores the imperative for the decision-making mechanisms of AI systems to be comprehensible and auditable by human stakeholders. This principle necessitates the development of explainable AI methodologies that provide insights into the reasoning behind AI outputs, thereby fostering trust, enabling accountability, and facilitating the identification of potential flaws or biases in the system's operation."
- **Example:** In a medical diagnosis AI that assists doctors in identifying diseases from medical images, transparency would involve the AI being able to provide explanations for its diagnosis. For instance, it might highlight specific regions in the image that contributed most significantly to its conclusion, allowing the doctor to understand the AI's reasoning and make an informed judgment. This transparency builds trust in the AI's recommendations and enables medical professionals to identify potential errors or limitations in the system's analysis.

3. Accountability:

- **Explanation:** Accountability in AI establishes that developers, deployers, and organizations are responsible for the actions and outcomes of their AI systems. This principle is essential for ensuring that there are mechanisms in place to address any negative consequences or unintended harms caused by AI. Accountability requires clear lines of responsibility, the ability to audit AI systems, and frameworks for redress when AI systems cause harm or make unfair decisions. It also involves considering the ethical implications throughout the entire AI lifecycle, from design to deployment and monitoring.
- "Accountability in Ethical AI mandates the establishment of clear lines of responsibility for the behavior and consequences of AI systems. This principle necessitates mechanisms

for auditing AI operations, tracing decision pathways, and providing avenues for redress in cases of harm or unfair outcomes. It underscores the ethical obligation of stakeholders across the AI lifecycle to ensure responsible development and deployment practices."

- **Example:** If a self-driving car causes an accident, determining accountability is a complex ethical and legal challenge. Ethical AI principles emphasize the need for clear accountability frameworks that specify the responsibilities of the vehicle manufacturer, the software developer, and potentially the owner or operator. This might involve detailed logging of the AI's decision-making process leading up to the accident, allowing for analysis and the assignment of responsibility. Establishing such accountability mechanisms is crucial for public trust and the responsible adoption of autonomous systems.

4. Privacy:

- **Explanation:** Privacy in the context of ethical AI necessitates the protection of individuals' personal data that is used by AI systems. AI often relies on large datasets, which may contain sensitive personal information. Ethical AI requires adherence to data privacy regulations, the implementation of robust security measures to prevent data breaches, and the responsible handling of personal data throughout the AI lifecycle. This includes obtaining informed consent for data collection and usage, anonymizing data where appropriate, and ensuring that AI systems are designed with privacy-preserving techniques.
- "Privacy in Ethical AI underscores the critical importance of safeguarding individuals' personal data utilized by AI systems. This principle demands strict adherence to data protection regulations, the implementation of robust security protocols, and the ethical handling of personal information throughout the AI lifecycle, including informed consent, anonymization techniques, and privacy-preserving system design."
- **Example:** An AI system used for personalized recommendations on an e-commerce platform relies on user purchase history and browsing behavior, which constitutes personal data. Ethical AI principles require that this data is collected with the user's consent, stored securely to prevent unauthorized access, and used in a way that respects the user's privacy preferences. Techniques like differential privacy might be employed to add noise to the data, protecting individual identities while still allowing the AI to learn useful patterns for recommendations.

5. Safety:

- **Explanation:** Safety in ethical AI means ensuring that AI systems do not cause harm to individuals or society, either intentionally or unintentionally. This includes physical safety in applications like robotics and autonomous vehicles, as well as safety from harmful biases, misinformation, or manipulation in virtual or informational AI systems. Achieving safety requires rigorous testing, validation, and monitoring of AI systems to identify and mitigate potential risks. It also involves considering the broader societal impact of AI and taking steps to prevent unintended negative consequences.
- "Safety in Ethical AI mandates the proactive prevention of harm to individuals and society resulting from the deployment of AI systems, whether physical or informational.

This principle necessitates rigorous testing, validation, and continuous monitoring to identify and mitigate potential risks, alongside a comprehensive consideration of the broader societal implications of AI technologies to avert unintended adverse outcomes."

- **Example:** An AI system used to control industrial robots in a factory must be designed and rigorously tested to ensure it operates safely and does not pose a risk of injury to human workers. This involves implementing safety protocols, fail-safe mechanisms, and continuous monitoring of the AI's performance. Similarly, AI algorithms used to filter news feeds should be designed to prevent the spread of misinformation or harmful content that could negatively impact individuals or society.

Moral Dilemmas in Artificial Intelligence: Navigating Autonomous Decisions with Conflicting Values

As artificial intelligence systems become increasingly sophisticated and capable of making autonomous decisions in complex, real-world scenarios, they inevitably encounter situations that present profound moral dilemmas. These dilemmas arise when AI is faced with choices that involve conflicting ethical values, potential for significant consequences (including life and death), considerations of human rights, and issues of fairness. The absence of human-like consciousness, empathy, and a comprehensive understanding of moral context makes navigating these dilemmas particularly challenging for AI.

"The burgeoning capacity of artificial intelligence to exercise autonomous decision-making in real-world environments precipitates the emergence of intricate moral dilemmas. These quandaries occur when AI systems are compelled to make choices that necessitate the reconciliation of competing ethical values and the navigation of potentially grave consequences, often involving fundamental considerations of human life, rights, and equitable treatment. The resolution of these dilemmas poses a significant challenge due to the inherent differences between artificial and human moral reasoning."

Examples of Moral Dilemmas in AI:

The following examples illustrate the types of ethical quandaries that AI systems might face:

1. Autonomous Vehicles:

- **Scenario:** Imagine an autonomous vehicle encountering an unavoidable collision scenario. Due to unforeseen circumstances, such as a sudden obstacle or a pedestrian unexpectedly entering the roadway, the vehicle's sensors and processing systems determine that a crash is imminent. The AI controlling the vehicle must instantaneously decide between two or more courses of action, each with potentially severe consequences. For instance, it might have to choose between swerving to avoid a pedestrian who is jaywalking, which could result in the vehicle crashing into a barrier and potentially harming its passengers, or continuing its current trajectory and colliding with the pedestrian. This scenario forces a decision involving life-and-death outcomes and raises fundamental ethical questions.

- **Ethical Question:** A central ethical question in this dilemma is: "Should the AI prioritize the safety of its passengers, who are the users of the technology, or should it prioritize minimizing harm to others, even if they are acting unsafely (e.g., jaywalking)?" This question probes the core values that should be embedded in autonomous systems.
- **Solution Approach:** Analyzing this dilemma often involves considering various ethical theories:
    - **Utilitarianism:** This approach would suggest that the AI should choose the action that maximizes overall well-being or minimizes overall harm. In this scenario, the AI might be programmed to calculate the potential number of casualties and the severity of injuries for each possible action and choose the one that results in the least total harm. However, this approach can lead to morally troubling outcomes, such as sacrificing one life to save multiple others.
    - **Deontological Ethics:** This perspective emphasizes adherence to specific moral rules or duties, regardless of the consequences. For example, a rule might be "always prioritize the safety of law-abiding individuals." Applying this could lead to different outcomes depending on how "law-abiding" is defined in the context of a jaywalking pedestrian.
    - **Virtue Ethics:** This approach focuses on the character of the decision-maker. For an AI, this would translate to programming it to act in a way that embodies virtuous traits, such as acting with a sense of care and responsibility. However, defining and implementing "virtue" in an AI is a complex challenge.

The ethical considerations surrounding autonomous vehicle decision-making remain largely unresolved, with ongoing debates about how to program these systems to navigate such tragic choices.

2. Healthcare AI:

- **Scenario:** Artificial intelligence is increasingly being used in healthcare systems for tasks such as diagnosing diseases from medical images or patient data. While these tools can enhance accuracy and efficiency, they are not infallible and may occasionally provide incorrect diagnoses. A moral dilemma arises when deciding the level of trust that should be placed in AI recommendations, especially when human lives are potentially at stake. Should a physician always override an AI diagnosis, even if the AI has a high accuracy rate? Conversely, should the AI's diagnosis be given significant weight, potentially leading to a doctor overlooking their own clinical judgment?
- **Ethical Question:** The core ethical question here is: "What is the appropriate level of autonomy for AI in critical healthcare decisions, and how should the responsibility for diagnostic errors be shared between the AI system and human medical professionals?"
- **Solution Approach:** A prevailing ethical approach in healthcare AI is to position AI as a tool to augment and support human decision-making, rather than to replace it entirely. This ensures that human doctors retain the ultimate authority and responsibility for diagnoses and treatment plans. AI can provide valuable insights and identify patterns that humans might miss, but human clinical judgment, informed by experience, empathy, and a holistic understanding of the patient, remains crucial. Implementing mechanisms that allow human doctors to review and override AI decisions, along with clear guidelines on

when and how to do so, is essential for ethical deployment. Furthermore, transparency about the AI's accuracy and limitations is vital for fostering appropriate levels of trust.

3. Criminal Justice AI:

- **Scenario:** In criminal justice systems, predictive algorithms are employed to assess the risk of an individual re-offending. These risk assessment tools are often trained on historical crime data. A significant moral dilemma arises because if this historical data reflects existing societal biases (e.g., over-policing of certain demographic groups), the AI system can learn and perpetuate these biases. For instance, if an AI is trained on data showing a higher arrest rate for a specific demographic group for certain crimes, it might incorrectly predict a higher risk of re-offending for individuals in that group, leading to unfair targeting in future policing, sentencing, or parole decisions.
- **Ethical Question:** The fundamental ethical question is: "How can we ensure that AI systems used in criminal justice do not perpetuate or amplify existing societal biases, and how can we guarantee fairness and equal treatment under the law when relying on these predictive tools?"
- **Solution Approach:** Ethical AI in criminal justice demands rigorous testing and auditing of these systems for fairness and bias. This involves analyzing the training data for potential biases, evaluating the model's predictions across different demographic groups, and implementing techniques to mitigate any identified unfairness. This might include using fairness metrics to ensure equitable outcomes, employing bias detection and correction algorithms, and ensuring transparency about the factors the AI considers in its risk assessments. It is crucial to recognize that AI should not be used to reinforce existing inequalities but rather to strive for a more just and equitable system. Human oversight and the ability to challenge AI-driven decisions are also essential safeguards.

Ethical Principles to Address Moral Dilemmas:

Several established ethical principles provide frameworks for analyzing and attempting to resolve moral dilemmas in AI:

- **Utilitarianism:** This ethical theory posits that the morally correct action is the one that produces the greatest good for the greatest number of people or minimizes overall harm. When applied to AI dilemmas, a utilitarian approach would involve weighing the potential consequences of different actions and choosing the one that maximizes positive outcomes or minimizes negative ones across all affected parties.
- **Deontological Ethics:** This perspective emphasizes duty and adherence to moral rules or principles, regardless of the consequences. In the context of AI, this might involve programming systems to follow specific ethical rules or guidelines, such as "do not intentionally harm a human being," even if violating the rule might lead to a seemingly better overall outcome in a specific situation.
- **Virtue Ethics:** This approach focuses on the character and moral virtues of the decision-maker. For AI, this translates to designing systems that embody virtuous traits like beneficence, non-maleficence, and justice. The challenge lies in defining and operationalizing these abstract virtues in algorithmic form.

Navigating moral dilemmas in AI is an ongoing and complex endeavor that requires interdisciplinary collaboration among AI researchers, ethicists, policymakers, and the public. As AI systems become more integrated into our lives, the careful consideration and ethical resolution of these dilemmas will be crucial for ensuring a future where AI serves humanity in a just and beneficial way.

AI and Human Rights

The advent and proliferation of artificial intelligence systems have ushered in an era of unprecedented technological capabilities. However, this technological advancement intersects with the fundamental principles of human rights in profound and often complex ways. Human rights, as the inherent dignity and inalienable entitlements of every individual, are brought into sharp focus by the data-driven nature, autonomous decision-making capacity, and widespread deployment of AI. This intersection raises critical questions concerning privacy, discrimination, freedom of expression, and the right to work, necessitating careful consideration and proactive measures to ensure that AI technologies are developed and utilized in a manner that respects and upholds these fundamental freedoms and protections.

"The integration of artificial intelligence into various facets of human life engenders a critical interface with the foundational tenets of human rights, those intrinsic freedoms and safeguards universally accorded to every individual. The data-intensive methodologies, autonomous decision-making capabilities, and pervasive deployment of AI systems necessitate a rigorous examination of their implications for privacy, non-discrimination, freedom of expression, and the right to gainful employment, demanding conscientious stewardship to ensure the preservation of these fundamental entitlements in the age of intelligent machines."

Examples of Human Rights Issues in AI:

The following examples illustrate specific areas where AI's deployment can pose challenges to established human rights:

1. Privacy:

- **Explanation:** AI systems, particularly those leveraging machine learning, often rely on the analysis of vast quantities of data to identify patterns, make predictions, and drive decision-making. A significant portion of this data frequently includes personal information, ranging from demographic details and online behavior to biometric data and communication content. The collection, storage, processing, and potential sharing of such personal data by AI systems can lead to severe violations of the right to privacy if not handled with the utmost care and adherence to ethical and legal standards. Misuse of data, inadequate security measures leading to data breaches, or the surreptitious collection of information without informed consent can severely undermine individuals' autonomy and control over their personal lives.
- **Example:** The widespread deployment of facial recognition systems for surveillance purposes exemplifies a potential infringement on the right to privacy. These systems can continuously monitor and track individuals' movements and associations in public spaces

without their knowledge or explicit consent. The collection and analysis of this biometric data, often stored indefinitely, can create detailed profiles of individuals' activities, potentially chilling freedom of assembly and expression, and raising concerns about potential misuse by state or private actors. The lack of transparency and control over this data collection process directly contradicts the principles of privacy and autonomy.

- **Solution Approach:** Ethical AI development and deployment must prioritize the protection of individuals' privacy rights. This necessitates the implementation of robust data governance frameworks that emphasize informed consent for data collection, the adoption of anonymization and pseudonymization techniques to minimize the identifiability of individuals, and the employment of strong security measures to safeguard data against unauthorized access and breaches. Furthermore, principles of data minimization, ensuring that only necessary data is collected and retained for specific purposes, are crucial for upholding privacy in AI systems.

2. Discrimination and Bias:

- **Explanation:** AI systems, particularly those trained on historical data, have the potential to unintentionally perpetuate or even exacerbate existing societal biases and discriminatory patterns. If the training data reflects historical inequalities or underrepresentation of certain demographic groups, the AI model will learn these biases and may subsequently make decisions that disproportionately harm these groups. This is particularly concerning in high-stakes applications such as hiring algorithms, loan approval systems, and risk assessment tools in the criminal justice system, where biased AI can lead to unfair and discriminatory outcomes, denying opportunities or reinforcing systemic disadvantages.
- **Example:** A hiring algorithm trained on historical hiring data from an industry with a long-standing gender imbalance might learn to associate certain keywords or qualifications predominantly found in male resumes with "successful" candidates. As a result, when presented with equally qualified female candidates, the AI might unfairly rank them lower or filter them out, not based on their actual skills or potential, but due to the patterns learned from the biased historical data. This perpetuates the existing gender imbalance in the industry and violates the principle of equal opportunity.
- **Solution Approach:** Addressing discrimination and bias in AI requires a multi-faceted approach. Firstly, meticulous attention must be paid to the composition and quality of training data, with efforts made to ensure diverse and representative datasets that accurately reflect the population. Secondly, AI systems should be rigorously audited for bias and fairness using appropriate metrics that assess the impact of the system's decisions across different demographic groups. Finally, techniques for bias detection and mitigation should be employed during the model development process to identify and remove discriminatory elements, striving for equitable outcomes and preventing the perpetuation of societal inequalities.

3. Freedom of Expression:

- **Explanation:** AI is increasingly employed as a tool for content moderation on social media platforms and other online environments. While the goal of this moderation is often to protect users from harmful content such as hate speech, incitement to violence, or misinformation, the overuse or flawed implementation of automated content moderation systems can inadvertently lead to censorship or the suppression of legitimate free speech. Algorithms that are not sufficiently nuanced or lack adequate contextual understanding may flag and remove content that is critical, satirical, or represents minority viewpoints, thus infringing on the fundamental human right to freedom of expression. The lack of transparency and accountability in these automated moderation processes can further exacerbate this issue.

- **Example:** An AI algorithm tasked with identifying and removing "offensive" content on a social media platform might be trained on data that reflects the dominant cultural norms and sensitivities. As a result, content that challenges these norms, expresses dissenting opinions, or uses language common within marginalized communities (but potentially flagged as offensive out of context) could be mistakenly removed, thereby silencing legitimate expression and limiting the diversity of online discourse.

- **Solution Approach:** Content moderation systems powered by AI must be developed and deployed with careful consideration for the right to freedom of expression. This requires ensuring transparency about the rules and algorithms used for moderation, providing clear and justifiable reasons for content removal, and implementing robust mechanisms for human oversight and appeal. Balancing the need to protect users from genuine harm with the imperative to safeguard free speech necessitates a nuanced approach that prioritizes contextual understanding and minimizes the risk of arbitrary censorship.

4. Right to Work:

- **Explanation:** The increasing automation of tasks traditionally performed by humans, driven by advancements in AI and robotics, raises significant concerns about potential job displacement and the fundamental human right to work and earn a livelihood. As AI systems become more capable in various industries, including manufacturing, retail, transportation, and services, there is a risk of widespread unemployment and economic disruption, potentially impacting individuals' ability to support themselves and their families, thus undermining their right to work and a decent standard of living.

- **Solution Approach:** Addressing the potential impact of AI on the right to work requires proactive and comprehensive policy responses from governments, organizations, and educational institutions. This includes investing in education and training programs that equip workers with the skills needed for jobs in the evolving economy, exploring social safety net mechanisms to support those displaced by automation, and considering policies that promote fair distribution of the economic benefits generated by AI. Facilitating the retraining and reskilling of workers, fostering innovation in job creation, and ensuring a just transition in the face of technological change are crucial for safeguarding individuals' right to work in the age of AI.

Accountability: Who is Responsible for the Actions of AI?

As artificial intelligence systems evolve towards greater autonomy, the question of accountability for their actions emerges as a critical ethical and legal challenge. When an AI system causes harm, makes a flawed decision, or violates ethical principles, determining who should bear the responsibility becomes a complex issue with far-reaching implications. The assignment of accountability is contingent upon a confluence of factors, including the extent of human involvement in the AI's creation and deployment, the level of autonomy exhibited by the AI, and the specific context in which the AI is utilized.

"The progressive autonomy of artificial intelligence systems precipitates a fundamental ethical and legal inquiry into the locus of responsibility for their actions. In instances where AI causes detriment, renders suboptimal decisions, or transgresses ethical norms, the attribution of accountability necessitates a nuanced consideration of the degree of human agency in the system's genesis and application, the level of operational independence exhibited by the AI, and the specific domain of its deployment."

Key Issues in Accountability:

Several key areas highlight the complexities of assigning responsibility for AI actions:

1. Developer Responsibility:

- **Explanation:** AI developers play a crucial role in shaping the capabilities, limitations, and ethical guardrails of AI systems. They are responsible for designing, training, and testing these systems to ensure they are safe, reliable, transparent, and aligned with ethical principles. If an AI system causes harm or makes an unethical decision due to flaws in its design, inadequate testing, or a failure to foresee and mitigate potential risks, the developers may be held accountable. This accountability can manifest in various forms, including legal liabilities, reputational damage, and professional sanctions.
- **Example:** If a self-driving car, due to a software bug or a flawed algorithm designed by its developers, causes an accident resulting in injury or death, legal action may be taken against the car manufacturer and the developers of the AI system that controlled the vehicle's autonomous driving functions. The investigation would likely focus on whether the developers adhered to industry best practices, conducted adequate safety testing, and appropriately addressed foreseeable risks in the design and implementation of the AI.
- **Solution Approach:** To ensure developer responsibility, ethical AI development practices must be rigorously implemented. This includes conducting thorough risk assessments to identify potential harms, implementing robust testing and validation procedures, ensuring transparency in the system's design and operation, and establishing clear ethical guidelines that developers must adhere to throughout the AI lifecycle. Regulatory frameworks and industry standards can also play a crucial role in defining the responsibilities and liabilities of AI developers.

2. AI's Autonomy and Accountability:

- **Explanation:** As AI systems become increasingly autonomous, capable of making decisions and taking actions without direct human intervention, the traditional models of assigning blame become more challenging. For instance, in scenarios involving highly autonomous systems like AI used in warfare, if a drone makes a targeting decision that results in unintended civilian casualties, the question arises as to who is ultimately responsible. Is it the manufacturer who designed the AI, the military operator who deployed it, or could the AI itself be considered responsible?

- **Solution Approach:** There is an ongoing and complex debate about whether highly autonomous AI systems should be granted some form of legal personhood, which could potentially entail a degree of responsibility for their actions. However, the prevailing view among most legal and ethical experts is that accountability should ultimately remain with the human creators, operators, and the organizations that deploy AI systems. This perspective emphasizes that humans are the moral agents who design, build, and utilize AI, and therefore, they should bear the responsibility for its consequences. Establishing clear lines of command and control for autonomous AI, along with robust oversight mechanisms, is crucial for maintaining human accountability.

3. AI in Military and Warfare:

- **Explanation:** The application of AI in military operations, such as autonomous drones and lethal autonomous weapons systems (LAWS), raises profound ethical and legal questions regarding responsibility for wartime decisions. If an AI system makes a targeting decision that leads to violations of international humanitarian law or results in unintended civilian deaths, determining who is legally and morally responsible becomes exceedingly complex. The chain of command, the level of human supervision over the AI's actions, and the inherent unpredictability of autonomous systems in dynamic battlefield environments all contribute to this complexity.

- **Example:** If an autonomous drone, operating with minimal human supervision, makes a targeting decision based on its algorithms that results in the unlawful killing of civilians, the question arises whether the responsibility lies with the military commander who deployed the drone, the AI developers who created its targeting algorithms, or the AI system itself. International legal frameworks, such as the Geneva Conventions, which traditionally assign responsibility to human actors in warfare, may need to be adapted or reinterpreted to address the unique challenges posed by autonomous weapons systems.

- **Solution Approach:** Addressing accountability for AI in military and warfare requires a concerted international effort to update and clarify legal frameworks and agreements, such as the Geneva Conventions, to explicitly address the use of AI in military operations. Establishing clear lines of human control and responsibility, prohibiting the development and deployment of fully autonomous weapons systems that lack meaningful human oversight in lethal decisions, and ensuring accountability for any actions that violate human rights or international law are crucial steps.

4. Corporate Responsibility:

- **Explanation:** Companies that develop, deploy, and utilize AI systems for various purposes, such as data mining, targeted advertising, customer service, and decision support, have a corporate responsibility to ensure the ethical implications of their AI applications are carefully considered and managed. If these AI systems violate users' privacy rights, perpetuate biases, or lead to unfair or discriminatory outcomes, the companies deploying them should be held accountable for these consequences. This accountability can manifest in regulatory fines, legal challenges, and damage to their reputation and public trust.

- **Solution Approach:** To ensure corporate responsibility for AI, companies should proactively adopt comprehensive ethical guidelines that emphasize transparency, fairness, accountability, and privacy protection in their AI systems. They should implement regular audits to assess the ethical impact of their AI applications, establish clear channels for addressing grievances and providing redress, and be transparent about how their AI systems function and the data they utilize. Regulatory oversight and industry-wide ethical standards can also play a significant role in holding corporations accountable for the ethical implications of their AI deployments.

Solutions for Accountability:

Establishing effective accountability mechanisms for AI requires a multi-pronged approach:

- **Establish Clear Legal Frameworks:** Governments and legal bodies must develop clear and adaptable regulations that define the roles, responsibilities, and liabilities of AI developers, users, and organizations. These frameworks should address issues such as data governance, algorithmic bias, and the potential for harm caused by AI systems.
- **Implement Robust Ethical Guidelines:** Organizations and professional bodies should adopt and enforce comprehensive ethical guidelines that ensure transparency, fairness, accountability, and safety in the design, development, and deployment of AI systems. These guidelines should provide practical guidance for practitioners and establish standards of conduct.
- **Foster AI Literacy:** Policymakers, developers, legal professionals, and the general public need to develop a deeper understanding of AI's capabilities, limitations, and ethical implications. This increased literacy will enable more informed decision-making regarding the regulation and use of AI, as well as a greater awareness of accountability issues.

30 MCQ questions with answers on the topics "Moral Dilemmas in AI," "AI and Human Rights," and "Accountability: Who is Responsible?"

Moral Dilemmas in AI

1. **Which of the following is a moral dilemma for AI in autonomous vehicles?**
   - A) Choosing between different colors of cars
   - B) Deciding whether to hit a pedestrian or swerve into a barrier
   - C) Optimizing fuel efficiency
   - D) Enhancing user interfaces
   - **Answer: B**
2. **In the context of AI, what does "the trolley problem" relate to?**
   - A) Ethical decision-making in AI systems
   - B) A transportation issue
   - C) The efficiency of AI systems

- o D) AI's ability to predict future events
- o **Answer: A**
3. **What ethical theory suggests that AI should make decisions that maximize overall happiness or minimize harm?**
   - o A) Deontological Ethics
   - o B) Virtue Ethics
   - o C) Utilitarianism
   - o D) Egoism
   - o **Answer: C**
4. **What would be the biggest moral dilemma if AI were used in warfare?**
   - o A) Deciding on the target to bomb
   - o B) Deciding on the color of the war uniform
   - o C) Deciding the type of fuel to use for drones
   - o D) Deciding on the best communication tools
   - o **Answer: A**
5. **Which of the following is NOT a moral dilemma that AI systems might face?**
   - o A) Determining fairness in decision-making
   - o B) Ensuring privacy of personal data
   - o C) Deciding how to prioritize emergency services
   - o D) Deciding the optimal storage size for data
   - o **Answer: D**
6. **What is the key ethical dilemma in AI's use in criminal justice systems?**
   - o A) Determining the programming language for AI
   - o B) Determining how to interpret data to predict recidivism
   - o C) Deciding whether AI systems should be trained by machine learning
   - o D) Deciding how many machines should be used
   - o **Answer: B**
7. **Which of these dilemmas is related to AI in healthcare?**
   - o A) Diagnosing diseases without human involvement
   - o B) Choosing the most cost-effective treatment plan
   - o C) Deciding on the ethical use of AI in patient data collection
   - o D) Determining the best software for hospitals
   - o **Answer: A**
8. **When an AI system makes a biased decision, which ethical principle is violated?**
   - o A) Fairness
   - o B) Transparency
   - o C) Accountability
   - o D) Privacy
   - o **Answer: A**
9. **What ethical dilemma arises from AI's ability to predict criminal behavior?**
   - o A) Transparency in decision-making
   - o B) Violation of privacy and human rights
   - o C) Misuse of AI in war
   - o D) Developing AI that is not accurate enough
   - o **Answer: B**
10. **Which is a key moral challenge for AI in decision-making processes?**
    - o A) Reproducing human emotions in machines
    - o B) Ensuring AI understands human ethics

- C) Making fair decisions without bias
- D) Making decisions with complete transparency
- **Answer: C**

AI and Human Rights

11. **Which human right is most directly affected by AI surveillance systems?**
    - A) Right to equality
    - B) Right to free speech
    - C) Right to privacy
    - D) Right to freedom of movement
    - **Answer: C**
12. **AI-based facial recognition technologies raise concerns about which human right?**
    - A) Right to free speech
    - B) Right to equality before the law
    - C) Right to privacy
    - D) Right to work
    - **Answer: C**
13. **AI systems used in hiring processes can affect which human right?**
    - A) Right to life
    - B) Right to equality
    - C) Right to education
    - D) Right to vote
    - **Answer: B**
14. **Which is a significant concern regarding AI in healthcare in relation to human rights?**
    - A) The availability of AI tools in hospitals
    - B) The risk of misdiagnosis leading to harm
    - C) The speed at which AI systems process data
    - D) The cost of implementing AI systems
    - **Answer: B**
15. **Which human right can be impacted by AI algorithms that prioritize profitability over fairness?**
    - A) Right to freedom of assembly
    - B) Right to an adequate standard of living
    - C) Right to non-discrimination
    - D) Right to free speech
    - **Answer: C**
16. **AI systems used to monitor online speech could infringe on which human right?**
    - A) Right to privacy
    - B) Right to free speech
    - C) Right to a fair trial
    - D) Right to education
    - **Answer: B**
17. **In what way can AI systems contribute to inequality in education?**
    - A) By offering biased recommendations in student admissions
    - B) By providing better learning resources to all students
    - C) By ensuring equal access to online education

- o D) By helping students with disabilities
- o **Answer: A**
18. **Which aspect of AI could violate the right to fair trials in legal contexts?**
    - o A) Predictive algorithms that influence sentencing
    - o B) Faster processing of court cases
    - o C) AI used to prepare legal documents
    - o D) AI used for case management
    - o **Answer: A**
19. **Which of the following AI applications would most directly affect human rights?**
    - o A) AI in customer service chatbots
    - o B) AI in healthcare diagnostics
    - o C) AI in autonomous vehicles
    - o D) AI in monitoring online content for hate speech
    - o **Answer: D**
20. **What is a potential violation of human rights in AI-based data collection?**
    - o A) Informed consent
    - o B) Data accuracy
    - o C) Data redundancy
    - o D) Data encryption
    - o **Answer: A**

Accountability: Who is Responsible?

21. **Who is generally held accountable for the actions of an AI system?**
    - o A) The AI itself
    - o B) The organization or developer behind the AI
    - o C) The AI's users
    - o D) The regulatory authorities
    - o **Answer: B**
22. **If an AI system causes harm, who should be responsible for its actions?**
    - o A) The AI
    - o B) The user who operated the AI
    - o C) The developers and creators of the AI system
    - o D) The regulatory bodies that allowed the AI's use
    - o **Answer: C**
23. **When AI systems cause harm, which of the following is a crucial question of accountability?**
    - o A) Whether the AI is autonomous or manually controlled
    - o B) Whether the AI system is transparent
    - o C) Who profits from the AI system
    - o D) How the AI was marketed
    - o **Answer: A**
24. **If an AI system causes a traffic accident, who should be held accountable?**
    - o A) The person riding in the vehicle
    - o B) The company that created the AI
    - o C) The traffic authorities
    - o D) The pedestrians involved

- o **Answer: B**
25. **Which ethical principle requires accountability for AI systems?**
    - o A) Privacy
    - o B) Fairness
    - o C) Transparency
    - o D) Integrity
    - o **Answer: C**
26. **In the case of an AI system making a biased decision, who should be accountable?**
    - o A) The organization using the AI system
    - o B) The user interacting with the AI
    - o C) The government regulating the AI
    - o D) The AI itself
    - o **Answer: A**
27. **Which of the following is NOT an accountability challenge in AI?**
    - o A) Determining who owns the AI system
    - o B) Deciding how to punish the AI for errors
    - o C) Assigning responsibility for AI's autonomous decisions
    - o D) Ensuring the transparency of AI's decision-making process
    - o **Answer: B**
28. **If an AI system violates privacy laws, who is legally accountable?**
    - o A) The AI system itself
    - o B) The organization deploying the AI
    - o C) The software developers
    - o D) The individuals whose privacy was violated
    - o **Answer: B**
29. **Which of the following is a responsibility of developers when creating AI systems?**
    - o A) Ensuring the system is unbiased
    - o B) Reducing the transparency of the system
    - o C) Making the system as complex as possible
    - o D) Limiting the system's impact on human rights
    - o **Answer: A**
30. **Which of the following is a critical factor in assigning accountability for AI in military use?**
    - o A) Whether AI has been tested in combat situations
    - o B) Who developed the AI system
    - o C) Who gave the AI the command
    - o D) Whether the AI complies with international law
    - o **Answer: D**

CHAPTER 6: AI AND HUMAN JOBS: THREAT OR TRANSFORMATION?

Artificial Intelligence (AI) has been the subject of debate for decades, and one of the most pressing concerns is its impact on human jobs. While some view AI as a threat that will take away jobs, others see it as a transformative force that can lead to the creation of new roles and industries. In this chapter, we will explore AI's impact on human jobs, how automation is reshaping the workforce, the skills needed for the AI era, and how we can reimagine work and society in an age of AI.

Automation and the Future of Careers

The increasing sophistication and pervasiveness of artificial intelligence are driving a wave of automation across numerous industries, fundamentally altering the landscape of work. Automation, in its essence, involves the deployment of technology to execute tasks that have historically been the domain of human labor. AI-powered automation, with its capacity for learning, adaptation, and complex problem-solving, holds the potential to reshape job roles and create entirely new industries. Understanding the multifaceted impact of this technological shift on the future of careers is crucial for individuals, organizations, and policymakers alike.

"Automation, within the context of technological advancement, signifies the utilization of machinery and computational systems to perform tasks previously requiring human exertion. The advent of artificial intelligence-driven automation introduces a transformative potential across a diverse spectrum of industries, from manufacturing and healthcare to education and customer service, enabling machines to execute functions such as data processing, equipment maintenance, diagnostic procedures, and customer interaction with escalating levels of sophistication and efficiency."

Step 1: Understanding Automation

- **Explanation:** Automation refers to the application of technological solutions to perform processes and tasks that traditionally necessitate human intervention. This can range from simple mechanical automation in manufacturing to complex AI-powered automation that involves intelligent decision-making and adaptive behavior. The integration of AI into automation systems significantly expands their capabilities, enabling machines to handle tasks requiring cognitive skills such as pattern recognition, learning from data, and problem-solving. This has profound implications for a wide array of industries, promising increased efficiency, productivity, and precision.
- "Automation denotes the employment of technological apparatus and computational systems to execute processes and tasks conventionally performed by human labor. The infusion of artificial intelligence into automation paradigms amplifies their functional scope, empowering machines to undertake tasks demanding cognitive proficiencies, including pattern recognition, data-driven learning, and problem resolution, thereby yielding substantial ramifications for efficiency, productivity, and accuracy across diverse industrial sectors."

- **Example:** In the realm of manufacturing, the deployment of AI-equipped robots exemplifies advanced automation. These robots, guided by AI algorithms, can perform intricate assembly tasks on production lines with a speed and accuracy that often surpasses human capabilities. Tesla's automotive factories, for instance, utilize sophisticated AI-powered robots to assemble vehicles, streamlining the manufacturing process and significantly reducing the reliance on manual labor for repetitive and physically demanding tasks.

Step 2: Job Losses Due to Automation

- **Explanation:** It is an undeniable consequence of AI-powered automation that certain job roles, particularly those involving routine, repetitive, and codifiable tasks, are susceptible to displacement. As machines become increasingly adept at performing these tasks with greater efficiency and lower cost, the demand for human labor in these specific areas is likely to decrease. This potential for job displacement raises concerns about the future of work and the need for societal adaptation.
- "A salient consequence of the proliferation of artificial intelligence-driven automation is the potential for occupational displacement within specific economic sectors. Job roles characterized by routine, repetitive, and algorithmically definable tasks are particularly vulnerable to automation, leading to a contraction in the demand for human labor in these domains."
- **Examples:**
  - **Manufacturing Workers:** The automation of assembly lines, packaging processes, and quality inspection tasks by robots can lead to a reduction in the number of human workers required in manufacturing plants.
  - **Customer Service Representatives:** The deployment of sophisticated chatbots and virtual assistants capable of handling a wide range of customer inquiries and tasks can diminish the need for human customer service agents in call centers and online support roles.
- **Nuance:** It is crucial to recognize that automation does not necessarily equate to a complete and absolute elimination of all jobs. Often, automation transforms the nature of work rather than simply eradicating it. While some specific roles may become obsolete, new roles emerge, and existing roles may evolve to focus on tasks that complement automated systems.

Step 3: Job Creation and Transformation

- **Explanation:** While automation leads to job displacement in certain areas, it also acts as a catalyst for the creation of new job opportunities in emerging sectors related to the development, implementation, and maintenance of AI and automation technologies. These new roles typically require more advanced skills, adaptability, and a deep understanding of the technological landscape. Furthermore, automation often transforms existing roles, requiring workers to acquire new skills to collaborate with and manage automated systems.
- "Concomitant with the displacement of certain occupations, the advancement and integration of artificial intelligence and automation also engender novel employment

opportunities within emergent technological sectors. These nascent roles typically necessitate advanced skill sets, adaptability to technological evolution, and a comprehensive understanding of the AI and automation landscape. Moreover, automation frequently precipitates a transformation of existing job roles, requiring incumbents to acquire new competencies to effectively collaborate with and oversee automated systems."

- **Examples:**
  - **AI Specialists:** The increasing adoption of AI across industries fuels a rapidly growing demand for AI engineers, data scientists, machine learning experts, and AI ethicists who possess the skills to develop, deploy, and manage intelligent systems.
  - **Robotics Technicians:** The widespread use of robots in automated processes creates a need for skilled technicians who can install, maintain, troubleshoot, and repair these complex machines.
  - **Healthcare Professionals in AI Management:** In the healthcare sector, the integration of AI-driven diagnostic tools and other applications creates new roles for healthcare professionals who can manage and interpret AI insights, integrate AI into clinical workflows, and ensure the ethical and effective use of these technologies, rather than simply being replaced by them.

Step 4: The Future of Careers in an AI World

- **Explanation:** The future of work in an era increasingly shaped by AI and automation is likely to be characterized by a dynamic interplay between human capabilities and artificial intelligence. Rather than a scenario of widespread human redundancy, a more probable future involves human-AI collaboration, where AI augments human abilities, enabling professionals to perform their tasks more efficiently and effectively. Human skills such as critical thinking, creativity, emotional intelligence, and complex problem-solving will remain highly valuable in this evolving landscape.
- "The prospective landscape of careers in an environment increasingly influenced by artificial intelligence and automation is anticipated to be defined by a synergistic relationship between human proficiencies and artificial intelligence. Rather than a paradigm of widespread human displacement, a more plausible trajectory involves human-AI collaboration, wherein AI serves to augment human capabilities, thereby enhancing professional efficiency and efficacy. Human attributes such as critical thinking, creativity, emotional intelligence, and complex problem-solving are projected to retain significant value in this evolving occupational milieu."
- **Example:** In the legal profession, AI tools are being developed to rapidly analyze and synthesize vast amounts of case law, legal precedents, and other relevant documents, significantly reducing the time lawyers spend on these tasks. However, the crucial aspects of legal practice, such as interpreting these insights, applying legal reasoning to specific cases, understanding the nuances of human interactions and emotions in legal disputes, and providing expert legal counsel to clients, will continue to require human expertise and judgment. The future likely involves lawyers leveraging AI as a powerful assistant to enhance their efficiency and effectiveness, rather than being entirely replaced by it.

New Skills for the AI Era: Navigating the Transforming Workforce

The accelerating evolution and integration of artificial intelligence across industries are fundamentally reshaping the demands of the labor market. Success in the future workforce will increasingly hinge on a new set of skills that complement and leverage the capabilities of AI. As AI-powered automation transforms traditional roles, a demand surge for professionals with advanced technological expertise and uniquely human capabilities will emerge. Adapting to this evolving landscape through the acquisition of new skills is paramount for individuals seeking career growth and relevance in the AI era.

"The progressive evolution and pervasive integration of artificial intelligence across diverse industrial sectors are instigating a fundamental recalibration of the requisite skill sets for workforce success. As AI-driven automation restructures traditional occupational roles, a burgeoning demand arises for professionals possessing advanced technological acumen and uniquely human proficiencies. Adapting to this dynamic landscape through the acquisition of novel skills is indispensable for individuals aspiring to career advancement and sustained relevance in the burgeoning AI era."

Step 1: The Need for New Skills

- **Explanation:** The continuous advancement and widespread adoption of AI are driving a significant transformation in the skills required for professional success. The labor market is undergoing a rapid evolution, with AI automation reshaping existing job roles and simultaneously creating entirely new ones. To thrive in this AI-powered economy, individuals must proactively develop skills that align with the new demands, encompassing both technical expertise in AI-related fields and uniquely human capabilities that AI cannot replicate.
- "The ongoing advancement and ubiquitous adoption of artificial intelligence are catalyzing a substantial transformation in the skill sets requisite for professional achievement. The labor market is experiencing a rapid evolution, with AI-driven automation reshaping extant occupational roles while concurrently generating entirely novel ones. To flourish in this AI-centric economic paradigm, individuals must proactively cultivate skills that harmonize with these emerging demands, encompassing both technical proficiency in AI-adjacent domains and uniquely human capabilities that transcend AI replication."
- **Example:** A data analyst in the pre-AI era might have primarily focused on manual data entry and basic statistical reporting. However, in the AI era, this role is evolving to require skills in understanding large datasets, utilizing AI-powered analytics tools, and interpreting the insights generated by machine learning algorithms to inform business decisions. The ability to work effectively with AI tools and derive meaningful conclusions from complex data will be a crucial differentiator.

Step 2: Technical Skills

- **Explanation:** As AI becomes increasingly integral to business operations and technological innovation, a range of technical skills directly related to AI development, deployment, and analysis will be in high demand. These skills form the foundation for building, maintaining, and leveraging intelligent systems.
- "As artificial intelligence assumes an increasingly pivotal role in business operations and technological innovation, a spectrum of technical proficiencies directly pertinent to AI development, deployment, and analysis will experience heightened demand. These skills constitute the foundational expertise for constructing, sustaining, and leveraging intelligent systems."
- **Key Technical Skills:**
    - **Data Science and Analytics:** A deep understanding of data, coupled with the ability to analyze, interpret, and extract meaningful insights from it, will be paramount. Professionals skilled in data mining, machine learning, statistical analysis, and data visualization will be highly sought after.
    - **Machine Learning and AI Development:** Expertise in machine learning algorithms, deep learning architectures, and natural language processing (NLP) will be essential for individuals seeking careers in the core AI development and research fields. This includes the ability to design, train, and deploy AI models for various applications.
    - **Robotics:** With the continued growth of robotics in manufacturing, logistics, healthcare, and other sectors, there will be a significant demand for experts in robotic programming, control systems, maintenance, and innovation. This includes skills in integrating AI with robotic hardware.
- **Example:** A professional proficient in Python programming and possessing a strong understanding of machine learning algorithms (such as regression, classification, and clustering) can build predictive models to forecast sales trends, identify customer churn risks, or personalize marketing campaigns. This skillset, combining programming with AI modeling capabilities, will be increasingly valuable as companies seek to leverage data-driven insights for strategic decision-making.

Step 3: Soft Skills

- **Explanation:** While technical expertise is crucial for working with and developing AI systems, uniquely human "soft skills" will retain, and even increase, their value in the AI era. AI, despite its advancements, cannot replicate human creativity, emotional intelligence, complex problem-solving abilities in unstructured environments, or nuanced ethical reasoning. These are areas where human professionals will continue to excel and provide indispensable value.
- "While technical proficiency forms a critical component of success in the AI era, uniquely human 'soft skills' will maintain, and indeed augment, their significance. Artificial intelligence, notwithstanding its advancements, lacks the capacity to replicate human creativity, emotional intelligence, complex problem-solving acumen in unstructured contexts, or nuanced ethical deliberation. These domains represent areas where human professionals will continue to excel and provide indispensable value."

- **Key Soft Skills:**
  - **Problem-solving:** The ability to creatively approach and solve complex, non-routine problems that may not have clear algorithmic solutions will be highly valued. This includes the capacity for innovation and adaptability in the face of novel challenges.
  - **Critical Thinking:** The ability to evaluate the outputs and recommendations of AI systems with sound judgment, understand their limitations and potential biases, and integrate AI insights with broader contextual awareness will be essential for effective decision-making.
  - **Communication:** The capacity to clearly and effectively communicate complex AI-related concepts and insights to diverse audiences, including those without a technical background, will be crucial for bridging the gap between AI development and its practical application in various fields. This includes storytelling with data and conveying the implications of AI findings.
- **Example:** In a business setting, an AI model might analyze vast amounts of market data and predict emerging consumer trends. However, it requires human business leaders with critical thinking skills to interpret this data within the context of their company's specific strategic goals, competitive landscape, and unique organizational challenges. Furthermore, effective communication skills are needed to convey these AI-driven insights to different stakeholders within the company and to formulate actionable strategies based on them.

Step 4: Lifelong Learning and Adaptability

- **Explanation:** The field of AI is characterized by rapid and continuous evolution. New technologies, algorithms, and applications are constantly emerging, requiring individuals to embrace a mindset of lifelong learning. The ability to continuously acquire new knowledge, upskill, and adapt to the changing demands of the AI landscape will be essential for sustained career growth and relevance in the future workforce.
- "The inherently dynamic and rapidly evolving nature of the artificial intelligence landscape necessitates that workers cultivate a commitment to lifelong learning. Embracing continuous education, proactively acquiring new knowledge, and demonstrating adaptability to the shifting demands of emerging technologies will be indispensable for sustained career progression and enduring relevance within the future workforce."
- **Example:** A marketing professional who has traditionally focused on print and broadcast advertising may need to upskill and learn about AI-powered digital marketing tools, such as predictive analytics for audience segmentation, AI-driven content personalization, and automated advertising platforms. By embracing lifelong learning and acquiring these new skills, the professional can remain competitive and effective in the evolving field of marketing, leveraging AI to enhance their strategies and reach target audiences more effectively.

Reimagining Work and Society in the Age of AI: A Transformative Shift

The continuous and accelerating integration of artificial intelligence into the fabric of our economies and daily lives necessitates a profound reimagining of fundamental concepts such as "work" and the very structure of society. As AI systems become increasingly capable of performing tasks previously exclusive to human labor, the traditional paradigms of employment, economic growth, human purpose, and societal responsibility are undergoing a significant transformation, demanding innovative approaches and thoughtful consideration.

"The persistent and escalating integration of artificial intelligence into the foundational structures of our economies and quotidian existence mandates a profound reconceptualization of core constructs such as 'work' and the very architecture of society. As AI systems progressively acquire the capacity to execute tasks historically confined to human labor, the conventional paradigms of employment, economic expansion, human purpose, and societal obligation are undergoing a substantial metamorphosis, necessitating inventive methodologies and judicious deliberation."

Step 1: The Changing Concept of Work

- **Explanation:** The relentless advancement of AI is not only automating tasks but also fundamentally altering our understanding of what constitutes "work." The traditional notion of work as a fixed, location-dependent, and time-bound activity is being challenged. AI-powered tools are enabling new models of work characterized by increased flexibility, autonomy, and global collaboration.
- "The inexorable advancement of artificial intelligence is not merely automating discrete tasks but is also fundamentally reshaping our comprehension of the very essence of 'work.' The conventional notion of work as a static, geographically constrained, and temporally defined activity is undergoing a significant challenge. AI-powered instruments are facilitating novel models of work characterized by heightened flexibility, autonomy, and global collaborative potential."
- **Examples:**
    - **Remote Work:** AI-powered collaboration platforms, coupled with automation of routine communication and administrative tasks, are empowering workers to contribute effectively from any geographical location. Tools like Zoom, Slack integrated with AI assistants, and sophisticated document management systems facilitate seamless teamwork across vast distances and time zones, offering increased flexibility in where and how work is performed.
    - **Flexible Work Hours:** AI systems can take over tasks requiring continuous human attention, such as monitoring systems or responding to routine inquiries, allowing human employees to work more flexibly. Instead of adhering to rigid schedules, individuals can focus their time and energy on higher-level strategic thinking, creative problem-solving, and decision-making, with AI handling the more time-consuming and less cognitively demanding aspects of their roles. AI-

driven scheduling tools can also optimize workflows and task allocation, further enhancing flexibility.

Step 2: AI-Driven Economic Growth

- **Explanation:** While the potential for job displacement due to AI automation is a significant concern, it is equally important to recognize AI's potential to be a powerful engine for economic growth. By optimizing production processes, fostering the emergence of entirely new industries, and enhancing overall business efficiency, AI can contribute to a significant expansion of the global economy. This growth can, in turn, generate new economic opportunities and improve overall societal well-being.
- "While the prospective displacement of certain occupational roles due to AI automation constitutes a significant concern, it is of equal import to acknowledge AI's inherent potential as a potent catalyst for economic expansion. By optimizing production methodologies, fostering the genesis of entirely novel industries, and augmenting overall business efficiency, AI can contribute to a substantial augmentation of the global economy. This expansion can, in turn, generate novel economic opportunities and enhance overall societal prosperity."
- **Examples:**
    - **New Job Categories:** As previously discussed, the development, deployment, and maintenance of AI and robotic systems are creating entirely new categories of jobs in fields like AI engineering, data science, machine learning research, AI ethics, and robotics maintenance. These roles often require specialized skills and offer significant growth potential.
    - **Increased Productivity:** AI's ability to automate mundane, repetitive tasks frees up human workers to concentrate on more complex, creative, and strategic activities. This augmentation of human capabilities by AI leads to increased productivity across various industries, allowing for the creation of more value with the same or fewer human resources. AI-powered optimization tools in logistics, supply chain management, and resource allocation further contribute to enhanced productivity.

Step 3: Redefining Human Purpose in Work

- **Explanation:** As AI increasingly assumes responsibility for routine and transactional tasks, humans may gain the opportunity to focus on work that aligns more closely with their intrinsic motivations, creativity, emotional intelligence, and desire for impactful contributions. This shift could lead to a fundamental re-evaluation of what constitutes meaningful and fulfilling work for individuals and society as a whole.
- "As artificial intelligence progressively assumes responsibility for routine and transactional tasks, human beings may gain the opportunity to dedicate their efforts to work that resonates more deeply with their intrinsic motivations, creative capacities, emotional intelligence, and aspiration for impactful contributions. This transition could precipitate a fundamental re-evaluation of what constitutes meaningful and fulfilling work for individuals and the collective societal fabric."

- **Example:** In the creative arts, AI tools can assist with the technical and time-consuming aspects of content creation, such as video editing software that uses AI for scene detection and color correction, music composition software that generates basic melodic structures, or graphic design tools that automate repetitive design elements. This frees up human artists to focus on the more original, imaginative, and emotionally resonant aspects of their artistic expression, allowing them to concentrate on the core creative vision and emotional depth of their work.

Step 4: Society's Role in Managing AI's Impact

- **Explanation:** While AI offers immense potential for societal and economic advancement, it is crucial that society proactively and thoughtfully manages its integration to mitigate potential negative consequences and ensure equitable benefits for all. This requires a collaborative effort involving governments, organizations, educational institutions, and individuals to adapt to the changing landscape.
- "While artificial intelligence presents substantial potential for societal and economic advancement, it is imperative that society proactively and judiciously manage its integration to mitigate potential adverse consequences and ensure an equitable distribution of benefits for all. This necessitates a collaborative endeavor involving governmental bodies, organizations, educational institutions, and individuals to adapt to the evolving landscape."
- **Examples:**
    - **Education and Training:** Governments, educational institutions, and businesses must collaborate to provide accessible and relevant training and upskilling opportunities that equip workers with the skills needed to navigate the AI-driven economy. This includes fostering digital literacy, promoting STEM education, and offering reskilling programs for individuals whose jobs are at risk of automation.
    - **Social Safety Nets:** Governments may need to explore and implement new social safety net policies to support workers who are displaced by automation and to ensure a basic standard of living in a potentially transformed labor market. Experiments with universal basic income (UBI), enhanced unemployment benefits, and job transition assistance programs are examples of such policy considerations. The ongoing experiments in countries like Finland and Canada with UBI aim to explore its feasibility and impact in an economy increasingly influenced by automation.

30 multiple-choice questions (MCQs) based on the topics **Automation and Future Careers**, **New Skills for the AI Era**, and **Reimagining Work and Society**, along with their answers:

Automation and Future Careers

1. **What is automation?**
    - a) The use of manual labor for repetitive tasks.

- o b) The use of machines and technology to perform tasks without human intervention.
- o c) The use of advanced machinery for creative work.
- o d) The process of hiring more workers for routine tasks.
- o **Answer:** b) The use of machines and technology to perform tasks without human intervention.

2. **Which sector is most likely to experience job displacement due to automation?**
   - o a) Creative industries
   - o b) Manufacturing
   - o c) Healthcare
   - o d) Education
   - o **Answer:** b) Manufacturing

3. **What kind of jobs are least likely to be automated?**
   - o a) Routine and repetitive tasks
   - o b) Creative roles requiring problem-solving
   - o c) Data entry positions
   - o d) Customer service via chatbots
   - o **Answer:** b) Creative roles requiring problem-solving

4. **AI-powered automation in healthcare can lead to:**
   - o a) More manual tasks for doctors
   - o b) Enhanced diagnostic accuracy
   - o c) Job loss in creative roles
   - o d) Reduced patient care
   - o **Answer:** b) Enhanced diagnostic accuracy

5. **Which industry is seeing the rise of AI-powered robots performing repetitive tasks?**
   - o a) Fashion
   - o b) Agriculture
   - o c) Manufacturing
   - o d) Construction
   - o **Answer:** c) Manufacturing

6. **What is an example of AI in customer service?**
   - o a) Human-only phone support
   - o b) Automated chatbots for customer queries
   - o c) Manual feedback collection
   - o d) Direct phone calls for every customer query
   - o **Answer:** b) Automated chatbots for customer queries

7. **How is automation impacting job roles in the logistics industry?**
   - o a) Reducing the need for data analysis
   - o b) Increasing reliance on human labor
   - o c) Introducing automated vehicles and drones
   - o d) Eliminating warehouses entirely
   - o **Answer:** c) Introducing automated vehicles and drones

8. **Which of the following tasks is most likely to be automated in the near future?**
   - o a) Writing novels
   - o b) Analyzing legal documents
   - o c) Creative advertising
   - o d) Human resource management
   - o **Answer:** b) Analyzing legal documents

9. **AI automation in factories can lead to:**

- o a) More manual supervision
- o b) Increased productivity and efficiency
- o c) Fewer machines used
- o d) Higher employee turnover
- o **Answer:** b) Increased productivity and efficiency

10. **What is the potential impact of AI automation on low-skill workers?**

- a) Creation of new, higher-paying low-skill jobs
- b) Complete job replacement
- c) No impact on their employment
- d) Opportunities to transition to new roles with adequate training
- **Answer:** d) Opportunities to transition to new roles with adequate training

New Skills for the AI Era

11. **Which of the following skills will be essential in the AI-driven workforce?**

- a) Basic administrative skills
- b) Machine learning and data science
- c) Basic computing knowledge
- d) Manual labor skills
- **Answer:** b) Machine learning and data science

12. **To work in AI development, what foundational skill is most important?**

- a) Writing fiction
- b) Knowledge of statistics and data analysis
- c) Customer service
- d) Traditional marketing
- **Answer:** b) Knowledge of statistics and data analysis

13. **Which programming language is most commonly used in AI development?**

- a) JavaScript
- b) Python
- c) C++
- d) HTML
- **Answer:** b) Python

14. **Which field is most associated with creating intelligent systems that can learn from data?**

- a) Robotics
- b) Machine Learning
- c) Ethical hacking
- d) Web development
- **Answer:** b) Machine Learning

15. **Which of the following is considered a soft skill that is highly valued in an AI-powered economy?**

- a) Data programming
- b) Team collaboration and communication
- c) Coding proficiency
- d) Hardware maintenance
- **Answer:** b) Team collaboration and communication

16. **Which of these professions is likely to see an increase in demand due to AI advancements?**

- a) Telemarketers
- b) Data scientists
- c) Physical laborers
- d) Travel agents
- **Answer:** b) Data scientists

17. **What kind of skills will be important for the future workforce in the AI era?**

- a) High-level programming skills only
- b) Ability to work with AI systems while retaining human judgment
- c) Traditional trade skills
- d) Knowledge of past technologies
- **Answer:** b) Ability to work with AI systems while retaining human judgment

18. **In the future, which new skill will be critical for understanding AI's decision-making processes?**

- a) Human relations
- b) AI ethics and transparency
- c) Basic office skills
- d) Marketing expertise
- **Answer:** b) AI ethics and transparency

19. **What role does creativity play in the AI-driven future?**

- a) None, AI will take over all creative roles.
- b) Creativity will be replaced by automation.
- c) Creativity will be needed to collaborate with AI in tasks such as design and content creation.
- d) Creativity will be irrelevant.
- **Answer:** c) Creativity will be needed to collaborate with AI in tasks such as design and content creation.

20. **Which of these is an important skill for AI professionals working with large datasets?**

- a) Public speaking
- b) Knowledge of data structures and algorithms
- c) Graphic design

- d) Typing speed
- **Answer:** b) Knowledge of data structures and algorithms

Reimagining Work and Society

21. **How does AI change the way we think about work?**

- a) It will eliminate all jobs.
- b) It will provide more opportunities for people to engage in creative and complex problem-solving.
- c) It will make workers more productive, but they will be working more hours.
- d) Work will no longer require human involvement.
- **Answer:** b) It will provide more opportunities for people to engage in creative and complex problem-solving.

22. **Which industry will likely see new types of jobs due to AI?**

- a) Manufacturing only
- b) Creative industries and AI-related fields
- c) Mining
- d) Fishing
- **Answer:** b) Creative industries and AI-related fields

23. **How does automation benefit the workforce in terms of productivity?**

- a) By making humans work harder
- b) By allowing humans to focus on tasks that require judgment, creativity, and complex problem-solving
- c) By replacing all jobs
- d) By reducing the number of working hours required
- **Answer:** b) By allowing humans to focus on tasks that require judgment, creativity, and complex problem-solving

24. **How will AI and automation impact societal inequality?**

- a) It will increase inequality by taking jobs from low-income workers
- b) It will make society more equal by providing access to more opportunities
- c) It will have no impact
- d) It will increase access to physical labor jobs
- **Answer:** b) It will make society more equal by providing access to more opportunities

25. **What new job sector could arise due to the increased use of AI in healthcare?**

- a) Data scientists working on AI-driven diagnostics
- b) Traditional medical practitioners
- c) Desk clerks in healthcare organizations

- d) Warehouse workers
- **Answer:** a) Data scientists working on AI-driven diagnostics

26. What is the main reason for the increase in remote work due to AI technologies?

- a) AI increases the need for face-to-face interaction.
- b) AI-powered tools help facilitate collaboration across time zones.
- c) AI reduces productivity when not in office.
- d) AI forces workers to travel.
- **Answer:** b) AI-powered tools help facilitate collaboration across time zones.

27. How can AI help in reimagining the future of work?

- a) By replacing human workers completely
- b) By improving collaboration and increasing efficiency, leaving humans with more creative tasks
- c) By creating more manual labor jobs
- d) By making humans obsolete
- **Answer:** b) By improving collaboration and increasing efficiency, leaving humans with more creative tasks

28. How will AI help workers in the future?

- a) By doing all the work for them
- b) By handling repetitive tasks, enabling workers to focus on higher-level decision-making
- c) By eliminating the need for jobs
- d) By reducing salaries
- **Answer:** b) By handling repetitive tasks, enabling workers to focus on higher-level decision-making

29. Which of the following will be a key feature of the workplace in an AI-driven economy?

- a) Increasing the number of low-skill jobs
- b) Automation replacing all office tasks
- c) A stronger emphasis on creative thinking, emotional intelligence, and problem-solving
- d) A decrease in the number of high-skilled jobs
- **Answer:** c) A stronger emphasis on creative thinking, emotional intelligence, and problem-solving

30. What is a potential risk of AI on jobs in society?

- a) Increased reliance on human decision-making
- b) Widening income inequality due to displacement of workers in certain sectors
- c) More jobs being created in non-technology sectors
- d) Reduced global connectivity
- **Answer:** b) Widening income inequality due to displacement of workers in certain sectors

CHAPTER 7: DEMYSTIFYING MACHINE LEARNING

Machine learning (ML) is a subset of artificial intelligence (AI) that enables machines to learn from data, identify patterns, and make decisions without explicit programming. This chapter aims to demystify the core concepts of machine learning and explain how the process works, step by step, using clear examples and concepts. We'll cover topics such as training, features and labels, patterns, and common issues like overfitting, underfitting, and generalization.

What Happens During "Training" in Machine Learning

"Training" is the foundational process in machine learning that empowers a model to learn patterns and relationships from data, enabling it to make predictions or decisions on new, unseen data. During training, a machine learning algorithm is presented with historical data, consisting of input features and their corresponding output labels, and iteratively adjusts its internal parameters to minimize the discrepancy between its predictions and the actual labels. This learning process allows the model to generalize from the training data and make accurate predictions on future instances.

"Training in the context of machine learning constitutes the fundamental iterative process through which a model acquires the capacity to generate predictions or make decisions based on input data. During this phase, a machine learning algorithm is exposed to historical data, comprising input features and their associated output labels, and systematically modifies its internal parameters to minimize the divergence between its generated predictions and the actual ground truth. This learning mechanism enables the model to extrapolate from the training data and produce accurate predictions on novel, previously unseen instances."

Step-by-Step Explanation of Training:

The training process in machine learning typically involves the following sequential steps:

1. Collecting Data:

- **Explanation:** The initial and crucial step in training a machine learning model is the acquisition of a relevant and representative dataset that encapsulates the problem we aim to solve. This dataset is typically structured into two key components: the **features** (the input variables or attributes that describe the data points) and the **labels** (the corresponding output or target variables that we want the model to predict). The quality and quantity of the training data significantly influence the performance of the trained model.
- "The initial and indispensable phase in training a machine learning model involves the acquisition of a pertinent and representative dataset that embodies the problem domain under investigation. This dataset is conventionally structured into two primary components: the **features** (the input variables or attributes characterizing the data

instances) and the **labels** (the corresponding output or target variables that the model is intended to predict). The caliber and volume of the training data exert a substantial influence on the efficacy of the resultant trained model."

- **Example:** Consider the task of building a machine learning model to predict house prices. The **features** in this dataset might include characteristics of the houses such as their size in square feet, the geographical location (e.g., neighborhood), the number of rooms and bathrooms, the age of the property, and proximity to amenities. The **label** for each house in the dataset would be its actual selling price. The model will learn the relationship between these features and the price during the training process.

2. Data Preparation:

- **Explanation:** Before the collected data can be effectively used for training, it often requires a series of preprocessing steps to ensure its quality and suitability for the chosen machine learning algorithm. This data preparation phase can involve several critical operations:
  - **Handling Missing Values:** Addressing incomplete data by either removing data points with missing values or imputing them using statistical techniques.
  - **Scaling Numerical Data:** Standardizing or normalizing numerical features to ensure that features with larger ranges do not disproportionately influence the learning process.
  - **Encoding Categorical Variables:** Converting categorical features (e.g., city names, types of materials) into a numerical format that the machine learning algorithm can process (e.g., one-hot encoding).
  - **Splitting the Dataset:** Dividing the dataset into at least two subsets: the **training set** (used to train the model) and the **testing set** (used to evaluate the model's performance on unseen data). Often, a third **validation set** is also used for hyperparameter tuning during training.
- "Prior to its effective utilization for training, the acquired data frequently necessitates a sequence of preprocessing steps to ascertain its quality and suitability for the selected machine learning algorithm. This data preparation phase can encompass several critical operations: addressing incomplete data through removal or imputation; scaling numerical features to prevent disproportionate influence; encoding categorical variables into a numerical format; and partitioning the dataset into at least a **training set** (for model learning) and a **testing set** (for evaluating generalization performance). Frequently, a third **validation set** is employed for hyperparameter optimization during the training process."
- **Example:** Continuing with the house price prediction example, the data preparation might involve: handling houses with missing information (e.g., if the number of rooms is not recorded for some houses); scaling the square footage and age of houses to a similar range; encoding the location (e.g., converting neighborhood names into numerical vectors); and splitting the entire dataset into a training set (e.g., 80% of the data) that the model will learn from, and a testing set (e.g., 20% of the data) that will be used later to assess how well the trained model predicts prices for houses it has never seen before.

3. Model Selection:

- **Explanation:** Choosing an appropriate machine learning algorithm is a crucial decision that depends on the nature of the problem (e.g., regression for predicting continuous values, classification for predicting discrete categories), the characteristics of the data, and the desired performance metrics. A wide variety of algorithms are available, each with its own underlying assumptions and strengths.
- "Selecting a suitable machine learning algorithm constitutes a pivotal decision contingent upon the nature of the problem (e.g., regression for continuous value prediction, classification for discrete category prediction), the inherent characteristics of the dataset, and the desired performance metrics. A diverse array of algorithms exists, each predicated on distinct underlying assumptions and exhibiting unique strengths."
- **Common Machine Learning Algorithms:**
  - **Linear Regression:** Primarily used for regression tasks where the goal is to model the linear relationship between the input features and a continuous output variable.
  - **Logistic Regression:** Primarily used for binary and multi-class classification tasks where the goal is to predict the probability of an instance belonging to a specific category.
  - **Decision Trees:** Tree-like structures that use a series of decisions based on feature values to classify or predict outcomes.
  - **Random Forests:** An ensemble learning method that combines multiple decision trees to improve prediction accuracy and robustness.
  - **Support Vector Machines (SVM):** Powerful algorithms used for both classification and regression tasks, aiming to find the optimal hyperplane that separates different classes or fits the data with a margin.

4. Training the Model:

- **Explanation:** This is the core phase of the machine learning process where the selected algorithm learns from the training data. The algorithm iteratively adjusts its internal parameters (e.g., weights in a linear model, split points in a decision tree) to find patterns and relationships between the input features and the corresponding output labels. The objective is to build a model that can accurately map the features to the labels.
- "This constitutes the central phase of the machine learning process wherein the selected algorithm learns from the training data. The algorithm iteratively modifies its internal parameters (e.g., weights in a linear model, split thresholds in a decision tree) to discern patterns and correlations between the input features and their associated output labels. The primary objective is to construct a model capable of accurately mapping the input features to the target labels."
- **Example:** In the house price prediction scenario using linear regression, the algorithm will attempt to find the "best-fitting" line (or hyperplane in higher dimensions with multiple features) that represents the linear relationship between the features (square footage, number of rooms, location, etc.) and the house price. The algorithm will adjust the coefficients associated with each feature to minimize the difference between its predicted prices and the actual selling prices in the training data.

5. Optimization:

- **Explanation:** Machine learning algorithms typically employ optimization techniques to minimize the error or loss function, which quantifies the discrepancy between the model's predictions and the actual labels in the training data. A common optimization algorithm is **gradient descent**, which iteratively adjusts the model's parameters in the direction that reduces the loss. The model is considered "trained" when the optimization process converges to a state where the model can make reasonably accurate predictions on the training data, as indicated by a sufficiently low loss value.
- "Machine learning algorithms typically employ optimization methodologies to minimize the error or loss function, which quantifies the divergence between the model's generated predictions and the actual labels within the training dataset. A prevalent optimization algorithm is **gradient descent**, which iteratively modifies the model's parameters in the direction that diminishes the loss. The model is deemed 'trained' when the optimization process converges to a state wherein the model can generate reasonably accurate predictions on the training data, as evidenced by a sufficiently low loss value."
- **Example:** During the training of the linear regression model for house prices, the gradient descent algorithm will iteratively adjust the coefficients associated with each feature. In each iteration, it calculates the error between the model's current price predictions and the actual prices in the training data. Based on this error, it slightly modifies the coefficients in a direction that reduces this error. This process continues over many iterations until the algorithm finds a set of coefficients that minimizes the overall prediction error on the training data.

6. Evaluation:

- **Explanation:** Once the model has been trained on the training data, it is crucial to evaluate its performance on unseen data, typically the **testing set**. This step assesses how well the model generalizes to new situations and whether it has learned meaningful patterns rather than simply memorizing the training data (overfitting). Various evaluation metrics are used depending on the task (e.g., mean squared error for regression, accuracy, precision, recall, F1-score for classification). If the model performs well on the testing set, it suggests that it is likely to make accurate predictions on new, real-world data and may be ready for deployment. If the performance is unsatisfactory, further tuning of the model architecture, hyperparameters, or retraining with more or different data may be necessary.
- "Subsequent to the model's training on the training dataset, it is imperative to evaluate its performance on previously unseen data, typically the **testing set**. This phase assesses the model's capacity to generalize to novel situations and ascertains whether it has learned meaningful underlying patterns rather than merely memorizing the training instances (overfitting). A variety of evaluation metrics are employed depending on the specific task (e.g., mean squared error for regression, accuracy, precision, recall, F1-score for classification). Satisfactory performance on the testing set suggests the model's potential for accurate predictions on new, real-world data and its readiness for deployment. Unsatisfactory performance may necessitate further refinement of the model architecture, hyperparameters, or retraining with an augmented or modified dataset."
- **Example:** After training the house price prediction model on the training set, we would use the testing set (the 20% of the data the model has never seen) to evaluate its

performance. We would compare the model's predicted prices for the houses in the testing set with their actual selling prices. Metrics like the mean absolute error or root mean squared error would be used to quantify the average prediction error. A low error on the testing set would indicate that the model has generalized well and is likely to provide reasonably accurate price predictions for new houses.

Features, Labels, and Patterns: The Core Vocabulary of Machine Learning

In the realm of machine learning, the concepts of features, labels, and patterns form the fundamental vocabulary that underpins the entire learning process. Features serve as the informational building blocks that the model uses as input, while labels represent the target outputs that the model strives to predict. The central objective of machine learning is to enable algorithms to discern and generalize the intricate patterns and relationships that exist between these features and labels within the training data.

 "Within the domain of machine learning, the concepts of features, labels, and patterns constitute the foundational lexicon upon which the entire learning process is predicated. Features function as the informational constituents that the model employs as input, while labels represent the target outputs that the model endeavors to predict. The principal objective of machine learning is to empower algorithms to discern and generalize the intricate patterns and correlations that exist between these features and labels within the training dataset."

1. Features:

- **Explanation:** Features are the set of input variables or attributes that provide the necessary information for a machine learning model to make predictions or classifications. They are the measurable characteristics or properties of the data points being analyzed. Features are also commonly referred to as independent variables, predictors, or attributes, as their values are considered independent of the output (label) that the model is trying to predict. The selection of relevant and informative features is a critical step in the machine learning pipeline, as the quality and nature of the features directly impact the model's ability to learn and generalize effectively.
- "Features represent the ensemble of input variables or attributes that furnish the requisite information for a machine learning model to generate predictions or classifications. They constitute the measurable characteristics or properties inherent to the data points under analysis. Features are also conventionally denoted as independent variables, predictors, or attributes, as their values are considered exogenous to the output (label) that the model aims to predict. The selection of pertinent and informative features constitutes a pivotal stage in the machine learning pipeline, as the quality and nature of the features exert a direct influence on the model's capacity to learn and generalize effectively."

- **Example:** In the context of a model designed to predict house prices, the features would be the various characteristics of a house that are believed to influence its price. These could include:
    - **Size of the house (in square feet):** A numerical feature representing the living area of the property.
    - **Number of bedrooms:** An integer feature indicating the quantity of sleeping rooms.
    - **Age of the house:** A numerical feature representing the number of years since the house was built.
    - **Location (neighborhood):** A categorical feature indicating the area where the house is situated. This might need to be encoded into a numerical format for many machine learning algorithms.

2. Labels:

- **Explanation:** Labels, also known as target variables, output variables, or dependent variables, represent the value or category that the machine learning model is trained to predict. In supervised learning tasks, each data point in the training set has an associated label that represents the ground truth or the actual outcome for that instance. The model learns the relationship between the features and these labels during the training process. For regression tasks, the label is a continuous numerical value, while for classification tasks, the label is a discrete category.
- "Labels, also designated as target variables, output variables, or dependent variables, represent the value or category that the machine learning model is trained to predict. In supervised learning paradigms, each data point within the training set possesses an associated label that embodies the ground truth or the actual outcome for that specific instance. The model learns the correlation between the features and these labels during the training phase. For regression tasks, the label assumes the form of a continuous numerical value, whereas for classification tasks, the label constitutes a discrete category."
- **Example:** Continuing with the house price prediction example, the label would be the **actual price of the house** at the time the data was collected. This is the continuous numerical value that the model will learn to predict based on the provided features of the house.

3. Patterns:

- **Explanation:** The fundamental goal of a machine learning model during the training process is to identify and learn the underlying patterns or relationships that exist between the input features and the output labels in the training data. These patterns can be complex and non-linear. For instance, a pattern might be a positive correlation between the size of a house and its price, or a tendency for houses in certain neighborhoods to have consistently higher prices than similar houses in other areas. Once the model has learned to recognize and generalize these patterns from the training data, it can then use these learned relationships to predict the label (e.g., house price) for new, unseen data points based on their features.

- "The principal objective of a machine learning model during the training process is to discern and learn the inherent patterns or correlations that exist between the input features and the output labels within the training dataset. These patterns can exhibit complexity and non-linearity. For instance, a pattern might manifest as a positive correlation between the size of a dwelling and its price, or a propensity for residences in specific neighborhoods to command consistently higher prices compared to comparable dwellings in alternative locales. Once the model has acquired the ability to recognize and generalize these patterns from the training data, it can subsequently leverage these learned correlations to predict the label (e.g., house price) for novel, previously unseen data points based on their respective features."
- **Example:** Through the training process on the house price dataset, the model might learn several patterns, such as:
    - **Larger houses (greater square footage) generally have a higher price:** This indicates a positive correlation between the 'size of the house' feature and the 'price' label.
    - **Houses in certain neighborhoods may have a premium price:** This suggests that the 'location' feature has a significant impact on the 'price' label, with certain neighborhood categories being associated with higher price ranges.
    - **Newer houses (lower age) might command a slightly higher price, all else being equal:** This indicates a potential inverse relationship between the 'age of the house' feature and the 'price' label.

The ability of machine learning models to automatically recognize and generalize these intricate patterns from data is what imbues them with their "intelligence" and predictive power. By learning these underlying relationships, the model can make informed predictions on new data where the label is unknown, effectively solving the task it was trained for.

Overfitting, Underfitting, and Generalization: The Balancing Act in Machine Learning

In the process of training a machine learning model, the ultimate goal is to create a model that exhibits strong **generalization**, meaning its ability to perform accurately on new, unseen data, rather than merely memorizing the specific instances it was trained on. Achieving this delicate balance is often challenged by two common pitfalls: **overfitting** and **underfitting**. Understanding these concepts and how to mitigate them is crucial for building robust and reliable machine learning models.

"During the training of a machine learning model, the paramount objective is to attain robust **generalization**, defined as the model's capacity to perform accurately on novel, previously unseen data, rather than exhibiting mere rote memorization of the training instances. Achieving this delicate equilibrium is frequently challenged by two prevalent pitfalls: **overfitting** and **underfitting**. Comprehending these concepts and the strategies to mitigate them is indispensable for constructing resilient and dependable machine learning models."

1. Overfitting:

- **Explanation:** Overfitting occurs when a machine learning model learns the training data too well, including the noise and random fluctuations present within that specific dataset. As a result, the model becomes excessively complex and tailored to the idiosyncrasies of the training data. While an overfit model may exhibit excellent performance on the training data itself, its ability to generalize to new, unseen data is significantly compromised because it has learned spurious correlations and noise that do not represent the underlying patterns. Essentially, the model has "memorized" the training set instead of learning the fundamental relationships between the features and the labels.

- "Overfitting transpires when a machine learning model learns the training data with excessive fidelity, encompassing the inherent noise and random variations specific to that dataset. Consequently, the model attains an unwarranted level of complexity and becomes excessively tailored to the peculiarities of the training data. While an overfit model may demonstrate exceptional performance on the training data itself, its capacity for **generalization** to novel, previously unseen data is substantially impaired because it has assimilated spurious correlations and noise that do not reflect the underlying patterns. In essence, the model has 'memorized' the training set rather than extracting the fundamental relationships between the features and the labels."

- **Example:** Imagine training a model to predict house prices based on a limited dataset. If the model becomes so complex that it perfectly predicts the price of every single house in the training set, even accounting for minor, irrelevant details specific to those houses (e.g., the exact shade of paint or the previous owner's pet's name, if included as features), it is likely overfitting. When presented with a new house with slightly different characteristics, the model's predictions might be wildly inaccurate because it has learned to rely on these irrelevant details that do not generalize to the broader population of houses.

- **Visual Example:** Consider fitting a curve to a scatter plot of data points. An overfit model would produce a highly convoluted curve that passes through every single data point, including any outliers or noise. This curve, while perfectly fitting the training data, is unlikely to accurately represent the underlying trend and will probably perform poorly on new data points that do not fall exactly on this intricate curve.

- **How to Avoid Overfitting:**
  - **Use cross-validation:** This technique involves splitting the training data into multiple subsets, training the model on some subsets, and evaluating its performance on the remaining subset(s). This provides a more robust estimate of the model's generalization ability.
  - **Regularize the model:** Regularization techniques, such as L1 (Lasso) and L2 (Ridge) regularization, add a penalty to the model's complexity during training, discouraging it from learning overly specific patterns.
  - **Use simpler models:** If the dataset is relatively small, using a less complex model with fewer parameters can reduce the risk of overfitting.
  - **Increase training data:** A larger and more diverse training dataset can help the model learn the underlying patterns more effectively and reduce its reliance on noise.

- **Feature selection/engineering:** Carefully selecting the most relevant features and engineering new, more informative features can reduce the dimensionality of the data and the potential for the model to learn spurious correlations.

2. Underfitting:

- **Explanation:** Underfitting occurs when a machine learning model is too simplistic to capture the underlying patterns and trends present in the training data. An underfit model fails to learn the important relationships between the features and the labels, resulting in poor performance not only on the unseen test data but also on the training data itself. This indicates that the model is not complex enough to represent the inherent structure of the data.
- "Underfitting transpires when a machine learning model exhibits excessive simplicity, rendering it incapable of capturing the fundamental patterns and trends inherent in the training data. An underfit model demonstrates subpar performance not only on the novel test data but also on the training data itself, indicating a deficiency in the model's complexity to represent the intrinsic structure of the data."
- **Example:** If we attempt to predict house prices using a simple linear model (a straight line) when the actual relationship between the features and the price is more complex (e.g., non-linear, involving interactions between location and size), the linear model will likely underfit the data. It will not be able to capture the nuances of the price variations, resulting in inaccurate predictions even for the houses in the training set.
- **Visual Example:** If we try to fit a straight line through a scatter plot of data points that clearly follow a curved trajectory, the straight line will be far from most of the points and will not accurately represent the underlying relationship. This is a visual representation of underfitting.
- **How to Avoid Underfitting:**
  - **Use more complex models:** Selecting a more sophisticated model with a greater capacity to learn complex relationships can help address underfitting.
  - **Add more features:** If the existing features do not adequately capture the underlying patterns, introducing new, relevant features might provide the model with more information to learn from.
  - **Train the model for longer:** Sometimes, an underfit model simply needs more training iterations to learn the existing patterns in the data.
  - **Use more data:** While primarily a solution for overfitting, increasing the training data can also sometimes help an underfit model by providing more examples of the underlying relationships.
  - **Feature engineering:** Creating more informative features from the existing ones can help the model better capture the underlying patterns.

3. Generalization:

- **Explanation:** Generalization is the ultimate goal in machine learning. It refers to the ability of a trained model to perform well on new, previously unseen data that was not used during the training process. A model that generalizes well has successfully learned the underlying patterns and relationships in the training data without memorizing the noise or becoming overly specific to that particular dataset. Such a model can make accurate predictions or classifications on real-world data, demonstrating its practical utility.

- "**Generalization** represents the ultimate objective in machine learning, denoting the capacity of a trained model to perform effectively on novel, previously unseen data that was not utilized during the training phase. A model that exhibits strong **generalization** has successfully learned the fundamental patterns and correlations within the training data without succumbing to the memorization of noise or becoming excessively specific to that particular dataset. Such a model demonstrates practical utility by generating accurate predictions or classifications on real-world data."

- **Example:** After training a house price prediction model on a large dataset of historical house sales, a model that generalizes well would be able to accurately predict the selling price of a new house that was not part of the training data, based on its features (size, location, etc.). This indicates that the model has learned the general principles that govern house prices rather than just remembering the prices of the houses it was trained on.

- **Visual Example:** A well-generalized model, when fitting a curve to data points, would strike a balance. The curve would follow the general trend of the data without being overly influenced by individual noisy points. It captures the essential relationship between the variables and is likely to perform well on new data points that follow a similar trend.

- **How to Improve Generalization:**
  - **Use regularization techniques:** Penalizing model complexity helps prevent overfitting and encourages the learning of more generalizable patterns.
  - **Increase the size of the training dataset:** Exposing the model to a wider variety of data helps it learn more robust and general patterns.
  - **Use ensemble methods:** Combining the predictions of multiple models (e.g., Random Forests, Gradient Boosting) can often lead to better generalization performance than using a single model.
  - **Careful hyperparameter tuning:** Optimizing the model's hyperparameters using a validation set can help find a configuration that balances bias and variance, leading to better generalization.
  - **Early stopping:** Monitoring the model's performance on a validation set during training and stopping the training process when the performance on the validation set starts to degrade can prevent overfitting and improve generalization.

In essence, building effective machine learning models is a constant balancing act between underfitting (being too simple to learn the underlying patterns) and overfitting (being too complex and memorizing the noise). The goal is to achieve good generalization, where the model has learned the true signal from the training data and can apply this knowledge accurately to new, unseen instances.

  -

Example of Overfitting, Underfitting, and Generalization: House Price Prediction in Detail

Let's delve deeper into the concepts of overfitting, underfitting, and generalization using the concrete example of building a machine learning model to predict the price of a house based on its features.

"To further elucidate the concepts of overfitting, underfitting, and generalization, let us consider the tangible example of constructing a machine learning model designed to predict the price of a residential property based on its constituent features."

Scenario: We have a dataset containing information about various houses, including their size (in square feet) and their corresponding selling prices. Our goal is to train a model that can accurately predict the price of a new house given its size.

1. Overfitting:

- **Step-by-Step Explanation:**
    1. **Model Selection:** We choose a highly complex model, such as a high-degree polynomial regression (e.g., a polynomial of degree 10). This model has a large number of parameters and can fit very intricate curves to the data.
    2. **Training:** We train this complex model on our training dataset of house sizes and prices. Due to its high degree, the polynomial regression can essentially "bend and twist" in such a way that it passes through or very close to every single data point in the training set. This results in extremely low error on the training data.
    3. **Evaluation:** When we evaluate this highly trained model on a separate validation or test dataset (containing house sizes and prices the model has never seen before), we observe a significantly higher error. The model's predictions for these new houses are often inaccurate and erratic.

-
    1. "**Model Selection:** We opt for a model of high complexity, such as a high-degree polynomial regression (e.g., a polynomial of the tenth order). This model possesses a substantial number of parameters, enabling it to fit highly intricate curves to the data."
    2. "**Training:** We subject this complex model to our training dataset of house sizes and prices. Owing to its elevated degree, the polynomial regression can effectively 'bend and twist' in a manner that allows it to pass through or in close proximity to every individual data point within the training set. This process culminates in exceptionally low error metrics on the training data."
    3. "**Evaluation:** Upon evaluating this extensively trained model on a distinct validation or test dataset (comprising house sizes and prices previously unseen by the model), we observe a markedly elevated error rate. The model's predictions for these novel residential properties are frequently inaccurate and erratic."
- **Symptoms:**

- High performance on training data: The model achieves very low error (e.g., very small difference between predicted and actual prices) on the data it was trained on.
- Poor performance on validation/test data: The model exhibits significantly higher error when predicting prices for new, unseen houses.
- Complex model with many parameters: The chosen model has a high degree of flexibility and can fit very intricate relationships, potentially capturing noise as well as the underlying signal.
- Visual Representation: If we were to plot the fitted curve, it would likely be a very wiggly line that closely follows each training data point, even if those points deviate slightly from a general trend.

2. Underfitting:

- **Step-by-Step Explanation:**
  1. **Model Selection:** We choose a very simple model, such as a linear regression (a straight line). This model has limited capacity to capture complex relationships between house size and price.
  2. **Training:** We train this simple linear regression model on our training dataset. The model attempts to find the best-fitting straight line through the data points. However, if the true relationship between house size and price is non-linear (e.g., the price increases at an increasing rate as size increases), the straight line will not be able to capture this complexity.
  3. **Evaluation:** When we evaluate this underfit model on both the training and the validation/test datasets, we observe high errors. The model's predictions are consistently far from the actual prices because it has failed to learn the underlying trend in the data.

-
  1. "**Model Selection:** We opt for a model of low complexity, such as a linear regression (a straight line). This model possesses a limited capacity to capture intricate relationships between house size and price."
  2. "**Training:** We subject this simple linear regression model to our training dataset. The model endeavors to find the optimal straight line that best approximates the data points. However, if the true relationship between house size and price is non-linear (e.g., the price increases at an accelerating rate with increasing size), the straight line will be unable to capture this complexity."
  3. "**Evaluation:** Upon evaluating this underfit model on both the training and the validation/test datasets, we observe elevated error rates. The model's predictions are consistently disparate from the actual prices because it has failed to learn the fundamental trend within the data."

- **Symptoms:**

  - High error on training data: The model's predictions are significantly different from the actual prices in the training set.
  - High error on validation/test data: The model also performs poorly on new, unseen houses, with predictions far from the actual prices.

- ○ **Simple model with few parameters:** The chosen model lacks the complexity to represent the underlying relationships in the data.
- ○ **Visual Representation:** If we were to plot the fitted line, it would be a straight line that does not closely follow the general curve or trend suggested by the data points.

3. Generalization:

- **Step-by-Step Explanation:**
  1. **Model Selection:** We choose a model with an appropriate level of complexity, such as a linear regression model with regularization (e.g., Ridge or Lasso regression) or a low-degree polynomial regression (e.g., degree 2 or 3). These models can capture the general trend in the data without being overly flexible.
  2. **Training:** We train this balanced model on our training dataset, using techniques like regularization to prevent it from overfitting to the noise. The model learns the general relationship between house size and price.
  3. **Evaluation:** When we evaluate this well-generalized model on both the training and the validation/test datasets, we observe relatively low and comparable errors. The model performs well on the data it was trained on and also makes accurate predictions for new, unseen houses.

-
  1. "**Model Selection:** We opt for a model with an appropriate level of complexity, such as a linear regression model incorporating regularization (e.g., Ridge or Lasso regression) or a polynomial regression of low degree (e.g., second or third order). These models possess the capacity to capture the general trend within the data without exhibiting excessive flexibility."
  2. "**Training:** We subject this balanced model to our training dataset, employing techniques such as regularization to mitigate the risk of overfitting to noise. The model learns the general correlation between house size and price."
  3. "**Evaluation:** Upon evaluating this well-generalized model on both the training and the validation/test datasets, we observe relatively low and comparable error rates. The model performs effectively on the data it was trained on and also generates accurate predictions for novel, previously unseen residential properties."

- **Symptoms:**

  - ○ **Reasonable performance on training data:** The model achieves a good fit to the training data without perfectly memorizing it.
  - ○ **Good performance on validation/test data:** The model maintains a similar level of accuracy when predicting prices for new, unseen houses.
  - ○ **Balanced model complexity:** The chosen model has enough parameters to capture the underlying trend but not so many that it fits the noise.
  - ○ **Visual Representation:** The fitted line or curve would follow the general trend of the data points, capturing the overall relationship between house size and price without being overly influenced by individual data points that might deviate slightly from the trend.

In essence, the goal of machine learning model building is to find that sweet spot of generalization. We want a model that is complex enough to learn the underlying patterns in the data (avoiding underfitting) but not so complex that it learns the noise and performs poorly on new data (avoiding overfitting). Evaluating the model's performance on unseen data (validation/test sets) is crucial for assessing its generalization ability and guiding the model selection and training process.

50 multiple-choice questions (MCQs) on the topics:

What Happens During "Training"? Features, Labels, and Patterns Overfitting, Underfitting, and Generalization

---

What Happens During "Training"?

1. **What is the first step in training a machine learning model?** a) Collecting and preprocessing data
   b) Model evaluation
   c) Hyperparameter tuning
   d) Cross-validation
   Answer: a) Collecting and preprocessing data
2. **Which of the following is used to evaluate the model's performance during training?** a) Test set
   b) Training set
   c) Validation set
   d) Data set
   Answer: c) Validation set
3. **In supervised learning, what is the primary role of the training process?** a) To test the model
   b) To adjust the weights and parameters
   c) To collect data
   d) To apply learned knowledge
   Answer: b) To adjust the weights and parameters
4. **Which technique is commonly used to reduce the error during model training?** a) Regularization
   b) Cross-validation
   c) Overfitting
   d) Model boosting
   Answer: a) Regularization
5. **What is the purpose of data splitting in training a model?** a) To create an equal distribution of data
   b) To evaluate model performance on unseen data
   c) To improve training speed
   d) To normalize data
   Answer: b) To evaluate model performance on unseen data
6. **Which of the following optimization techniques is used in the training process to minimize errors?** a) Gradient descent
   b) Random forest

c) Data augmentation
d) Feature scaling
Answer: a) Gradient descent

7. **During training, what does a machine learning model adjust to improve performance?** a) Parameters and hyperparameters
   b) Features and labels
   c) Loss function
   d) Cross-validation set
   Answer: a) Parameters and hyperparameters

8. **In the training phase, what is the role of the loss function?** a) To measure how well the model performs
   b) To select the optimal model
   c) To split the data
   d) To identify features
   Answer: a) To measure how well the model performs

9. **Which of the following is an essential component in the training of a supervised learning model?** a) Labels
   b) Randomness
   c) Test data
   d) Hyperparameters
   Answer: a) Labels

10. **How does the model "learn" from the data during training?** a) By adjusting its parameters to minimize the loss
    b) By ignoring the training data
    c) By making random predictions
    d) By copying patterns from the data
    Answer: a) By adjusting its parameters to minimize the loss

Features, Labels, and Patterns

11. **In a supervised machine learning model, which of the following represents the "input" data?**
    a) Labels
    b) Features
    c) Weights
    d) Loss function
    Answer: b) Features

12. **In supervised learning, which of the following is considered the "output"?** a) Labels
    b) Features
    c) Model parameters
    d) Training data
    Answer: a) Labels

13. **What is the relationship between features and labels in supervised learning?** a) Features are the input, and labels are the target or output.
    b) Features are the output, and labels are the input.
    c) Features and labels are unrelated.

d) Labels are used for feature extraction.
Answer: a) Features are the input, and labels are the target or output.

14. **Which of the following is an example of a feature in a house price prediction model?** a) House price
b) Location of the house
c) House size
d) Both b and c
Answer: d) Both b and c

15. **What do machine learning models aim to find between features and labels?** a) The relationship or pattern
b) The number of features
c) The complexity of the model
d) The data distribution
Answer: a) The relationship or pattern

16. **Which of the following describes the pattern the model learns in supervised learning?** a) A fixed rule
b) A relationship between features and labels
c) Random errors
d) A predefined output
Answer: b) A relationship between features and labels

17. **Which technique is commonly used to process and extract relevant features from raw data?** a) Data cleaning
b) Feature engineering
c) Model tuning
d) Label encoding
Answer: b) Feature engineering

18. **Which of the following is an example of a label in a supervised learning model?** a) The temperature in a weather prediction model
b) The brand of a car
c) The price of a house
d) The age of an individual
Answer: c) The price of a house

19. **In machine learning, what does a "pattern" refer to?** a) A constant value in the dataset
b) A repeatable structure or relationship in the data
c) A random set of numbers
d) A unique identifier for data points
Answer: b) A repeatable structure or relationship in the data

20. **When a model recognizes a pattern between features and labels, what can it do?** a) Make predictions on new, unseen data
b) Ignore new data
c) Increase the model complexity
d) Adjust the features of the data
Answer: a) Make predictions on new, unseen data

21. **What does overfitting refer to in a machine learning model?** a) The model performs well on both training and test data

    b) The model memorizes the training data too well, leading to poor performance on new data

    c) The model underperforms on both training and test data

    d) The model is too simple to learn from the data

    Answer: b) The model memorizes the training data too well, leading to poor performance on new data

22. **Which of the following best describes underfitting in a machine learning model?** a) The model performs well on new data but poorly on training data

    b) The model is too complex

    c) The model is too simple to capture the underlying patterns in the data

    d) The model performs well on both training and test data

    Answer: c) The model is too simple to capture the underlying patterns in the data

23. **How can overfitting be reduced in machine learning models?** a) By increasing the complexity of the model

    b) By adding more noise to the data

    c) By using regularization techniques

    d) By using fewer training samples

    Answer: c) By using regularization techniques

24. **Which of the following can lead to overfitting?** a) Using a simple model

    b) Having a small amount of data

    c) Having a large and varied dataset

    d) Cross-validation

    Answer: b) Having a small amount of data

25. **Which of the following is true about underfitting?** a) The model is unable to capture the patterns in the data

    b) The model performs perfectly on all data

    c) The model memorizes the training data

    d) The model performs well on test data

    Answer: a) The model is unable to capture the patterns in the data

26. **Which of the following strategies can help reduce underfitting?** a) Use more complex models

    b) Use more data

    c) Apply regularization

    d) Remove irrelevant features

    Answer: a) Use more complex models

27. **What does generalization refer to in machine learning?** a) The ability of the model to perform well on training data

    b) The ability of the model to make accurate predictions on new, unseen data

    c) The process of adding more features to the model

    d) The ability to memorize data

    Answer: b) The ability of the model to make accurate predictions on new, unseen data

28. **How can we improve the generalization of a machine learning model?** a) By overfitting the training data

    b) By using simpler models with more features

    c) By increasing the training data and using cross-validation

d) By reducing the amount of data used

Answer: c) By increasing the training data and using cross-validation

29. **What is the effect of a highly complex model on generalization?** a) It enhances generalization

    b) It has no effect on generalization

    c) It can lead to poor generalization if overfitting occurs

    d) It improves the model's interpretability

    Answer: c) It can lead to poor generalization if overfitting occurs

30. **What is a good strategy to prevent overfitting while maintaining generalization?** a) Using a large training dataset

    b) Adding more noise to the data

    c) Reducing the model complexity

    d) Using more features

    Answer: a) Using a large training dataset

31. **Which of the following is an indication of a model being overfit?** a) High accuracy on both training and test data

    b) Low accuracy on test data but high accuracy on training data

    c) Low accuracy on both training and test data

    d) Consistent performance on training data only

    Answer: b) Low accuracy on test data but high accuracy on training data

32. **Which of the following is a common sign of underfitting?** a) The model performs well on both training and test data

    b) The model performs poorly on both training and test data

    c) The model performs well on test data but not on training data

    d) The model has a high variance

    Answer: b) The model performs poorly on both training and test data

33. **What is the main challenge in achieving good generalization in machine learning?** a) Finding the right dataset

    b) Avoiding overfitting and underfitting

    c) Increasing model complexity

    d) Reducing the training time

    Answer: b) Avoiding overfitting and underfitting

34. **Which of the following is used to detect overfitting during training?** a) Monitoring performance on the validation set

    b) Increasing the complexity of the model

    c) Reducing the training data

    d) Using a different algorithm

    Answer: a) Monitoring performance on the validation set

35. **Which of the following is a typical result of overfitting?** a) The model performs well on unseen data

    b) The model performs poorly on unseen data

    c) The model requires fewer training samples

    d) The model generalizes well

    Answer: b) The model performs poorly on unseen data

36. **Which technique can help in balancing overfitting and underfitting?** a) Regularization

    b) Data augmentation

    c) Cross-validation

    d) Hyperparameter tuning

    Answer: d) Hyperparameter tuning

37. **How does cross-validation help with overfitting?** a) It helps select the best model
    b) It reduces the amount of data used for training
    c) It ensures that the model generalizes well on unseen data
    d) It speeds up the training process
    Answer: c) It ensures that the model generalizes well on unseen data
38. **What does a model with high variance typically indicate?** a) The model is underfitting
    b) The model is generalizing well
    c) The model is overfitting
    d) The model has low accuracy
    Answer: c) The model is overfitting
39. **Which of the following is the goal of reducing bias in a model?** a) To ensure the model can capture complex patterns in the data
    b) To simplify the model
    c) To prevent overfitting
    d) To make the model interpret easily
    Answer: a) To ensure the model can capture complex patterns in the data
40. **How can increasing the training data help in avoiding overfitting?** a) It makes the model more complex
    b) It improves the model's ability to generalize
    c) It increases the computation time
    d) It removes irrelevant features
    Answer: b) It improves the model's ability to generalize
41. **In the context of training a model, what is regularization used for?** a) To improve model interpretability
    b) To prevent overfitting by penalizing large weights
    c) To increase the model's complexity
    d) To add more features to the model
    Answer: b) To prevent overfitting by penalizing large weights
42. **Which of the following best describes the term "bias-variance tradeoff"?** a) The balance between model complexity and training time
    b) The balance between model accuracy and complexity
    c) The balance between underfitting and overfitting
    d) The balance between features and labels
    Answer: c) The balance between underfitting and overfitting
43. **What could happen if a model is underfitted?** a) It will perform well on test data
    b) It will fail to capture important patterns in the data
    c) It will make highly accurate predictions
    d) It will be too complex
    Answer: b) It will fail to capture important patterns in the data
44. **Which of the following is most likely to help a model generalize well?** a) Using a very complex model
    b) Having a very small training dataset
    c) Using cross-validation
    d) Using only one feature
    Answer: c) Using cross-validation
45. **How does feature scaling help during training?** a) It reduces overfitting
    b) It speeds up the training process
    c) It improves generalization

d) It ensures that all features contribute equally

Answer: d) It ensures that all features contribute equally

46. **What is one key sign that a model is underfitting the data?** a) High bias
    b) High variance
    c) Low complexity
    d) High training error and high test error
    Answer: d) High training error and high test error

47. **Which of the following strategies helps prevent underfitting?** a) Increasing model complexity
    b) Reducing training data
    c) Using simpler models
    d) Regularization
    Answer: a) Increasing model complexity

48. **Which of the following is the most critical factor in determining whether a model is overfitting or underfitting?** a) The amount of training data
    b) The accuracy of predictions on test data
    c) The number of features used
    d) The training time
    Answer: b) The accuracy of predictions on test data

49. **What does it mean when a model is said to "generalize well"?** a) It can predict accurately on unseen data
    b) It is overfitted
    c) It is underfitted
    d) It has low bias
    Answer: a) It can predict accurately on unseen data

50. **Which of the following is most effective in dealing with overfitting?** a) Increasing the number of features
    b) Using a large validation set
    c) Adding regularization terms to the cost function
    d) Reducing the size of the dataset
    Answer: c) Adding regularization terms to the cost function

CHAPTER 8: EXPLORING DEEP LEARNING AND NEURAL NETWORKS

In this chapter, we delve into the fascinating world of deep learning and neural networks, two key pillars of modern artificial intelligence. These systems are designed to mimic the human brain's functioning and have revolutionized many fields, including image recognition, natural language processing, and even medical diagnostics. We'll explore how they work, how their biological counterparts differ from artificial neurons, and how they are used to solve complex real-world problems.

How Neurons Work: Biological vs. Artificial

To understand the fascinating world of neural networks and artificial intelligence, it's essential to first grasp the fundamental unit of computation: the neuron. This concept draws inspiration from the biological neurons that form the intricate network of the human brain. Let's embark on a detailed exploration of how both biological and artificial neurons function, highlighting their similarities and key differences.

"The cornerstone of both biological intelligence and artificial neural networks lies in the concept of the neuron, a fundamental unit responsible for processing and transmitting information. To appreciate the power and potential of artificial intelligence, we must first delve into the workings of its biological inspiration and its mathematical counterpart. This chapter will provide a comprehensive understanding of how both biological and artificial neurons function, illuminating their structural components and the mechanisms by which they process and relay signals."

1. Biological Neurons: The Brain's Building Blocks

- **Step 1: Understanding the Neuron's Role:** Biological neurons are specialized cells that serve as the primary communication units within the nervous system, including the brain. Their primary function is to receive, process, and transmit electrical signals, enabling rapid communication throughout the body. These signals are crucial for everything we do, from thinking and feeling to movement and sensation.
- "Biological neurons are specialized cells that constitute the fundamental communication units within the nervous system, most notably the brain. Their principal role is to receive, process, and transmit electrical signals, facilitating rapid communication across the entirety of the organism. These signals are indispensable for all aspects of biological function, encompassing cognition, emotion, motor control, and sensory perception."
- **Step 2: Dissecting the Structure of a Biological Neuron:** A typical biological neuron comprises several key structural components, each playing a vital role in its function:
  - **Cell Body (Soma):** This is the central part of the neuron, containing the nucleus and other essential cellular machinery. The soma integrates the various electrical signals received from other neurons through the dendrites. Think of it as the neuron's command center, where incoming information is processed.
  - **Dendrites:** These are branched, tree-like extensions emanating from the cell body. Dendrites act as the primary receivers of signals from other neurons. They are covered with receptors that bind to neurotransmitters, converting chemical

signals into electrical signals. Imagine them as the neuron's antennas, capturing incoming messages.

- o **Axon:** This is a long, slender projection that extends from the cell body. The axon is responsible for transmitting electrical signals, known as action potentials, away from the cell body towards other neurons, muscles, or glands. It's like the neuron's transmission cable, carrying the processed information. Some axons are covered by a myelin sheath, which acts as an insulator and speeds up signal transmission.
- o **Synapse:** This is the crucial junction where communication occurs between the axon terminal of one neuron and the dendrite or cell body of another neuron. There is a small gap at the synapse called the synaptic cleft. The electrical signal traveling down the axon cannot directly cross this gap. Instead, it triggers the release of chemical messengers called neurotransmitters.

- "A prototypical biological neuron is composed of several key structural elements, each fulfilling a critical function in its operation:
  - o **Cell Body (Soma):** The central component of the neuron, housing the nucleus and other essential cellular organelles. The soma serves as the integration center for the diverse electrical signals received from other neurons via the dendrites, akin to a command center where incoming information is processed.
  - o **Dendrites:** Branched, arbor-like extensions emanating from the cell body, acting as the primary recipients of signals from other neurons. Their surfaces are equipped with receptors that bind to neurotransmitters, transducing chemical signals into electrical impulses, much like antennas capturing incoming messages.
  - o **Axon:** A long, slender projection extending from the cell body, responsible for transmitting electrical signals, known as action potentials, away from the soma towards other neurons, muscles, or glands, functioning as the neuron's transmission cable carrying processed information. Some axons are ensheathed in myelin, an insulating layer that accelerates signal propagation.
  - o **Synapse:** The critical junction facilitating communication between the axon terminal of a presynaptic neuron and the dendrite or cell body of a postsynaptic neuron. A narrow gap, the synaptic cleft, separates these neurons. Electrical signals cannot directly traverse this gap; instead, they trigger the release of chemical messengers termed neurotransmitters."

- **Step 3: How a Biological Neuron Fires (Signal Transmission):** The process by which a biological neuron transmits information involves a sequence of electrical and chemical events:

  0. **Signal Reception:** When a neuron receives signals from other neurons, these signals arrive at its dendrites. The neurotransmitters released by the sending neurons bind to receptors on the dendrites of the receiving neuron, causing a change in the electrical potential across the receiving neuron's membrane.
  1. **Integration at the Cell Body:** The electrical signals received by the dendrites are then conducted towards the cell body (soma). The soma acts as an integrator, summing up the excitatory and inhibitory signals it receives.
  2. **Action Potential Generation (Firing):** If the sum of the incoming signals at the axon hillock (a specialized region of the cell body where the axon originates) exceeds a certain threshold, the neuron generates a rapid, short-lasting electrical

impulse called an action potential. This is the "firing" of the neuron. It's an all-or-none event – the action potential either occurs at full strength or not at all.

3. **Signal Propagation along the Axon:** The action potential travels rapidly along the axon, away from the cell body, towards the axon terminals.

4. **Neurotransmitter Release at the Synapse:** When the action potential reaches the axon terminal, it triggers the release of neurotransmitters (chemical messengers) into the synaptic cleft. These neurotransmitters are stored in vesicles at the axon terminal.

5. **Activation of the Next Neuron:** The released neurotransmitters diffuse across the synaptic cleft and bind to specific receptors on the dendrites or cell body of the postsynaptic neuron (the receiving neuron). This binding causes a change in the electrical potential of the postsynaptic neuron, either making it more likely to fire its own action potential (excitatory signal) or less likely to fire (inhibitory signal). The cycle then continues with the next neuron in the network.

- "The process by which a biological neuron transmits information involves a sequence of electro-chemical events:

  0. **Signal Reception:** Upon receiving signals from other neurons, these signals arrive at its dendrites. Neurotransmitters released by presynaptic neurons bind to receptors on the postsynaptic neuron's dendrites, inducing a change in the electrical potential across its membrane.

  1. **Integration at the Cell Body:** The electrical signals received by the dendrites propagate towards the cell body (soma). The soma functions as an integrator, summing the excitatory and inhibitory signals it receives.

  2. **Action Potential Generation (Firing):** If the aggregate of incoming signals at the axon hillock (a specialized region of the soma at the axon's origin) surpasses a specific threshold, the neuron generates a rapid, transient electrical impulse termed an action potential – the 'firing' of the neuron. This is an all-or-none phenomenon; the action potential occurs at full amplitude or not at all.

  3. **Signal Propagation along the Axon:** The action potential propagates rapidly along the axon, away from the cell body, towards the axon terminals.

  4. **Neurotransmitter Release at the Synapse:** Upon reaching the axon terminal, the action potential triggers the release of neurotransmitters (chemical messengers) into the synaptic cleft. These neurotransmitters are stored within vesicles at the axon terminal.

  5. **Activation of the Next Neuron:** The released neurotransmitters diffuse across the synaptic cleft and bind to specific receptors on the dendrites or cell body of the postsynaptic neuron (the receiving neuron). This binding induces a change in the postsynaptic neuron's electrical potential, either increasing the likelihood of it firing its own action potential (excitatory signal) or decreasing this likelihood (inhibitory signal). The cycle then perpetuates with the subsequent neuron in the neural network."

2. Artificial Neurons (in Neural Networks): Mathematical Mimicry

- **Step 1: The Artificial Neuron as a Mathematical Construct:** Artificial neurons, also known as nodes or units, are the fundamental building blocks of artificial neural networks

(ANNs). Unlike their biological counterparts, they are mathematical functions designed to simulate the signal processing behavior of biological neurons. They take numerical inputs, perform a computation, and produce a numerical output.

- "Artificial neurons, also referred to as nodes or units, constitute the fundamental building blocks of artificial neural networks (ANNs). In contrast to their biological counterparts, they are mathematical functions engineered to emulate the signal processing behavior of biological neurons. They accept numerical inputs, perform a mathematical operation, and generate a numerical output."
- **Step 2: Components of an Artificial Neuron:** An artificial neuron is typically characterized by the following components:
    - **Input:** An artificial neuron receives one or more numerical input values. These inputs can represent features from a dataset (e.g., size of a house, number of bedrooms) or the outputs from other artificial neurons in the network. This is analogous to the signals received by the dendrites of a biological neuron.
    - **Weights:** Each input connection to an artificial neuron has an associated weight. These weights are numerical values that represent the strength or importance of the corresponding input. A higher weight indicates a stronger influence of that input on the neuron's output. Weights are analogous to the strength of synaptic connections in a biological neuron.
    - **Bias:** A bias term is a constant value that is added to the weighted sum of the inputs. The bias allows the neuron to be activated even when all inputs are zero, providing an additional degree of freedom in the neuron's activation. It's like a baseline activation level for the neuron.
    - **Activation Function:** This is a mathematical function that determines the output of the artificial neuron based on the weighted sum of the inputs plus the bias. The activation function introduces non-linearity into the network, allowing it to learn complex relationships in the data. Common activation functions include sigmoid, ReLU (Rectified Linear Unit), tanh (hyperbolic tangent), and others. This function mimics the non-linear firing behavior of a biological neuron.
- "An artificial neuron is typically characterized by the following components:
    - **Input:** An artificial neuron accepts one or more numerical input values. These inputs can represent features from a dataset (e.g., house size, number of bedrooms) or the outputs from other artificial neurons within the network, analogous to the signals received by a biological neuron's dendrites.
    - **Weights:** Each input connection to an artificial neuron is associated with a weight, a numerical value representing the strength or importance of the corresponding input. A larger weight signifies a greater influence of that input on the neuron's output, akin to the strength of synaptic connections in a biological neuron.
    - **Bias:** A bias term is a constant value added to the weighted sum of the inputs. The bias enables the neuron to activate even when all inputs are zero, providing an additional degree of freedom in the neuron's activation, similar to a baseline activation level.
    - **Activation Function:** A mathematical function that determines the output of the artificial neuron based on the weighted sum of the inputs and the bias. The activation function introduces non-linearity into the network, enabling it to learn

complex relationships within the data, mimicking the non-linear firing behavior of a biological neuron. Common activation functions include sigmoid, ReLU (Rectified Linear Unit), tanh (hyperbolic tangent), and others."

- **Step 3: The Process of an Artificial Neuron Working:** The operation of an artificial neuron can be broken down into a sequence of mathematical computations:

  0. **Input Reception:** The artificial neuron receives its input values.
  1. **Weighted Sum and Bias:** Each input value is multiplied by its corresponding weight. These weighted inputs are then summed together, and the bias term is added to this sum. This step is analogous to the integration of signals in the biological neuron's cell body. Mathematically, this can be represented as:

  ```
  2. z = (w₁ * x₁) + (w₂ * x₂) + ... + (w<0xE2><0x82><0x99> *
     x<0xE2><0x82><0x99>) + b
  ```

  where (x_i) are the inputs, (w_i) are the corresponding weights, (n) is the number of inputs, and (b) is the bias.

  3. **Activation:** The result of the weighted sum and bias ((z)) is then passed through the activation function (f). The output of the activation function becomes the output of the artificial neuron. Mathematically:

  ```
  4. y = f(z)
  ```

  where (y) is the output of the neuron.

- "The operation of an artificial neuron can be delineated into a sequence of mathematical computations:

  0. **Input Reception:** The artificial neuron receives its input values.
  1. **Weighted Sum and Bias:** Each input value is multiplied by its corresponding weight. These weighted inputs are then summed together, and the bias term is added to this sum. This step is analogous to the integration of signals in the biological neuron's cell body. Mathematically, this can be represented as:

  ```
  2. z = \sum_{i=1}^{n} (w_i \cdot x_i) + b
  ```

  where (x_i) are the inputs, (w_i) are the corresponding weights, (n) is the number of inputs, and (b) is the bias.

  3. **Activation:** The result of the weighted sum and bias ((z)) is then passed through the activation function (f). The output of the activation function becomes the output of the artificial neuron. Mathematically:

  ```
  4. y = f(z)
  ```

  where (y) is the output of the neuron."

- **Example:** Consider an artificial neuron with one input (x = 2), a weight (w = 0.5), and a bias (b = 1). If the activation function (f) is the ReLU (Rectified Linear Unit) function, defined as (f(z) = \max(0, z)), the output (y) of the neuron is computed as follows:
  0. **Weighted Sum and Bias:** (z = (0.5 \cdot 2) + 1 = 1 + 1 = 2)

1.   **Activation:** $(y = f(2) = \max(0, 2) = 2)$

Therefore, the output of this artificial neuron for the given input, weight, and bias with the ReLU activation function is 2.

- **Step 4: Neural Networks: Stacking Artificial Neurons:** Just as the human brain consists of billions of interconnected biological neurons, artificial neural networks are formed by stacking multiple layers of interconnected artificial neurons. These layers typically include an input layer (receiving the initial data), one or more hidden layers (performing intermediate computations), and an output layer (producing the final prediction or classification). The connections between neurons in different layers also have associated weights. By adjusting these weights during the training process, the network learns complex patterns and relationships in the data, enabling it to perform sophisticated tasks like image recognition, natural language processing, and more.
- "Analogous to the human brain's vast network of interconnected biological neurons, artificial neural networks are constructed by stacking multiple layers of interconnected artificial neurons. These layers typically comprise an input layer (receiving the initial data), one or more hidden layers (performing intermediate computations), and an output layer (generating the final prediction or classification). The connections between neurons in different layers are also associated with weights. By adjusting these weights during the training process, the network learns intricate patterns and relationships within the data, enabling it to execute sophisticated tasks such as image recognition, natural language processing, and beyond."

2. Layers, Activation Functions, and Learning Rates: How Neural Networks are Built and Learn

Think of a neural network like a processing factory. Data enters one end, goes through different stages, and then the final result comes out the other end. These stages are the **layers**.

- **Input Layer: Where the Data Enters** This is the first step. It's where your raw data gets fed into the network. Imagine it as the receiving dock of the factory. Each piece of information (each feature) has its own entry point here. For our house price prediction, the size goes in one spot, the number of bedrooms in another, and so on.
- **Hidden Layers: The Brain of the Operation** These are the layers in between the input and the final output. They're where the magic happens. Each neuron in these layers takes information from the previous layer, does some math on it, and then passes the result to the next layer. The more hidden layers you have, the more complex stuff the network can figure out. Think of these as the different assembly lines in the factory, each transforming the raw materials in a specific way. They're "hidden" because we don't directly see what they're doing; they're just changing the data into a more useful form.
- **Output Layer: The Final Product** This is the last layer. It spits out the network's answer. What this layer looks like depends on what you're trying to predict. If you're saying "yes" or "no" (like spam or not spam), you might have one neuron here. If you're picking from a bunch of options (like cat, dog, or bird), you'll have one neuron for each option. If you're predicting a number (like a house price), you'll likely have one neuron

giving you that number. This is like the shipping department, where the final product is packaged and sent out.

Activation Functions: Making Decisions Inside the Neurons

Inside each neuron (except in the input layer), there's a little switch called the **activation function**. This function decides if the neuron should "fire" or not, meaning whether it should pass its result on to the next layer. Without these switches, the whole network would just be doing simple linear math, and it wouldn't be able to learn anything complicated. Activation functions introduce non-linearity, which is what allows neural networks to learn complex patterns.

- **Sigmoid:** This squishes the output to be between 0 and 1, like a probability.
  - **Example:** In the output layer, if you're trying to predict if something is true or false (like a cat being in a picture), a sigmoid can output the probability of it being true.
- **ReLU (Rectified Linear Unit):** This is a simple one: if the input is negative, the output is 0; if it's positive, the output is just the input. It's fast and works well in many cases.
  - **Example:** Often used in the hidden layers to help the network learn faster.
- **Tanh (Hyperbolic Tangent):** Similar to sigmoid, but it squishes the output to be between -1 and 1.
  - **Example:** You might see this in networks that need to handle both positive and negative information.
- **Softmax:** If you have multiple categories you're trying to predict (like cat, dog, bird), softmax takes the raw scores and turns them into probabilities that add up to 1. So, it might say there's a 70% chance it's a cat, 20% a dog, and 10% a bird.
  - **Example:** Used in the output layer when you have more than two things you're classifying.

Think of activation functions as the decision-makers within each assembly line worker. They look at what they've processed and decide whether to pass it on strongly, weakly, or not at all.

Learning Rates: How Fast the Network Learns

The **learning rate** is like the knob that controls how much the network adjusts its internal settings (the weights) each time it learns from the data. If you set it too high, the network might make big, clumsy adjustments and miss the sweet spot, like someone turning a dial too quickly and skipping the right setting. If you set it too low, it will make tiny, careful adjustments, which might take forever to learn, like someone turning a dial a tiny bit at a time.

- **Too High:** The network might learn too fast and end up with a bad solution or even fail to learn at all. It's like trying to learn to ride a bike by making huge, jerky movements – you'll probably fall.
- **Too Low:** The network might take ages to learn, or it might get stuck in a bad spot without realizing there's a better solution nearby. It's like trying to learn to ride a bike by making such small adjustments you never really get going.

A good strategy is often to start with a moderate learning rate and then adjust it as the training goes on. This is like starting with bigger movements when learning to ride a bike and then making finer adjustments as you get better. This dynamic adjustment is called **learning rate scheduling**.

So, layers organize the processing, activation functions make decisions within the neurons, and the learning rate controls how quickly and effectively the network learns from the data. These are key ingredients in building and training powerful neural networks.

3. 3. Convolutional and Recurrent Neural Networks (CNNs and RNNs): Special Neural Network Tools

While regular neural networks are great for lots of things, CNNs and RNNs are like specialized tools in a toolbox, perfect for particular jobs. CNNs are your go-to for anything involving images and videos, while RNNs shine when dealing with sequences like text or time-based data.

Convolutional Neural Networks (CNNs): Seeing Patterns in Images

Imagine trying to teach a computer to see a cat in a picture. You wouldn't just feed it all the pixel values directly into a regular network. It would be like trying to describe a picture by listing the color of every single dot – it wouldn't understand the shapes or the overall image. CNNs work differently; they're designed to automatically find patterns in images, just like our eyes and brain do.

- **Step 1: Convolution Layer - Finding the Important Bits:** Think of this layer as using a special magnifying glass (called a **filter** or **kernel**) to slide over the image, looking for specific features like edges, corners, or simple textures. This filter is a small grid of numbers. As it moves across the image, it does some math with the pixel values underneath it. The result is a new, smaller image called a **feature map** that highlights where those specific features are present.
  - **Example:** The first layer might have filters that are good at detecting horizontal lines. When this filter moves over the image, it will produce a feature map where bright spots indicate areas with strong horizontal lines. Another filter might detect vertical lines, and so on.
- **Step 2: Pooling Layer - Shrinking and Simplifying:** After the convolution layer finds these features, the pooling layer comes in to make things simpler and less overwhelming. It reduces the size of the feature maps while keeping the important information. Think of it as summarizing the findings from the magnifying glass.
  - **Max Pooling:** This is like looking at a small square in the feature map and just remembering the brightest spot (the maximum value) in that square. This helps keep the most important activations.
  - **Average Pooling:** Instead of the brightest spot, this takes the average of all the values in the small square.
- **Step 3: Fully Connected Layer - Making the Final Decision:** After going through several rounds of convolution and pooling (where the network learns more and more complex features like cat ears or eyes), the final step is the fully connected layer. Here,

all the processed information from the previous layers is flattened into a single long list of numbers, and then it's treated like the input to a regular neural network. This layer makes the final classification or prediction (like "This is a cat!"). Every neuron in this layer is connected to every neuron in the layer before it.

- **Example:** For our cat image, the CNN might work like this:

  0. **First Convolution Layer:** Detects basic things like edges and curves in the fur.
  1. **Pooling Layer:** Makes those edge maps smaller and more manageable.
  2. **Second Convolution Layer:** Combines the edges to find more complex shapes, like the outline of an ear.
  3. **Pooling Layer:** Shrinks those shape maps.
  4. **Third Convolution Layer:** Detects even more complex features like the texture of the fur or the shape of an eye.
  5. **Pooling Layer:** Shrinks again.
  6. **Fully Connected Layer:** Takes all these high-level features and decides, "Yep, based on these ears, eyes, and fur texture, this is a cat!"

Recurrent Neural Networks (RNNs): Remembering Sequences

Now, imagine trying to understand a sentence. The order of the words matters a lot! "The cat sat on the mat" is different from "The mat sat on the cat." Regular neural networks process each input independently, but RNNs are designed to handle data where the order is important – sequences. They have a kind of memory that allows them to remember information from previous steps in the sequence.

- **Step 1: RNN Cells - Processing One Step at a Time with Memory:** At each step in the sequence (like each word in a sentence), an RNN takes two things as input: the current item in the sequence and a "hidden state" from the previous step. This hidden state is like the network's memory of what it has seen so far in the sequence. The RNN cell processes these two inputs and produces two outputs: a new hidden state (which gets passed on to the next step) and an output for the current step (like a prediction).
- **Step 2: Long Short-Term Memory (LSTM) - Remembering the Long Game:** Regular RNNs can have trouble remembering things from very far back in a long sequence. LSTMs are a special type of RNN designed to overcome this "long-term dependency" problem. They have extra mechanisms called "gates" that help them decide what information to keep in their memory and what to forget. Think of these gates as little controllers that manage the flow of information in the hidden state.
  - **Example:** For speech recognition, an LSTM can remember the beginning of a sentence to correctly understand words that come much later, even if there are many words in between.
- **Step 3: GRU (Gated Recurrent Unit) - A Simpler Memory:** GRUs are like a simplified version of LSTMs. They also have gating mechanisms to help with long-term dependencies but have fewer parts, which can make them a bit faster to train. They achieve a similar goal of remembering information over longer sequences.
- **Example:** For a language model trying to predict the next word, an RNN (like an LSTM or GRU) would process the words one by one. After seeing "big" and "red," the hidden

state would contain information about these words. When it sees the next (blank) space, it uses its hidden state to predict the most likely next word, which might be "house." It remembers the context from the beginning of the sentence.

So, CNNs are like having specialized vision, able to automatically pick out patterns in images. RNNs are like having a memory, allowing them to understand and process sequences of data where the order matters. They're both powerful tools for tackling specific types of problems that regular neural networks might struggle with.

50 multiple-choice questions (MCQs) with answers based on the topics:

How Neurons Work (Biological vs. Artificial)

1. **Which part of a biological neuron receives signals from other neurons?**
   - o a) Axon
   - o b) Dendrites
   - o c) Cell Body
   - o d) Synapse
   Answer: b) Dendrites
2. **What is the primary function of the axon in a biological neuron?**
   - o a) To receive signals
   - o b) To store neurotransmitters
   - o c) To transmit electrical impulses to other neurons
   - o d) To generate electrical impulses
   Answer: c) To transmit electrical impulses to other neurons
3. **What is the name of the junction where one neuron communicates with another?**
   - o a) Dendrite
   - o b) Axon terminal
   - o c) Synapse
   - o d) Soma
   Answer: c) Synapse
4. **Which of the following best describes the function of the activation function in an artificial neuron?**
   - o a) To generate electrical impulses
   - o b) To determine the output based on the weighted inputs
   - o c) To receive the inputs
   - o d) To store the results for later use
   Answer: b) To determine the output based on the weighted inputs
5. **In an artificial neural network, the inputs to a neuron are multiplied by which of the following?**
   - o a) Bias
   - o b) Weights
   - o c) Outputs
   - o d) Activation functions
   Answer: b) Weights
6. **What is the purpose of the bias in an artificial neuron?**
   - o a) To modify the weights of the neuron

- o b) To introduce non-linearity to the output
- o c) To shift the activation function
- o d) To adjust the activation threshold
  Answer: c) To shift the activation function
7. **Which of the following activation functions is commonly used in hidden layers of deep networks?**
   - o a) ReLU
   - o b) Sigmoid
   - o c) Softmax
   - o d) Linear
     Answer: a) ReLU
8. **Which is a key difference between biological neurons and artificial neurons?**
   - o a) Biological neurons can only process linear data
   - o b) Artificial neurons can learn from data
   - o c) Artificial neurons do not have a synaptic gap
   - o d) Biological neurons do not have activation functions
     Answer: b) Artificial neurons can learn from data
9. **Which of the following is NOT a component of a biological neuron?**
   - o a) Dendrites
   - o b) Axon
   - o c) Activation function
   - o d) Soma
     Answer: c) Activation function
10. **Which of these is an example of a commonly used activation function in artificial neural networks?**
    - o a) ReLU
    - o b) Gamma
    - o c) Inverse
    - o d) RNN
      Answer: a) ReLU

Layers, Activation Functions, and Learning Rates

11. **What is the function of the output layer in a neural network?**
    - o a) To receive the input features
    - o b) To compute the error
    - o c) To produce the final output or prediction
    - o d) To perform feature extraction
      Answer: c) To produce the final output or prediction
12. **Which layer is responsible for learning the features from the raw data in deep learning?**
    - o a) Output layer
    - o b) Hidden layer
    - o c) Input layer
    - o d) Pooling layer
      Answer: b) Hidden layer
13. **Which of the following activation functions outputs values between 0 and 1?**

- o a) ReLU
- o b) Sigmoid
- o c) Tanh
- o d) Softmax
  Answer: b) Sigmoid
14. **What happens if the learning rate is too high during the training of a neural network?**
    - o a) The model converges too slowly
    - o b) The model might converge to a suboptimal solution or fail to converge
    - o c) The model gets stuck in a local minimum
    - o d) The training becomes easier
    Answer: b) The model might converge to a suboptimal solution or fail to converge
15. **Which activation function is used in the output layer for multi-class classification?**
    - o a) ReLU
    - o b) Sigmoid
    - o c) Softmax
    - o d) Tanh
    Answer: c) Softmax
16. **What is the primary function of a learning rate in neural network training?**
    - o a) To speed up the training
    - o b) To control how much the weights are updated with each iteration
    - o c) To improve the activation function
    - o d) To balance the training data
    Answer: b) To control how much the weights are updated with each iteration
17. **Which activation function is known for being computationally efficient and commonly used in hidden layers?**
    - o a) ReLU
    - o b) Tanh
    - o c) Sigmoid
    - o d) Softmax
    Answer: a) ReLU
18. **Which of the following layers in a neural network is responsible for reducing the dimensionality of the feature maps?**
    - o a) Fully connected layer
    - o b) Convolutional layer
    - o c) Pooling layer
    - o d) Recurrent layer
    Answer: c) Pooling layer
19. **What is the primary benefit of using the Tanh activation function over Sigmoid?**
    - o a) It outputs values between -1 and 1, which helps with negative values
    - o b) It has a faster convergence rate
    - o c) It is less computationally expensive
    - o d) It is always preferred for classification problems
    Answer: a) It outputs values between -1 and 1, which helps with negative values
20. **Which of the following methods is used to adjust the learning rate during training?**
    - o a) Learning rate scheduler
    - o b) Backpropagation
    - o c) Weight regularization

o d) Activation function adjustment
Answer: a) Learning rate scheduler

Convolutional and Recurrent Neural Networks (CNNs and RNNs)

21. **What is the main purpose of Convolutional Neural Networks (CNNs)?**
    - o a) To process sequential data
    - o b) To perform image and video recognition tasks
    - o c) To generate natural language text
    - o d) To perform time-series prediction
    Answer: b) To perform image and video recognition tasks

22. **Which layer in a CNN is responsible for applying filters to the input data?**
    - o a) Fully connected layer
    - o b) Convolutional layer
    - o c) Pooling layer
    - o d) Output layer
    Answer: b) Convolutional layer

23. **What does a convolutional layer do in a CNN?**
    - o a) It reduces the size of the data
    - o b) It extracts features from the input data using filters
    - o c) It creates new dimensions for data
    - o d) It classifies the data
    Answer: b) It extracts features from the input data using filters

24. **What does the pooling layer in a CNN do?**
    - o a) Increases the dimensionality of the data
    - o b) Reduces the size of the feature maps while retaining important information
    - o c) Performs convolution operations
    - o d) Connects neurons across layers
    Answer: b) Reduces the size of the feature maps while retaining important information

25. **Which of the following is the primary function of Recurrent Neural Networks (RNNs)?**
    - o a) To handle spatial data like images
    - o b) To handle sequential data such as time-series or text
    - o c) To reduce the dimensionality of data
    - o d) To perform non-linear transformations
    Answer: b) To handle sequential data such as time-series or text

26. **Which of the following architectures is commonly used to model long-term dependencies in sequences?**
    - o a) CNN
    - o b) LSTM (Long Short-Term Memory)
    - o c) Fully connected networks
    - o d) Linear regression
    Answer: b) LSTM (Long Short-Term Memory)

27. **In an RNN, what type of data is best suited for processing?**
    - o a) Static images
    - o b) Time-series or sequential data
    - o c) Non-linear data

- o d) Tabular data

Answer: b) Time-series or sequential data

28. **Which of the following layers in a CNN is responsible for combining features extracted from different regions of an image?**
    - o a) Pooling layer
    - o b) Convolutional layer
    - o c) Fully connected layer
    - o d) Recurrent layer

    Answer: c) Fully connected layer

29. **Which of the following is a key advantage of RNNs over traditional neural networks?**
    - o a) Ability to process non-sequential data
    - o b) Memory of past inputs
    - o c) Faster training times
    - o d) Simpler architecture

    Answer: b) Memory of past inputs

30. **In CNNs, what is the primary purpose of using multiple convolutional layers?**
    - o a) To increase computational complexity
    - o b) To learn hierarchical features of the data
    - o c) To reduce overfitting
    - o d) To optimize the learning rate

    Answer: b) To learn hierarchical features of the data

31. **What is a characteristic feature of LSTM cells in RNNs?**
    - o a) They forget past data entirely
    - o b) They can maintain and update memory across time steps
    - o c) They are used for feature extraction in images
    - o d) They have a fixed memory size

    Answer: b) They can maintain and update memory across time steps

32. **What does the term "filter" refer to in the context of CNNs?**
    - o a) A method for adjusting the learning rate
    - o b) A function for reducing the dimensionality of data
    - o c) A set of weights used to detect specific features in an image
    - o d) A process for normalizing inputs

    Answer: c) A set of weights used to detect specific features in an image

33. **Which of the following is a common application of CNNs?**
    - o a) Speech recognition
    - o b) Image classification
    - o c) Time-series forecasting
    - o d) Text generation

    Answer: b) Image classification

34. **What is the role of the "forget gate" in an LSTM?**
    - o a) To decide which information should be discarded from the cell state
    - o b) To update the cell state
    - o c) To control the learning rate
    - o d) To filter input data

    Answer: a) To decide which information should be discarded from the cell state

35. **Which of the following neural network architectures is best for modeling data that requires sequential processing?**
    - o a) CNN

- o b) RNN
- o c) GAN
- o d) SVM
   Answer: b) RNN

Advanced Questions

36. **Which method in CNN helps prevent overfitting by randomly disabling certain neurons during training?**
    - o a) Max-pooling
    - o b) Dropout
    - o c) Batch normalization
    - o d) L2 regularization
      Answer: b) Dropout
37. **What does the output of an RNN cell depend on?**
    - o a) Only the current input
    - o b) Only the previous output
    - o c) Both the current input and the previous output
    - o d) Only the hidden state
      Answer: c) Both the current input and the previous output
38. **Which method is commonly used to optimize the weights in both CNNs and RNNs?**
    - o a) Gradient descent
    - o b) K-means clustering
    - o c) Decision trees
    - o d) Naive Bayes
      Answer: a) Gradient descent
39. **What is the main purpose of the softmax activation function in the final layer of a CNN for classification tasks?**
    - o a) To ensure outputs are between 0 and 1
    - o b) To compute probabilities of different classes
    - o c) To reduce the dimensionality of the output
    - o d) To scale the input values
      Answer: b) To compute probabilities of different classes
40. **Which layer in a CNN is used to down-sample the feature map size?**
    - o a) Fully connected layer
    - o b) Convolutional layer
    - o c) Pooling layer
    - o d) Recurrent layer
      Answer: c) Pooling layer
41. **Which neural network architecture would be most appropriate for speech-to-text conversion?**
    - o a) CNN
    - o b) RNN
    - o c) GAN
    - o d) KNN
      Answer: b) RNN
42. **Which of the following is a limitation of traditional RNNs compared to LSTMs?**
    - o a) They have shorter memory

- o b) They are more computationally expensive
- o c) They handle sequential data poorly
- o d) They require more layers

   Answer: a) They have shorter memory

43. **In a convolutional operation, what is the role of the stride parameter?**
    - o a) To adjust the size of the output feature map
    - o b) To control the pooling operation
    - o c) To control the overlap between consecutive receptive fields
    - o d) To initialize weights

   Answer: c) To control the overlap between consecutive receptive fields

44. **What is the key feature of a "recurrent" network?**
    - o a) It has a fixed number of neurons
    - o b) It can process both sequential and non-sequential data
    - o c) It can reuse information from previous time steps
    - o d) It performs feature extraction in images

   Answer: c) It can reuse information from previous time steps

45. **What is the primary function of the cell state in LSTMs?**
    - o a) To store temporary results during the computation
    - o b) To regulate the flow of information across time steps
    - o c) To calculate gradients for optimization
    - o d) To control the learning rate

   Answer: b) To regulate the flow of information across time steps

46. **Which of the following is NOT typically used in CNNs?**
    - o a) Convolutional layers
    - o b) Fully connected layers
    - o c) Recurrent layers
    - o d) Pooling layers

   Answer: c) Recurrent layers

47. **Which architecture is preferred for modeling long-term dependencies in sequences?**
    - o a) CNN
    - o b) RNN
    - o c) LSTM
    - o d) MLP

   Answer: c) LSTM

48. **Which method helps improve the performance of deep learning models by normalizing the inputs to a layer?**
    - o a) Batch normalization
    - o b) ReLU
    - o c) Dropout
    - o d) Gradient clipping

   Answer: a) Batch normalization

49. **In CNNs, what is the primary function of the "ReLU" activation function?**
    - o a) To handle negative values in the data
    - o b) To introduce non-linearity into the model
    - o c) To normalize the data
    - o d) To adjust the learning rate

   Answer: b) To introduce non-linearity into the model

50. **Which type of neural network is specifically designed to handle images as input?**
    - o a) RNN
    - o b) CNN
    - o c) GAN
    - o d) MLP

   Answer: b) CNN

CHAPTER 9: UNDERSTANDING NATURAL LANGUAGE PROCESSING (NLP)

Natural Language Processing (NLP) is a branch of artificial intelligence (AI) that focuses on the interaction between computers and humans through natural language. The goal is to enable machines to read, understand, interpret, and respond to human languages in a way that is both meaningful and useful. NLP involves multiple tasks that range from basic language understanding to complex reasoning about the text and context.

How Machines Understand Human Language: Decoding Our Words

Getting a machine to understand human language is a tricky business. It's not like teaching it math where everything is precise. Our language is messy, full of slang, different ways of saying the same thing, and context that's often implied. So, machines go through a few key stages to try and make sense of it all.

1. Text Preprocessing: Cleaning Up the Mess

Before a machine can even start to understand the meaning, it needs to clean up the text and break it down into manageable pieces. Think of it like preparing ingredients before you can cook.

- **Step 1: Tokenization - Chopping into Pieces:** This is the first step where the machine takes a chunk of text and chops it up into smaller bits called **tokens**. These tokens are usually words, but they can also be punctuation marks or even parts of words.
  - **Example:** Text: "Let's go to the park, okay?" Tokens: ["Let", "'s", "go", "to", "the", "park", ",", "okay", "?"]
- **Step 2: Stopword Removal - Getting Rid of the Fluff:** Our sentences are full of common words like "the," "is," "a," "of" that don't really add much to the core meaning. These are called **stopwords**. The machine often removes them to focus on the more important words.
  - **Example:** Text: "The big dog is running very fast." Stopwords removed: ["big", "dog", "running", "very", "fast"] (Words like "the," "is" are gone)
- **Step 3: Stemming and Lemmatization - Finding the Root:** Words can appear in different forms (running, ran, runs) but they all relate to the same basic meaning ("run"). **Stemming** and **lemmatization** are ways to reduce these words to their root form.
  - **Stemming:** This is a simpler process that just chops off the ends of words based on some rules. It might not always give you a real word.
    - "Playing" → "Play"
    - "Happily" → "Happi" (not a real word, but the root idea is there)
  - **Lemmatization:** This is a more sophisticated process that tries to find the actual dictionary form of the word (the **lemma**), taking into account the word's meaning and context.
    - "Better" → "Good"
    - "Running" → "Run"

- "Cacti" → "Cactus"

2. Word Embeddings: Giving Words Meaning in Numbers

Once the text is cleaned up and broken down, the machine needs a way to understand what the words actually *mean*. It can't just treat them as random symbols. **Word embeddings** are a clever way to represent words as lists of numbers (vectors) in a high-dimensional space. The idea is that words with similar meanings will have vectors that are close to each other in this space.

- **Word2Vec:** One popular technique for creating word embeddings. It learns these numerical representations by looking at how words appear together in tons of text. Words that are often used in similar contexts end up with similar vectors.
  - **Example:** The Word2Vec vectors for "king" and "queen" would be more similar (closer in the numerical space) than the vectors for "king" and "bicycle" because "king" and "queen" are related concepts. You could even do cool math with these vectors: the vector for "king" minus "man" plus "woman" might end up being very close to the vector for "queen"!

3. Syntax and Grammar Analysis: Understanding the Structure

Just knowing the meaning of individual words isn't enough. The order of words and how they relate to each other in a sentence is crucial for understanding the overall meaning. This is where syntax and grammar analysis comes in.

- **Part-of-Speech Tagging (POS Tagging):** The machine identifies the grammatical role of each word in a sentence, like whether it's a noun (person, place, thing), a verb (action), an adjective (describing word), etc.
  - **Example:** Sentence: "The cat chased the mouse." Analysis: "The" (determiner) "cat" (noun) "chased" (verb) "the" (determiner) "mouse" (noun)
- **Dependency Parsing:** This goes a step further and tries to understand the relationships *between* the words in a sentence. It figures out which words depend on other words and how. This helps the machine understand the structure of the sentence and who is doing what to whom.
  - **Example:** Sentence: "The big dog barked loudly." Analysis (simplified): "barked" (head verb) → "dog" (subject, depends on "barked") → "The" (determiner, depends on "dog") → "big" (adjective, depends on "dog") → "loudly" (adverb, depends on "barked")

4. Sentiment Analysis: Feeling the Emotion

Sometimes, we don't just want the machine to understand the literal meaning of words; we want it to understand the *feeling* behind them – whether the text is positive, negative, or neutral. This is called **sentiment analysis**.

- The machine looks at the words used and the way they're combined to try and figure out the emotional tone. Some words have a strong positive or negative connotation.

- **Example:** Text: "This is an amazing movie!" Sentiment: Positive (words like "amazing" give it away)

  Text: "I am so disappointed with this service." Sentiment: Negative (words like "disappointed" are key)

Advanced sentiment analysis can even detect more specific emotions like joy, sadness, anger, or fear.

So, it's a multi-stage process. Machines first clean up the language, then represent words with numerical meaning, then analyze the structure of sentences, and finally try to understand the underlying sentiment. It's not perfect, and human language is still full of nuances that machines struggle with, but these steps are how they're learning to "understand" us better and better.

---

1. Sentiment Analysis: Figuring Out How People Feel

Sentiment analysis is all about teaching computers to understand the emotion or opinion expressed in a piece of text. Is someone happy, sad, angry, or just neutral about something they wrote? Machines can learn to figure this out.

- **Steps:**
  1. **Data Collection: Gathering Opinions:** First, you need a bunch of text examples where humans have already said what the sentiment is (positive, negative, neutral, etc.). Think of it like creating a labeled training set for the machine to learn from.
     - **Example:** You might collect customer reviews for a product and manually label each review as "positive," "negative," or "neutral."
  2. **Preprocessing: Cleaning the Text:** Just like before, you need to clean up the text so the machine can work with it better. This involves:
     - **Tokenization:** Breaking the text into individual words or pieces.
       - Text: "This movie was absolutely amazing!"
       - Tokens: ["This", "movie", "was", "absolutely", "amazing", "!"]
     - **Stopword Removal:** Getting rid of common, less important words.
       - Tokens: ["This", "movie", "was", "absolutely", "amazing", "!"]
       - Stopwords Removed: ["movie", "absolutely", "amazing", "!"] (Words like "this" and "was" are gone)
     - **Stemming/Lemmatization:** Reducing words to their base form.
       - "Amazing" → "Amaze"
       - "Movies" → "Movie"
  3. **Feature Extraction: Turning Words into Numbers:** Machines understand numbers, not words. So, you need to convert the processed text into numerical features that the machine learning model can use. Some common ways to do this are:

- **Bag of Words:** You create a list of all the unique words in your training data. Then, for each piece of text, you count how many times each word appears in that text. This count becomes the numerical feature.
  - **TF-IDF (Term Frequency-Inverse Document Frequency):** This is similar to Bag of Words, but it also considers how rare a word is across all the text examples. Words that appear frequently in one text but rarely in others are considered more important.
  - **Word Embeddings:** Like we talked about before, these represent words as dense vectors that capture their meaning. You can use the average of the word embeddings in a text as its overall numerical representation.
4. **Model Training: Teaching the Machine to Feel:** You take the numerical features you created and the sentiment labels (positive, negative, etc.) and feed them into a machine learning model. The model learns the relationship between the features (the word numbers) and the sentiments. Common models used include:
   - **Support Vector Machines (SVM):** Good at finding the best boundary between different sentiment categories.
   - **Random Forests:** An ensemble of decision trees that can handle complex relationships.
   - **Neural Networks:** Can learn very intricate patterns in the text and are often used for more advanced sentiment analysis.
5. **Prediction: Guessing the Feeling of New Text:** Once the model is trained, you can give it a new piece of text it has never seen before. It will go through the same preprocessing and feature extraction steps, and then the trained model will predict the sentiment of that text (positive, negative, neutral, etc.).

- **Example:** Text: "The food was terrible and the service was slow." The sentiment analysis model, after going through the steps, would likely predict this as **negative** because of words like "terrible" and "slow."

2. Chatbots: Talking to Machines

Chatbots are AI systems designed to have conversations with humans, like a digital customer service agent or a virtual assistant.

- **Two Main Types:**
  - **Rule-Based Chatbots: Following the Script:** These chatbots are like robots that follow a strict set of rules. If you say something specific, they have a pre-programmed answer. They often use decision trees (if you say X, then answer Y) or try to match your input to known patterns.
    - **Example:** User: "What are your operating hours?" Chatbot: "Our operating hours are 9 AM to 5 PM, Monday to Friday." This chatbot likely has a rule that says if the user asks about operating hours, it should give this specific answer. It wouldn't be able to handle more complex or unexpected questions very well.
  - **AI-Based Chatbots: Actually Understanding (Trying To):** These chatbots are more sophisticated. They use machine learning models (especially those that

understand language, like the ones we talked about earlier) to understand the *meaning* and context of what you're saying. This allows them to generate more natural and flexible responses, even if you don't use the exact phrases they were programmed for.

- **Example:** User: "I'm really frustrated because my order hasn't arrived yet." Chatbot: "I understand your frustration. Can you please provide your order number so I can look into this for you?" This chatbot likely understood the emotion ("frustrated") and the topic ("order hasn't arrived") and gave a relevant and helpful response, even though the user didn't use a specific pre-programmed question.

3. Language Translation: Speaking Across Languages

Machine translation is the task of automatically translating text from one human language to another. Think Google Translate or other translation tools.

- **Steps (Simplified for Modern Systems):**
  1. **Tokenization:** The sentence in the original language is broken down into tokens (words, punctuation).
     - Example: "Hello, how are you?" → ["Hello", ",", "how", "are", "you", "?"]
  2. **Model Training (Neural Machine Translation):** Modern translation systems, like Google Translate, mostly use **Neural Machine Translation (NMT)** models. These are complex neural networks that are trained on massive amounts of text that has already been translated by humans (parallel corpora). The network learns the complex relationships between words and phrases in different languages.
  3. **Translation:** When you give the trained model a new sentence in the source language, it processes the tokens and generates the corresponding sentence in the target language.
     - Example: Input: "Hello, how are you?" → Output: "Hola, ¿cómo estás?"
- **Sequence-to-Sequence (Seq2Seq) Models:** Many modern translation systems use a specific type of neural network architecture called **Sequence-to-Sequence (Seq2Seq)**. These models have two main parts:

  o **Encoder:** This part reads the input sentence (the sequence of words) and converts it into a condensed representation, kind of like a thought or a summary of the sentence's meaning in a numerical form.
  o **Decoder:** This part takes that condensed representation from the encoder and uses it to generate the translated sentence, word by word, in the target language. It learns to predict the next word based on the encoded meaning and the words it has already generated.

So, Sentiment Analysis helps machines understand feelings, Chatbots let us have conversations (simple or complex), and Language Translation breaks down language barriers – all using the power of machine learning and understanding human language.

The Rise of Large Language Models (like ChatGPT!): Machines That Talk Like Us

You've probably heard of ChatGPT. It can chat with you, write stories, answer questions – it feels almost human. These abilities come from a new breed of AI called **Large Language Models (LLMs)**. They're a huge leap forward in how machines understand and generate human language.

What Are Large Language Models? Big Brains for Text

Think of LLMs as super-smart AI that have read a massive amount of text – practically the entire internet and a whole lot of books! Because they've seen so much text, they've learned all sorts of patterns and relationships between words, how sentences are structured, and even a bit about the world the text describes. Models like GPT (which powers ChatGPT) are the rockstars of this field.

- **Training Process: Learning by Reading Everything:** LLMs learn in a way called **unsupervised learning**. This means they aren't explicitly told "this is a positive sentence," or "this word follows that word." Instead, they are just fed huge amounts of raw text, and they learn by trying to predict the next word in a sequence. It's like learning to speak a language by just listening to tons and tons of conversations and trying to guess what comes next. Over time, they get really good at figuring out these patterns.
  - **Example:** Imagine feeding an LLM the sentence "The cat sat on the...". It will try to guess the next word based on all the text it has seen. Because "mat" is a common word to follow that phrase, the model will learn to assign a high probability to "mat" being the next word.
- **Architecture: How They're Built - The Transformer Power:** The secret sauce behind the success of LLMs like GPT is their architecture, called **Transformer**. Older models like RNNs and LSTMs (we talked about them earlier for sequences) had trouble with very long pieces of text because they processed words one after the other. Transformers are different. They can process all the words in a sentence at the same time, in **parallel**. This makes them much faster and better at understanding the relationships between words that are far apart in a sentence. They use a clever mechanism called "attention" that allows them to focus on the most important words in the input when trying to understand or generate text.
  - **Example:** In the sentence "The dog chased its tail," the "attention" mechanism helps the model understand that "its" refers back to "dog," even though they aren't right next to each other.

How ChatGPT Works: Having a Conversation

ChatGPT, built by OpenAI, is a specific example of a powerful LLM that's designed for conversations. Here's how it works when you chat with it:

- **Step 1: Input Processing - You Say Something:** First, you type in your question, request, or statement – this is the **prompt** or **query**. ChatGPT takes this input text.

- o **Example:** You type: "Tell me a short story about a robot who wants to be a painter."
- **Step 2: Context Understanding - Remembering What You Said:** ChatGPT doesn't just look at your current message in isolation. It tries to understand the **context** of the entire conversation, including what you've said before. This helps it give responses that make sense in the flow of the chat. It also tries to understand the nuances in your text, like the tone or implied meaning.
  - o **Example:** If you previously said you like science fiction, ChatGPT is more likely to generate a sci-fi story about the robot painter.
- **Step 3: Response Generation - Predicting What to Say Next:** This is where the LLM magic really happens. ChatGPT generates its response by predicting the most likely **next word** (or sequence of words) based on the input it received and the context it has understood. It has learned probability distributions for which words tend to follow other words. It doesn't "think" like a human, but it's incredibly good at statistically figuring out what a human would likely say next in a similar situation. It keeps generating words, one after another, until it forms a complete response.
  - o **Example:** After your prompt about the robot painter, ChatGPT might first predict the word "Once," then "upon," then "a," and so on, building the story word by word based on the patterns it learned during its massive training.

Applications of Large Language Models: What Can They Do?

Because LLMs are so good at understanding and generating human-like text, they have a ton of potential applications:

- **Text Generation:** They can write articles, stories, poems, scripts, emails, and all sorts of other written content, sometimes even with a specific style or tone.
- **Question Answering:** You can ask them questions on a wide range of topics, and they can often provide informative and coherent answers by drawing on the vast knowledge they've learned.
- **Personal Assistants:** They can help with tasks like setting reminders, summarizing information, drafting emails, and retrieving information from the web.
- **Code Generation:** Surprisingly, LLMs can even write and debug computer code in various programming languages, making them a potential tool for developers.

The rise of LLMs like ChatGPT is changing how we interact with computers and opening up new possibilities for automating tasks and creating intelligent systems that can understand and generate human language in impressive ways. They're like a new kind of digital brain that has learned to speak our language by reading almost everything we've ever written.

50 multiple-choice questions (MCQs) based on the topics:

How Machines Understand Human Language

1. **What is the first step in Natural Language Processing (NLP)?**

- A) Tokenization
- B) Lemmatization
- C) Named Entity Recognition
- D) Stopword Removal
- **Answer**: A) Tokenization

2. **Which technique is used for converting words into a numerical representation?**
   - A) Clustering
   - B) Word Embeddings
   - C) Decision Trees
   - D) Bag of Words
   - **Answer**: B) Word Embeddings

3. **Which of the following is used to eliminate common words like "is", "the", and "of"?**
   - A) Tokenization
   - B) Stopword Removal
   - C) Named Entity Recognition
   - D) Lemmatization
   - **Answer**: B) Stopword Removal

4. **Which of the following is an example of stemming?**
   - A) Running → Run
   - B) Running → Ran
   - C) Better → Good
   - D) Happiness → Happy
   - **Answer**: A) Running → Run

5. **Which model is commonly used for converting words into vector space representations?**
   - A) K-means
   - B) Word2Vec
   - C) Naive Bayes
   - D) SVM
   - **Answer**: B) Word2Vec

6. **What does POS tagging stand for?**
   - A) Part of Speech tagging
   - B) Processing of Sentences
   - C) Parsing of Syntax
   - D) Pattern Optimization for Speech
   - **Answer**: A) Part of Speech tagging

7. **Which method is used to detect the relationship between words in a sentence?**
   - A) Dependency Parsing
   - B) Word Embedding
   - C) Named Entity Recognition
   - D) Tokenization
   - **Answer**: A) Dependency Parsing

8. **What is the goal of named entity recognition (NER)?**
   - A) To classify the sentiment of a sentence
   - B) To detect names of people, organizations, and locations
   - C) To predict the next word in a sentence
   - D) To convert text into numerical values
   - **Answer**: B) To detect names of people, organizations, and locations

9. **Which technique involves analyzing the tone of a sentence, such as positive, negative, or neutral?**
    - A) Sentiment Analysis
    - B) Named Entity Recognition
    - C) POS Tagging
    - D) Speech Recognition
    - **Answer**: A) Sentiment Analysis
10. **Which of the following techniques is NOT typically used in text preprocessing?**
    - A) Tokenization
    - B) Stopword Removal
    - C) Sentiment Analysis
    - D) Lemmatization
    - **Answer**: C) Sentiment Analysis

Sentiment Analysis, Chatbots, and Language Translation

11. **Which of the following is an example of sentiment analysis?**
    - A) Classifying text into categories such as positive, negative, or neutral
    - B) Translating a sentence from one language to another
    - C) Generating random text
    - D) Categorizing parts of speech
    - **Answer**: A) Classifying text into categories such as positive, negative, or neutral
12. **Which type of chatbot uses pre-defined rules to respond to user inputs?**
    - A) Rule-Based Chatbots
    - B) AI-Based Chatbots
    - C) Neural Network Chatbots
    - D) Recurrent Neural Network Chatbots
    - **Answer**: A) Rule-Based Chatbots
13. **Which of the following is an example of an AI-based chatbot?**
    - A) ChatGPT
    - B) Siri
    - C) Alexa
    - D) All of the above
    - **Answer**: D) All of the above
14. **What does machine translation (MT) focus on?**
    - A) Recognizing entities in text
    - B) Translating text between languages
    - C) Summarizing text
    - D) Performing sentiment analysis
    - **Answer**: B) Translating text between languages
15. **Which of the following techniques is used in modern neural machine translation systems?**
    - A) K-means clustering
    - B) Sequence-to-sequence (Seq2Seq) models
    - C) Support Vector Machines
    - D) Naive Bayes classifier
    - **Answer**: B) Sequence-to-sequence (Seq2Seq) models

16. **Which of the following is true about AI chatbots?**
    - ○ A) They do not require data to function
    - ○ B) They can only answer predefined questions
    - ○ C) They can be trained to understand and respond to various queries
    - ○ D) They cannot learn from previous conversations
    - ○ **Answer:** C) They can be trained to understand and respond to various queries
17. **Which task is NOT typically associated with sentiment analysis?**
    - ○ A) Detecting sarcasm in a sentence
    - ○ B) Classifying opinions as positive, negative, or neutral
    - ○ C) Translating text from one language to another
    - ○ D) Analyzing the emotion conveyed in the text
    - ○ **Answer:** C) Translating text from one language to another
18. **Which model is used in machine translation for training a neural network on language pairs?**
    - ○ A) LSTM
    - ○ B) Transformer
    - ○ C) CNN
    - ○ D) RNN
    - ○ **Answer:** B) Transformer
19. **What is the primary function of a chatbot?**
    - ○ A) To analyze and summarize text
    - ○ B) To simulate human-like conversation
    - ○ C) To translate text between languages
    - ○ D) To generate creative writing
    - ○ **Answer:** B) To simulate human-like conversation
20. **Which AI technique helps in translating websites and apps into multiple languages automatically?**
    - ○ A) Speech Recognition
    - ○ B) Machine Translation
    - ○ C) Sentiment Analysis
    - ○ D) Named Entity Recognition
    - ○ **Answer:** B) Machine Translation

The Rise of Large Language Models (like ChatGPT!)

21. **Which of the following describes the core function of large language models (LLMs)?**
    - ○ A) Generating random text
    - ○ B) Understanding and generating human-like text
    - ○ C) Recognizing objects in images
    - ○ D) Performing complex mathematical calculations
    - ○ **Answer:** B) Understanding and generating human-like text
22. **Which architecture is commonly used in large language models such as GPT?**
    - ○ A) Convolutional Neural Networks (CNN)
    - ○ B) Transformer
    - ○ C) Recurrent Neural Networks (RNN)
    - ○ D) Support Vector Machines (SVM)
    - ○ **Answer:** B) Transformer

23. **What is the major advantage of using transformers in language models like GPT?**
    - o A) They can handle sequential data efficiently
    - o B) They are computationally efficient
    - o C) They can process words in parallel
    - o D) They require less data for training
    - o **Answer**: C) They can process words in parallel
24. **Which type of learning is primarily used in training large language models?**
    - o A) Supervised Learning
    - o B) Unsupervised Learning
    - o C) Reinforcement Learning
    - o D) Transfer Learning
    - o **Answer**: B) Unsupervised Learning
25. **What is the primary source of data used for training large language models?**
    - o A) Labeled datasets with predefined responses
    - o B) Large corpus of text from books, websites, and articles
    - o C) Audio and video data
    - o D) Data from IoT devices
    - o **Answer**: B) Large corpus of text from books, websites, and articles
26. **Which of the following models is a direct precursor to ChatGPT?**
    - o A) BERT
    - o B) GPT-3
    - o C) LSTM
    - o D) XGBoost
    - o **Answer**: B) GPT-3
27. **Which of the following is NOT a typical application of large language models?**
    - o A) Text generation
    - o B) Image recognition
    - o C) Sentiment analysis
    - o D) Question answering
    - o **Answer**: B) Image recognition
28. **Which feature of GPT-3 enables it to perform diverse tasks such as translation, summarization, and question answering?**
    - o A) Multi-task learning
    - o B) Reinforcement learning
    - o C) Data augmentation
    - o D) Transfer learning
    - o **Answer**: A) Multi-task learning
29. **How does ChatGPT generate human-like responses?**
    - o A) By memorizing responses from a large database
    - o B) By using preprogrammed decision rules
    - o C) By predicting the next word in a sequence based on context
    - o D) By performing statistical calculations
    - o **Answer**: C) By predicting the next word in a sequence based on context
30. **Which of the following is a key feature of GPT-based models?**
    - o A) They are good at recognizing patterns in images
    - o B) They are capable of real-time data collection
    - o C) They generate coherent text based on input prompts
    - o D) They analyze human speech in real-time

- o **Answer**: C) They generate coherent text based on input prompts

---

Applications and Challenges

31. **Which challenge is commonly faced by language models when processing ambiguous text?**
    - o A) Data scarcity
    - o B) Handling sarcasm and irony
    - o C) Lack of computational power
    - o D) Real-time performance
    - o **Answer**: B) Handling sarcasm and irony
32. **Which of the following applications is most suitable for large language models like GPT?**
    - o A) Image classification
    - o B) Speech-to-text conversion
    - o C) Text summarization and generation
    - o D) Object detection
    - o **Answer**: C) Text summarization and generation
33. **What is a common limitation of machine translation systems?**
    - o A) They can only translate short texts
    - o B) They always produce grammatically correct translations
    - o C) They often fail to capture the nuances and context of the original language
    - o D) They cannot process multiple languages
    - o **Answer**: C) They often fail to capture the nuances and context of the original language
34. **What is one of the ethical concerns related to large language models?**
    - o A) They may reinforce harmful biases from the data they were trained on
    - o B) They are too expensive to use
    - o C) They cannot generate meaningful text
    - o D) They are unable to adapt to different languages
    - o **Answer**: A) They may reinforce harmful biases from the data they were trained on
35. **Which of the following best describes the GPT-3 model's behavior in generating text?**
    - o A) It selects a single correct answer for a question
    - o B) It generates text based on context without true understanding
    - o C) It can independently learn new tasks without any training data
    - o D) It only responds with pre-programmed sentences
    - o **Answer**: B) It generates text based on context without true understanding
36. **What does fine-tuning a language model like GPT typically involve?**
    - o A) Training the model from scratch using a new dataset
    - o B) Adjusting the model using domain-specific data to improve performance
    - o C) Reducing the model's size for faster performance
    - o D) Applying data augmentation techniques to increase data size
    - o **Answer**: B) Adjusting the model using domain-specific data to improve performance
37. **Which of the following is a direct use of language models in customer service?**
    - o A) Sentiment analysis on reviews
    - o B) Speech-to-text conversion
    - o C) Automating chat responses through chatbots
    - o D) Translating website content
    - o **Answer**: C) Automating chat responses through chatbots

38. **In which scenario is a pre-trained language model particularly useful?**
    - o A) Recognizing images
    - o B) Predicting the stock market
    - o C) Generating code from text
    - o D) Generating creative writing or poetry
    - o **Answer**: D) Generating creative writing or poetry
39. **What is one of the limitations of using large language models in real-world applications?**
    - o A) They require vast amounts of labeled data for training
    - o B) They need a massive amount of computational power
    - o C) They are unable to perform basic text classification
    - o D) They perform better than humans in all tasks
    - o **Answer**: B) They need a massive amount of computational power
40. **Which factor contributes to the success of large language models like GPT in text generation?**
    - o A) A smaller number of parameters
    - o B) Extensive pre-training on diverse text sources
    - o C) Pre-defined rules for every response
    - o D) Use of external databases for real-time knowledge
    - o **Answer**: B) Extensive pre-training on diverse text sources

Ethical and Social Implications

41. **What is one potential risk of widespread use of AI chatbots like ChatGPT?**
    - o A) They might never provide accurate answers
    - o B) They might be exploited to generate misleading or harmful content
    - o C) They will eliminate jobs in all sectors
    - o D) They will require less computational power than traditional software
    - o **Answer**: B) They might be exploited to generate misleading or harmful content
42. **Which aspect is most important when considering the ethical use of AI language models?**
    - o A) Their ability to generate creative writing
    - o B) Ensuring transparency and fairness in their outputs
    - o C) Reducing the cost of deployment
    - o D) Making the models smaller and faster
    - o **Answer**: B) Ensuring transparency and fairness in their outputs
43. **Which of the following is a challenge in ensuring the fairness of language models?**
    - o A) Ensuring the model understands text correctly
    - o B) Eliminating all biases in the training data
    - o C) Making the models smaller for better performance
    - o D) Ensuring that the model can translate text in real-time
    - o **Answer**: B) Eliminating all biases in the training data
44. **Which of the following is a common criticism of AI-based text generation models like GPT?**
    - o A) They cannot generate any text
    - o B) They often reproduce societal biases
    - o C) They always produce grammatically incorrect text
    - o D) They have no capability of improving over time
    - o **Answer**: B) They often reproduce societal biases
45. **How can the ethical implications of AI be addressed in language models?**

- A) By reducing the size of the models
- B) By using diverse and representative datasets for training
- C) By making the models fully autonomous
- D) By limiting their usage to a few specific areas
- **Answer:** B) By using diverse and representative datasets for training

---

The Future of Language Models

46. **What is the most likely future application of large language models in everyday life?**
    - A) Improving image classification
    - B) Enhancing virtual assistants and chatbots
    - C) Developing hardware for better processing
    - D) Replacing human teachers entirely
    - **Answer:** B) Enhancing virtual assistants and chatbots

47. **Which of the following is essential for improving language models?**
    - A) Increasing the training dataset size and diversity
    - B) Reducing model complexity
    - C) Making the model smaller
    - D) Sticking to pre-existing rules
    - **Answer:** A) Increasing the training dataset size and diversity

48. **What does the future hold for AI language models in terms of creativity?**
    - A) They will be able to write novels on their own
    - B) They will always struggle with creativity
    - C) They will help humans become more creative by suggesting ideas
    - D) They will create entirely new art forms from scratch
    - **Answer:** C) They will help humans become more creative by suggesting ideas

49. **Which field is expected to benefit the most from the evolution of large language models?**
    - A) Image processing
    - B) Autonomous vehicles
    - C) Healthcare and medical research
    - D) Sports analytics
    - **Answer:** C) Healthcare and medical research

50. **What is the ultimate goal for improving AI language models?**
    - A) Making them fully autonomous
    - B) Enabling them to understand and generate human-like language with accuracy
    - C) Reducing their computational costs
    - D) Making them capable of reasoning and critical thinking
    - **Answer:** B) Enabling them to understand and generate human-like language with accuracy

CHAPTER 10: AI IN EVERYDAY LIFE

Artificial Intelligence (AI) has evolved rapidly and is now integrated into many aspects of our everyday lives. From smartphones to healthcare systems, AI is reshaping the way we interact with technology and each other. In this chapter, we will explore how AI is impacting various sectors, including smartphones, smart homes, smart cities, healthcare, education, finance, and entertainment.

---

1. Smartphones: AI in Your Pocket

Your smartphone isn't just for calls and social media anymore. AI is baked right into many of its features, making it more intuitive and helpful.

a. Personal Assistants (Siri, Google Assistant, Alexa): Your Voice-Activated Helper

These assistants are like having a digital sidekick that you can talk to.

- **Example:** When you ask Siri on your iPhone "What's the weather like today?", it uses AI to understand you and give you the forecast.
- **Step-by-step Process:**
    1. **Voice Input:** You say "Hey Siri" or press a button to wake up the assistant. Your phone records your voice.
    2. **Speech Recognition:** The phone's AI uses special models (acoustic models) to turn the sounds of your voice into text. It figures out what words you're saying.
    3. **Natural Language Processing (NLP):** The AI then analyzes the text to understand what you actually *meant* by your question. It figures out the intent – you want to know the weather.
    4. **Action:** The assistant connects to a weather service online, gets the current forecast for your location, and then speaks or displays the answer back to you.

b. Camera Enhancements: Making Your Photos Look Pro

Ever wonder how your phone takes such good pictures even in bad lighting? AI plays a big role here.

- **Example:** Google's Night Sight on Pixel phones can take surprisingly bright and clear photos in almost complete darkness using AI. Apple's Smart HDR can balance the light and dark parts of a photo to make everything look more detailed.
- **Step-by-step Process:**
    1. **Image Capture:** You press the button, and the phone's camera sensor captures an image.
    2. **Image Processing:** Right after taking the shot, AI algorithms kick in. They analyze the image, identifying things like faces, objects (trees, buildings), and how much light there is in different parts of the scene.

3. **Enhancement:** Based on this analysis, the AI intelligently adjusts things like how bright the image is overall (exposure), the difference between light and dark areas (contrast), and reduces grainy noise, especially in low-light photos. For faces, it might subtly smooth the skin or enhance features.
4. **Final Image:** The result is a processed image that often looks much better than what the raw camera data would have produced – brighter in the dark, more balanced in tricky lighting, and sharper overall.

c. Predictive Text and Auto-Correction: Helping You Type Faster and Better

Those helpful suggestions and automatic fixes when you're typing? That's AI at work.

- **Example:** When you start typing a word, your phone suggests the word you're likely trying to type. If you make a typo, it often corrects it automatically.
- **Step-by-step Process:**
    1. **Typing Input:** You start typing letters on the keyboard.
    2. **Prediction:** The phone's AI models, which have learned from huge amounts of text data (how people usually write), predict the word or phrase you're most likely going to type next based on the letters you've already entered and the context of your message.
    3. **Correction:** If the AI detects a common misspelling based on language patterns and your typing history, it suggests a correction. Sometimes it even auto-corrects without you having to do anything.

2. Smart Homes: AI Making Your Living Space Intelligent

Smart homes use AI to make your life easier, safer, and more energy-efficient by automating various tasks.

a. Smart Thermostats (like Nest): Learning Your Comfort Zone

These thermostats don't just follow a schedule; they learn what temperatures you like and when.

- **Example:** A Nest thermostat learns when you usually turn up the heat in the morning and when you lower it at night, and then starts doing it automatically.
- **Step-by-step Process:**
    1. **Learning Preferences:** For the first few days or weeks, you manually set the temperature to what feels comfortable at different times.
    2. **Data Collection:** The thermostat constantly records these temperature settings, along with the time of day, whether people are home (using sensors), and even the outside weather.
    3. **Automation:** AI algorithms analyze this collected data to figure out your preferred temperature patterns. Over time, it starts predicting what temperature you'll want at a specific time and adjusts it automatically, without you touching it.

b. Smart Security Systems (like Ring Doorbell): Your AI-Powered Watchdog

These systems use AI to understand what's happening at your doorstep.

- **Example:** A Ring doorbell can tell the difference between a person, a car driving by, and a pet walking on the sidewalk. It can also recognize familiar faces.
- **Step-by-step Process:**
    1. **Video Capture:** When the doorbell detects motion or someone presses the button, it starts recording video.
    2. **Object Recognition:** AI algorithms analyze the video feed in real-time to identify different types of objects, like people, animals, and vehicles.
    3. **Face Recognition:** If the AI detects a person, it can compare their face to a database of faces you've stored (like family members) to identify them.
    4. **Notification:** The system sends an alert to your phone if it detects an unfamiliar person or when a recognized visitor arrives.

c. Smart Lighting (like Philips Hue): Lights That Adapt to Your Life

Smart lights can do more than just turn on and off with your voice. AI can make them adjust automatically.

- **Example:** Philips Hue lights can be set to gradually brighten in the morning to gently wake you up, mimicking a sunrise. They can also turn off automatically when you leave a room.
- **Step-by-step Process:**
    1. **Motion Detection:** Sensors in the room detect when someone enters.
    2. **Lighting Adjustment:** AI algorithms determine the appropriate brightness and color of the lights based on factors like the time of day (brighter during the day, warmer at night) and your saved preferences.
    3. **Automation:** The system can be set up so that when the sensors no longer detect motion for a certain period, the AI tells the lights to turn off, saving energy automatically.

---

3. Smart Cities: Making Urban Life Better with AI and the Internet of Things

Smart cities are all about using technology, especially AI and the Internet of Things (IoT) (everyday objects connected to the internet), to make cities run more smoothly, be more sustainable, and respond better to the needs of their citizens.

a. Traffic Management Systems: Untangling Traffic Jams with AI

Nobody likes being stuck in traffic. Smart cities use AI to try and make traffic flow more efficiently.

- **Example:** Many cities are now using AI to control traffic lights in real-time based on how many cars are actually there.

- **Step-by-step Process:**
  1. **Data Collection:** Traffic cameras installed at intersections and sensors embedded in the roads constantly collect data about the number of vehicles, their speed, and direction of travel.
  2. **Analysis:** AI algorithms analyze this massive stream of real-time data to understand current traffic flow patterns. They can identify bottlenecks and predict where congestion might build up.
  3. **Optimization:** Based on this analysis, the AI system dynamically adjusts the timing of traffic lights. For example, if one street has a long line of cars, the light might stay green longer, while a less busy street gets a shorter green light. This helps reduce waiting times and improve the overall flow of traffic.

b. Waste Management: Smarter Trash Collection with AI

Collecting trash can be inefficient. Smart cities are using AI to make it more streamlined.

- **Example:** Some cities are using smart bins with sensors that tell the city when they're full, so trucks only go where they're needed.
- **Step-by-step Process:**
  1. **Data Collection:** Waste bins are equipped with IoT sensors that continuously monitor the level of fullness inside the bin. This data is sent wirelessly to a central system.
  2. **Analysis:** AI models analyze the data from all the smart bins, looking at patterns in how quickly they fill up in different areas and at different times of the week or year.
  3. **Scheduling:** Based on these predictions of when bins will be full, the system optimizes the routes and schedules for the trash collection trucks. This means trucks don't waste fuel going to empty bins, and full bins are collected promptly, making the process more efficient and environmentally friendly.

4. Healthcare: AI as a Health Ally

AI is bringing big changes to healthcare, helping doctors diagnose illnesses, personalize treatments, and improve how patients are cared for.

a. Diagnostic Assistance (like IBM Watson Health): AI as a Doctor's Helper

AI can help doctors sift through tons of medical information to make better diagnoses.

- **Example:** IBM Watson Health (though its focus has shifted) was designed to analyze patient records, research papers, and other medical data to help doctors understand complex cases.
- **Step-by-step Process:**
  1. **Data Collection:** A patient's medical records, their history of illnesses, test results (like blood tests and scans), and even relevant medical research papers are gathered and fed into the AI system.

2. **Analysis:** AI algorithms analyze this vast amount of data, looking for patterns, correlations, and connections that might be relevant to the patient's current condition.
3. **Diagnosis:** Based on the patterns it finds and its knowledge from analyzing countless previous cases and medical literature, the AI can suggest possible diagnoses to the doctor. This doesn't replace the doctor's expertise but acts as a powerful tool to help them consider all possibilities and make more informed decisions.

b. Personalized Medicine: Tailoring Treatment to Your Genes with AI

We're learning that the best medicine isn't one-size-fits-all. AI can help tailor treatments to an individual's unique makeup.

- **Example:** AI can analyze a patient's genetic information to predict how they might respond to different cancer treatments, helping doctors choose the most effective option with fewer side effects.
- **Step-by-step Process:**
    1. **Data Collection:** Genetic data from the patient, usually obtained through genetic testing, is collected.
    2. **Analysis:** AI algorithms analyze this complex genetic data, looking for specific genes or mutations that are known to influence how the body processes drugs or how likely a patient is to respond to certain therapies.
    3. **Treatment Recommendation:** Based on this detailed genetic analysis, the AI can suggest personalized treatment plans that are more likely to be effective for that specific patient, potentially leading to better outcomes and fewer adverse reactions.

c. Virtual Health Assistants: AI Chatbots for Health Advice

Just like chatbots for customer service, AI can power virtual assistants for health-related questions.

- **Example:** Many healthcare providers offer AI-powered chatbots on their websites or apps that can answer common health questions, help you schedule appointments, or remind you to take your medication.
- **Step-by-step Process:**
    1. **User Input:** You type or speak a question to the chatbot, like "What are the symptoms of a cold?" or "Remind me to take my pills at 8 PM."
    2. **Data Processing:** The chatbot uses Natural Language Processing (NLP) to understand what you're asking. It identifies the key words and the intent behind your query.
    3. **Response:** The chatbot accesses a database of medical knowledge or its training data to provide an answer. It might give you information about cold symptoms, set a reminder on your phone, or suggest next steps, like seeing a doctor if your symptoms are severe.

In both smart cities and healthcare, AI acts as a powerful tool for analyzing large amounts of data, identifying patterns, and making intelligent decisions that can lead to more efficient systems, better services, and improved outcomes for everyone.

---

5. Education: AI as Your Personalized Tutor and Efficient Helper

AI is stepping into the classroom and beyond, offering tailored learning experiences for students and making administrative tasks easier for educators.

a. Personalized Learning Platforms (like Duolingo): Learning That Adapts to You

Imagine a teacher who knows exactly what you're struggling with and adjusts the lessons just for you. That's what AI-powered learning platforms aim to do.

- **Example:** Duolingo, the language learning app, uses AI to figure out which words and grammar rules you're finding difficult and then gives you more practice in those specific areas.
- **Step-by-step Process:**
  1. **User Input:** You start learning a new language on Duolingo, working through various exercises and lessons.
  2. **Progress Tracking:** The AI constantly monitors your performance. It keeps track of which questions you answer correctly, how quickly you answer, and the types of mistakes you make.
  3. **Personalized Content:** Based on this detailed tracking, the AI adapts the lessons. If you consistently struggle with a certain verb tense, for example, the app will give you more exercises focusing on that tense until you show improvement. It might also speed you through areas you're mastering quickly.

b. Automated Grading Systems: AI as Your Tireless Grader

Grading papers and exams can take up a lot of teachers' time. AI is helping to automate this process, especially for certain types of assignments.

- **Example:** AI systems can grade math problems by checking if the final answer is correct and even analyzing the steps taken to get there. They can also grade coding assignments by running the code and checking if it produces the correct output.
- **Step-by-step Process:**
  1. **Student Submission:** Students submit their work digitally, whether it's a math worksheet, a coding project, or even an essay (though essay grading is more complex and still evolving).
  2. **AI Analysis:** The AI system compares the student's submission to a pre-defined set of correct answers, an expected output for code, or specific evaluation criteria (for more structured writing tasks). For math, it can check the numerical answers

and sometimes even the logical steps. For code, it can run the submitted program against test cases.

3. **Feedback:** Based on its analysis, the AI can automatically provide a grade and even give specific feedback, like pointing out which parts of a math problem were incorrect or where a piece of code failed to execute properly. This frees up teachers to focus on more personalized instruction.

6. Finance: AI as Your Financial Guardian and Trading Brain

The world of finance deals with huge amounts of data and fast-paced decisions. AI is proving to be incredibly valuable in this domain.

a. Fraud Detection (like PayPal): AI as Your Financial Sherlock Holmes

Protecting your money online is crucial, and AI plays a key role in spotting suspicious activity.

- **Example:** PayPal uses AI algorithms to monitor millions of transactions in real-time, looking for patterns that might indicate fraudulent activity.
- **Step-by-step Process:**
    1. **Transaction Monitoring:** Every time you make a transaction on PayPal, AI systems analyze various details like the amount, the location, the recipient, your past transaction history, and the device you're using.
    2. **Pattern Recognition:** The AI compares this current transaction to vast amounts of historical data on both legitimate and fraudulent transactions. It looks for unusual patterns or anomalies that deviate from your normal behavior or match known fraud patterns. For example, a large transaction from a new location you've never used before might be flagged.
    3. **Alert:** If the AI detects a transaction that looks suspicious based on these patterns, it can automatically alert you, the user, and might even temporarily block the transaction until you can verify its legitimacy. This helps prevent financial losses.

b. Algorithmic Trading: AI Making Split-Second Investment Decisions

In the fast-paced world of stock markets, AI can analyze data and execute trades much faster than humans.

- **Example:** Investment firms use AI models to constantly analyze stock prices, news articles, social media sentiment, and other market data to predict which stocks might go up or down. Based on these predictions, the AI can automatically buy or sell stocks.
- **Step-by-step Process:**
    1. **Data Collection:** The AI system continuously gathers massive amounts of real-time data from stock exchanges, financial news outlets, economic indicators, and even social media.
    2. **Analysis:** Sophisticated AI algorithms process this data, looking for trends, correlations, and potential signals that might indicate future price movements.

These algorithms can be incredibly complex, taking into account a multitude of factors.

3. **Execution:** Based on the predictions made by the AI models, the system can automatically execute trades – buying or selling stocks – often in fractions of a second. The goal is to capitalize on small price fluctuations and maximize profits based on the learned patterns.

From personalized learning that caters to your individual needs to sophisticated systems that protect your finances and make lightning-fast investment decisions, AI is rapidly changing the landscape of education and finance, making them more efficient, tailored, and secure right here in Ranchi and across the globe.

---

7. Entertainment: AI as Your Personal Curator and Intelligent Game Master

AI isn't just for serious stuff; it's also making our leisure time more enjoyable, from suggesting what to watch next to making video game characters feel more alive.

a. Content Recommendation (like Netflix, Spotify): AI as Your Taste Matchmaker

Ever wonder how Netflix or Spotify always seems to know exactly what you want to watch or listen to next? That's AI at work, acting like your personal entertainment guru.

- **Example:** Netflix uses AI to analyze your viewing history and suggest movies and TV shows that you're likely to enjoy.
- **Step-by-step Process:**
    1. **User Behavior Tracking:** Netflix keeps a close eye on what you watch, when you watch it, what you search for, how you rate shows, and even when you pause or rewind. Spotify does something similar with the music you listen to, the playlists you create, and the artists you follow.
    2. **Data Analysis:** AI algorithms then crunch all this data, looking for patterns in your preferences. They try to understand what genres you like, which actors or directors you prefer, what kind of mood you're usually in when you watch certain things, and even what other users with similar tastes have enjoyed.
    3. **Personalized Recommendations:** Based on this analysis, the AI suggests movies, TV shows, or music that it thinks you'll find interesting. These recommendations are often displayed in various categories like "Because You Watched...", "Top Picks for You," or personalized playlists. It's like having a friend who knows your taste inside and out suggesting what to check out next.

b. AI in Video Games: Making Virtual Worlds Feel Real

Remember those video game characters that just stood around waiting for you? AI is making them much smarter and more interactive, creating more immersive game worlds.

- **Example:** In modern video games, non-playable characters (NPCs) can have complex behaviors, react realistically to your actions, and even seem to have their own routines.
- **Step-by-step Process:**
    1. **Game Environment:** The AI system within the game constantly processes information about the virtual world – where the player is, what they're doing, what other objects and characters are nearby, and what events are happening.
    2. **NPC Behavior:** AI algorithms control how these NPCs act. Instead of just following simple scripts, they can make decisions based on their surroundings, their programmed personalities, and the player's actions. For instance, an NPC might run away if they see the player drawing a weapon, or a shopkeeper might greet the player when they enter their store.
    3. **Adaptation:** The AI can adapt the NPC's behavior in response to what the player does. If you help an NPC, they might become friendly and offer you rewards later. If you attack them, they might become hostile and try to defend themselves. This dynamic interaction makes the game world feel more alive and your actions feel like they have real consequences within the game.

50 multiple-choice questions (MCQs) with answers related to **Smartphones, Smart Homes, Smart Cities, Healthcare, Education, Finance, and Entertainment**:

Smartphones

1. **Which AI feature helps in improving speech recognition in smartphones?** a) Image processing
   b) Natural Language Processing (NLP)
   c) Voice synthesis
   d) Data mining
   Answer: b) Natural Language Processing (NLP)
2. **Which smartphone assistant uses AI to provide voice-based assistance?** a) Cortana
   b) Siri
   c) Google Assistant
   d) All of the above
   Answer: d) All of the above
3. **What feature of smartphones uses AI to adjust camera settings automatically?** a) Autofocus
   b) Smart HDR
   c) GPS
   d) Image recognition
   Answer: b) Smart HDR
4. **Which of the following is a key technology in smartphones for detecting faces in photos?** a) Facial recognition
   b) Object detection
   c) Gesture recognition
   d) Sound recognition
   Answer: a) Facial recognition
5. **What is the primary purpose of AI-powered predictive text on smartphones?** a) To make phone calls
   b) To suggest the next word while typing
   c) To enhance voice clarity

d) To recognize handwriting
Answer: b) To suggest the next word while typing

Smart Homes

6. **Which device in a smart home helps in controlling the temperature automatically?** a) Smart thermostat
   b) Smart lightbulb
   c) Smart speaker
   d) Smart refrigerator
   Answer: a) Smart thermostat
7. **Which of the following is a key feature of smart home security systems?** a) Voice recognition
   b) Motion detection
   c) Temperature control
   d) Facial recognition
   Answer: b) Motion detection
8. **What is the purpose of AI in smart lighting systems?** a) To improve Wi-Fi speed
   b) To adjust lighting based on occupancy
   c) To measure temperature
   d) To play music
   Answer: b) To adjust lighting based on occupancy
9. **Which technology is primarily used in smart homes for voice-controlled assistance?** a) Bluetooth
   b) Zigbee
   c) Wi-Fi
   d) Voice recognition
   Answer: d) Voice recognition
10. **Which of the following AI systems helps to monitor the health of elderly individuals in a smart home?** a) Smart light system
    b) Smart fridge
    c) Smart wearable devices
    d) Smart vacuum cleaner
    Answer: c) Smart wearable devices

Smart Cities

11. **How do smart cities improve traffic management?** a) By using manual traffic signals
    b) By using AI-based traffic optimization
    c) By reducing public transportation
    d) By increasing speed limits
    Answer: b) By using AI-based traffic optimization
12. **What is the role of IoT in smart cities?** a) To improve battery life
    b) To connect everyday devices and manage city infrastructure
    c) To enhance the visual appeal of buildings

d) To improve public transportation only

Answer: b) To connect everyday devices and manage city infrastructure

13. **Which AI feature in smart cities helps monitor waste management systems?** a) Facial recognition

b) IoT sensors

c) GPS tracking

d) Smart parking

Answer: b) IoT sensors

14. **What is the main benefit of smart grids in smart cities?** a) Reducing electricity bills

b) Optimizing energy distribution

c) Enhancing internet connectivity

d) Increasing traffic speed

Answer: b) Optimizing energy distribution

15. **How do smart cities improve the environment?** a) By using AI to monitor pollution levels

b) By encouraging non-automobile transportation

c) By increasing the number of vehicles

d) Both a and b

Answer: d) Both a and b

Healthcare

16. **How does AI assist in healthcare diagnostics?** a) By making automatic decisions without any human input

b) By analyzing medical data to support doctors' decisions

c) By replacing doctors in the diagnostic process

d) By generating new diseases

Answer: b) By analyzing medical data to support doctors' decisions

17. **Which AI application is used for personalizing treatment based on genetic data?** a) Machine learning algorithms

b) Genetic modification tools

c) Electronic health records

d) Predictive analytics

Answer: a) Machine learning algorithms

18. **What is the role of AI-powered chatbots in healthcare?** a) To perform surgery

b) To provide medication recommendations

c) To assist with routine inquiries and appointment scheduling

d) To develop medical equipment

Answer: c) To assist with routine inquiries and appointment scheduling

19. **How do AI systems help in drug discovery?** a) By automating the drug production process

b) By predicting potential drug candidates based on data analysis

c) By manufacturing drugs

d) By testing drugs on humans

Answer: b) By predicting potential drug candidates based on data analysis

20. **AI in telemedicine primarily helps with:** a) Physical examination of patients

b) Video consultations and remote patient monitoring

c) Distributing medicines

d) Designing hospital buildings
Answer: b) Video consultations and remote patient monitoring

Education

21. **How does AI personalize learning in education?** a) By giving all students the same lessons
b) By tracking students' progress and suggesting custom learning paths
c) By automating teacher evaluations
d) By grading students without a human teacher
Answer: b) By tracking students' progress and suggesting custom learning paths

22. **Which AI application can help students improve their language skills?** a) Image recognition tools
b) Language learning apps (like Duolingo)
c) Virtual reality tools
d) Speech-to-text software
Answer: b) Language learning apps (like Duolingo)

23. **How can AI help in grading assignments?** a) By automating subjective assessments
b) By comparing assignments to predefined criteria and generating grades
c) By assigning grades randomly
d) By replacing teachers' input completely
Answer: b) By comparing assignments to predefined criteria and generating grades

24. **What is a key feature of AI tutors in education?** a) To replace human teachers
b) To provide personalized feedback and lessons
c) To monitor students' physical activities
d) To manage school finances
Answer: b) To provide personalized feedback and lessons

25. **Which technology does AI in education use to analyze student performance?** a) Facial recognition
b) Natural Language Processing
c) Data analytics
d) Virtual reality
Answer: c) Data analytics

Finance

26. **AI-powered fraud detection systems in finance primarily use:** a) Basic rule-based systems
b) Machine learning algorithms to detect unusual patterns
c) Human judgment
d) Paper-based systems
Answer: b) Machine learning algorithms to detect unusual patterns

27. **Which of the following AI technologies is used in algorithmic trading?** a) Supervised learning
b) Natural language processing
c) Predictive analytics
d) Data encryption
Answer: c) Predictive analytics

28. **In the context of banking, AI chatbots are used for:** a) Depositing money
    b) Personalized financial advice
    c) Conducting physical transactions
    d) Preparing tax returns
    Answer: b) Personalized financial advice
29. **AI helps banks in customer service by:** a) Automating transactions
    b) Identifying customer queries and providing quick responses
    c) Increasing interest rates
    d) Managing the stock market
    Answer: b) Identifying customer queries and providing quick responses
30. **How does AI contribute to financial forecasting?** a) By creating random predictions
    b) By analyzing historical financial data to predict future trends
    c) By increasing customer spending
    d) By reducing the amount of data used
    Answer: b) By analyzing historical financial data to predict future trends

Entertainment

31. **How does AI enhance content recommendations on platforms like Netflix?** a) By automatically creating new movies
    b) By analyzing user viewing habits and suggesting content accordingly
    c) By allowing users to skip ads
    d) By developing scripts for movies
    Answer: b) By analyzing user viewing habits and suggesting content accordingly
32. **Which AI technology is used in video game NPC behavior?** a) Image recognition
    b) Natural language processing
    c) Pathfinding algorithms
    d) Deep learning
    Answer: c) Pathfinding algorithms
33. **How does AI help in music recommendations on platforms like Spotify?** a) By creating new music for users
    b) By analyzing user preferences and suggesting songs based on listening history
    c) By developing music genres
    d) By automatically playing songs at random
    Answer: b) By analyzing user preferences and suggesting songs based on listening history
34. **AI in film production can be used for:** a) Directing movies
    b) Scriptwriting
    c) Analyzing audience reactions and predicting hits
    d) Cooking meals for the crew
    Answer: c) Analyzing audience reactions and predicting hits
35. **Which AI feature is used to improve the image quality in videos?** a) Motion blur
    b) Image upscaling
    c) Noise reduction
    d) Pixelation
    Answer: b) Image upscaling

Miscellaneous

36. **Which AI application is used in real-time language translation in smartphones?** a) Google Translate
    b) Microsoft Office
    c) Adobe Acrobat
    d) Microsoft Excel
    Answer: a) Google Translate

37. **What is the role of AI in mobile gaming?** a) Generating storylines automatically
    b) Enhancing NPC behavior and game difficulty
    c) Automatically designing game levels
    d) Writing scripts for gaming content
    Answer: b) Enhancing NPC behavior and game difficulty

38. **Which technology helps in the automation of repetitive tasks in smart homes?** a) Internet of Things (IoT)
    b) Augmented reality
    c) 3D printing
    d) Virtual reality
    Answer: a) Internet of Things (IoT)

39. **Which is a key function of AI in self-driving cars?** a) To navigate through cities without human input
    b) To play music automatically
    c) To maintain the car's engine
    d) To ensure the car's paint job remains intact
    Answer: a) To navigate through cities without human input

40. **What is the primary advantage of AI-powered personal assistants like Siri and Alexa?** a) They provide weather updates
    b) They perform complex calculations
    c) They help in managing schedules and tasks through voice commands
    d) They order groceries automatically
    Answer: c) They help in managing schedules and tasks through voice commands

Additional Questions (Healthcare, Education, Finance, Entertainment)

41. **What is the role of AI in predicting disease outbreaks?** a) Data collection
    b) Predictive analytics based on patterns
    c) Testing vaccines
    d) Providing treatment directly
    Answer: b) Predictive analytics based on patterns

42. **Which AI system helps in online education by providing personalized feedback to students?** a) Learning Management System (LMS)
    b) AI-powered tutor systems
    c) Video conferencing software
    d) Physical classroom tools
    Answer: b) AI-powered tutor systems

43. **AI-powered algorithms in banking help to assess:** a) Interest rates
    b) Loan eligibility based on credit scores and financial behavior
    c) Staff performance
    d) Market trends
    Answer: b) Loan eligibility based on credit scores and financial behavior
44. **Which entertainment platform primarily uses AI to suggest content to users?** a) YouTube
    b) Facebook
    c) Instagram
    d) All of the above
    Answer: d) All of the above
45. **What is the role of AI in improving content recommendations in entertainment?** a) Generating new content automatically
    b) Personalizing suggestions based on user data and preferences
    c) Streaming content at faster speeds
    d) Editing content
    Answer: b) Personalizing suggestions based on user data and preferences

Healthcare/Finance/Entertainment

46. **How does AI impact financial customer service?** a) By automating investment decisions
    b) By analyzing financial data to offer personalized services
    c) By preventing customers from making transactions
    d) By creating fake financial products
    Answer: b) By analyzing financial data to offer personalized services
47. **Which AI application is used for the detection of fraudulent activities in banking?** a) Data mining tools
    b) Fraud detection algorithms
    c) Personal assistants
    d) Chatbots
    Answer: b) Fraud detection algorithms
48. **Which technology in smartphones helps improve healthcare monitoring?** a) GPS
    b) Mobile sensors
    c) Face recognition
    d) Wi-Fi
    Answer: b) Mobile sensors
49. **In entertainment, AI is used to:** a) Direct movies automatically
    b) Create automated dialogues for actors
    c) Analyze audience preferences and create personalized content
    d) Replace human actors
    Answer: c) Analyze audience preferences and create personalized content
50. **How does AI help in making smart cities more sustainable?** a) By promoting more car use
    b) By optimizing resource use such as water, energy, and waste management
    c) By building more skyscrapers
    d) By increasing traffic congestion
    Answer: b) By optimizing resource use such as water, energy, and waste management

CHAPTER 11: AI IN CREATIVITY AND THE ARTS

The integration of Artificial Intelligence (AI) in creative fields such as **music**, **painting**, and **literature** has sparked numerous discussions about the potential of machines to produce works of art traditionally attributed to human creativity. AI is being utilized in various artistic disciplines, and its role in creativity has evolved significantly over the years. This chapter explores how AI is used in the arts, its implications, and the fundamental question: **Can AI Be an Artist?**

---

1. AI in Music: The Digital Composer and Producer

AI's role in music is evolving from simple automated beats to sophisticated systems that can compose original pieces and even help in the intricate process of music production. At its heart, AI's musical talent comes from **Machine Learning (ML)**. It's trained on vast libraries of music to understand the underlying rules, harmonies, rhythms, and stylistic nuances.

a) Neural Networks in Music: The AI Brain That Learns Melodies

Neural networks, particularly **Recurrent Neural Networks (RNNs)** and their more advanced cousin, **Long Short-Term Memory (LSTM) networks**, are key players in AI music generation. These networks can listen to (analyze) huge collections of musical pieces and then learn to create new music that sounds similar in style. Think of it like an AI that's listened to so much Bollywood music that it can now compose its own Bollywood-style song.

- **Example: OpenAI's MuseNet** is a prime example. It's an AI model that has been trained on thousands of musical compositions across various genres like classical (think Beethoven), jazz (think Miles Davis), and pop (think recent chart-toppers). You can give MuseNet some starting parameters, like a specific genre, a desired mood (happy, sad), and the instruments you want in the piece (piano, guitar, drums), and it can generate a completely new and unique musical piece in that style. Imagine it composing a new instrumental track that sounds like a blend of Indian classical music with a touch of contemporary electronic elements, all based on the parameters you set.

b) AI-Generated Music Platforms: Your Personal AI Music Creator

Platforms powered by AI, such as **AIVA (Artificial Intelligence Virtual Artist)** and **Amper Music** (now part of Shutterstock), put the power of AI music creation directly into the hands of users, even if they don't have deep musical knowledge. These platforms use deep learning models trained on diverse musical styles to produce original music with minimal user input. They're great for creating background scores for videos, podcasts, or even just for exploring new sonic landscapes.

- **Example: AIVA** has even composed symphonic music that has been used in films and advertisements. As a user, you might tell AIVA you need a "uplifting" and "fast-paced" track for a short video you're making. You can also specify the instrumentation, perhaps wanting strings and percussion. AIVA will then generate a unique musical piece that fits those parameters. Imagine a local filmmaker in Ranchi using AIVA to create an original, royalty-free soundtrack for their documentary about the city's vibrant culture.

c) AI in Music Production: Refining Existing Sounds with AI

AI isn't just about creating new music from scratch; it's also becoming a valuable tool in the nitty-gritty of music production – the process of taking recorded tracks and making them sound their absolute best. AI can assist in tasks like mixing (balancing the levels of different instruments) and mastering (the final polish that makes a track sound good on all playback systems). It does this by analyzing frequency patterns, equalization (adjusting different frequencies), and dynamics (controlling the loudness and softness).

- **Example:** Platforms like **LANDR** use AI to automate the mastering process. Traditionally, mastering is a skilled and often expensive process done by experienced audio engineers. LANDR's AI analyzes your mixed song, compares it to a vast library of professionally mastered tracks, and then applies adjustments to make it sound more balanced, louder, and ready for distribution on streaming services. This makes professional-sounding mastering more accessible to independent musicians right here in Ranchi who might be recording in their home studios. They can upload their track to LANDR, and the AI will handle the mastering, giving their music a polished, professional finish.

In essence, AI in music is like having a tireless, knowledgeable collaborator who can compose original pieces in various styles, help you create custom soundtracks, and even assist in making your recordings sound their best. It's a rapidly evolving field that's opening up exciting new possibilities for musicians and music lovers alike, right here in our local music scene and globally.

2. AI in Painting and Visual Arts: The Digital Brush and Creative Partner

AI is no longer just about crunching numbers; it's also making significant strides in the realm of visual arts, capable of generating original paintings, transforming photos in artistic styles, and even assisting human artists in pushing creative boundaries. A key technology behind this artistic AI is **Generative Adversarial Networks (GANs)**. Think of GANs as a creative duo – a generator trying to create art and a discriminator trying to tell if it's real or fake.

a) GANs in Art Creation: The AI as the Artist

GANs are a type of deep learning architecture that involves two neural networks working against each other.

- **The Generator:** This network acts like the artist, taking random noise as input and trying to create images – be it a portrait, a landscape, or an abstract piece. Initially, its creations are usually pretty abstract and nonsensical.
- **The Discriminator:** This network acts like the art critic, trained on a dataset of real artwork (e.g., classical portraits or modern abstract paintings). Its job is to look at the images produced by the generator and distinguish between real artwork from the training data and the AI-generated images.

Over time, through this constant back-and-forth, the generator learns to create images that become increasingly realistic or creatively compelling, often mimicking famous art styles or even inventing entirely new visual concepts that can fool the discriminator.

- **Example 1: "Edmond de Belamy"**: Remember that portrait created by the Paris-based art collective Obvious using a GAN? This piece, which had a distinct resemblance to classical portraiture with a slightly eerie, unfinished quality, was actually generated by AI. It was then printed on canvas and sold at a prestigious auction house for a significant sum. This event sparked a lot of discussion about the definition of art, artistic ownership, and the value of AI-generated creations. Imagine an AI in Ranchi being trained on local Madhubani paintings and then generating its own unique interpretations of that style.
- **Example 2: DeepArt.io**: This online platform showcases another fascinating application of GANs (or related neural networks). You can upload your own photo, and DeepArt.io uses AI trained on the styles of famous artists like Vincent van Gogh, Pablo Picasso, or Claude Monet to transform your photo into an image that looks like it was painted by that artist. For instance, you could upload a picture of the Jagannath Temple in Ranchi and have it rendered in the swirling brushstrokes of Van Gogh's "Starry Night."

b) AI as a Tool for Artists: The AI as the Collaborator

Instead of completely taking over the creative process, AI can also serve as a powerful tool for human artists, helping them explore new styles and push their artistic boundaries.

- **Neural Style Transfer:** This technique, often powered by AI, allows artists to take the content of one image (say, a photograph) and apply the artistic style of another image (say, Van Gogh's brushstrokes or the vibrant colors of a Ravi Varma painting). This blending of content and style can lead to entirely new and innovative forms of art that combine human vision with machine interpretation. Imagine a local artist in Ranchi taking a photo of the Hundru Falls and then using AI to render it in the intricate style of a traditional Santhal painting.
- **Example: Refik Anadol's "Machine Hallucinations"**: Artist Refik Anadol is renowned for his stunning visual installations that blend machine learning and media art. He uses AI and data-driven algorithms to create dynamic and generative environments. For example, "Machine Hallucinations" involves training AI on vast datasets of architectural images. The AI then "hallucinates" and generates dreamlike, ever-evolving visual landscapes that explore the relationship between human perception and artificial intelligence. These immersive experiences showcase AI as a powerful tool for visualizing and interpreting complex data in artistic and thought-provoking ways. Imagine a similar

installation in Ranchi, visualizing the city's growth and cultural shifts through AI-generated abstract forms.

c) AI in Art Curation: The AI as the Art Analyst

AI's analytical capabilities are also being applied to the world of art curation and analysis.

- **Pattern and Style Recognition:** AI tools can be trained to identify patterns, styles, and even the subtle characteristics of different artists' works. This can help in authenticating artworks, understanding art history trends, and organizing art collections more effectively. Imagine an AI system being used by a museum in Ranchi to categorize and analyze its collection of tribal art, identifying common motifs and stylistic evolutions over time.
- **Market Value Prediction:** Some AI tools are even being developed to predict the potential market value of a piece of artwork based on factors like the artist's reputation, the style, the size, the historical context, and past auction data. While art valuation is complex and subjective, AI can provide data-driven insights to assist art collectors and investors.

---

3. AI in Literature: The Digital Bard and Author's Assistant

AI's presence in literature is becoming increasingly noticeable, not just in the realm of automated content creation but also as a creative partner for human writers. At the heart of this is AI's ability to understand and generate human language, largely powered by sophisticated language models.

a) Text Generation: The AI Storyteller and Poet

AI can now be used to generate various forms of text, from short stories and poems to even longer narratives. Language models, like the powerful GPT series developed by OpenAI (the same technology behind ChatGPT), are capable of producing coherent and contextually relevant text based on the prompts they receive. They've learned the rules of grammar, sentence structure, and even some aspects of storytelling by being trained on massive amounts of written material.

- **Example 1: GPT-3 Writing a Short Story**: Imagine giving a language model like GPT-3 a simple prompt: "Write a story about a mysterious forest on the outskirts of Ranchi where strange things happen at night." The AI could then generate a story with characters, a plot unfolding within that setting, descriptive language, and thematic elements, all while adhering to proper grammar and sentence structure. It might describe rustling leaves with no wind, faint whispers carried on the breeze, or perhaps an encounter with an unusual creature that only appears after sunset near the local Hatia Dam.
- **Example 2: "The Day A Computer Writes a Novel"**: This was an actual project where a novel was largely generated by AI and presented at the Tokyo International Literature

Festival. While it might not have been hailed as a literary masterpiece by human critics, it demonstrated the potential of AI to construct a longer narrative with elements of plot, character development, and thematic exploration. It showed that AI could string together coherent sentences and paragraphs to form a larger story, even if the nuances of human emotion and experience were still somewhat lacking.

b) AI-Assisted Writing Tools: The AI Editor and Muse

AI isn't just trying to replace human authors; it's also proving to be a valuable assistant, helping writers improve their work and overcome creative blocks.

- **Grammar and Style Enhancement:** Tools like Grammarly and ProWritingAid utilize AI to analyze a writer's text and suggest improvements to grammar, spelling, punctuation, style, and overall flow. They can catch errors that human eyes might miss and offer suggestions for more effective phrasing, helping writers from Ranchi refine their articles, stories, or academic papers.
- **Idea Generation:** AI can also help authors brainstorm and develop their ideas. Tools like Plot Factory (an AI-powered platform) can assist writers in creating plot outlines based on initial concepts. You might give it a basic premise, like "A young woman in Ranchi discovers a hidden talent," and the AI can suggest potential plot points, character arcs, and conflicts to help structure a novel. AI could even help generate character names or suggest different dialogue options based on the characters' personalities and the situation.

c) AI in Poetry: The Algorithmic Verse Maker

AI can also be trained to compose poetry in various styles, from the structured form of a haiku to the more free-flowing nature of free verse. The approach here is often based on learning the statistical patterns of language and the structural elements of different poetic forms from large datasets of existing poems.

- **Example: The Poem "Sunspring"**: This poem was written entirely by AI using a neural network and then adapted into a short film. The resulting poem, and subsequently the film, is often described as nonsensical and abstract. It doesn't necessarily convey deep human emotions or cultural references in the way a human-written poem might. Instead, it showcases the AI's ability to generate sequences of words and phrases that statistically follow the patterns it has learned, even if the meaning isn't always clear to a human reader. It's more of an exploration of the creative potential of AI through language, even if the output is unconventional. Imagine an AI trained on the lyrical beauty of Jharkhandi folk songs attempting to generate its own verses, perhaps capturing the rhythm and some of the imagery but with a unique, almost dreamlike quality.

In the realm of literature, AI is acting as both a potential new form of creative expression and a valuable tool for human authors. While AI-generated novels or poems might not yet capture the full depth and nuance of human experience, the technology is rapidly advancing, and AI-assisted tools are already helping writers in Ranchi and around the world to craft better stories and express their ideas more effectively. It's an exciting and evolving intersection of technology and the art of storytelling.

---

4. Can AI Be an Artist? The Million-Dollar Question

The exciting advancements in AI art and music naturally lead us to ponder: can these sophisticated machines genuinely be considered artists in their own right? It's a question that sparks a lot of debate among philosophers, artists, and technologists.

Philosophical Considerations: The Missing Human Touch?

One major viewpoint revolves around the core elements that we traditionally associate with art and the artistic process. These often include:

- **Consciousness:** The awareness of oneself and one's surroundings.
- **Emotions:** Feelings like joy, sorrow, anger, which can drive artistic expression.
- **Intentions:** A deliberate purpose or goal behind creating a work of art, often to communicate an idea, feeling, or perspective.
- **Human Experience:** The culmination of our personal histories, cultural influences, and interactions with the world, which deeply informs our creative output.

Critics argue that AI systems, as complex as they are, are fundamentally designed to mimic human cognition through algorithms and vast datasets. They lack the lived experience, emotional depth, and conscious intent that many believe are intrinsic to true artistic creation.

- **Example:** An AI can generate a stunning painting that might evoke a sense of awe or wonder in a viewer, perhaps even resembling a traditional Paitkar painting from Jharkhand in its style and color palette. However, did the AI *intend* to evoke those specific emotions? Did it create the artwork as a form of personal expression or to communicate a specific cultural narrative in the way a human Paitkar artist does, drawing upon generations of tradition and personal experience? Many argue that the AI's creation, however beautiful, lacks this intrinsic human element of intention and emotional depth, making it more of a sophisticated mimicry than true art born from personal experience.

AI as a Tool vs. Artist: The Extended Human Hand?

Another perspective views AI not as an independent artist but rather as a powerful tool that can be used by human artists to enhance their creative process. In this sense, the AI becomes an extension of the artist's vision, enabling them to explore new forms of art and push creative boundaries that might have been impossible with traditional methods alone.

- **Example:** Think back to David Cope, the composer who used AI to generate classical music in the styles of masters like Bach and Mozart. In this scenario, Cope, the human artist, directed the AI, set parameters, and ultimately decided which of the AI's outputs were worth pursuing or refining. The AI acted as a sophisticated assistant, capable of generating musical ideas in a specific style, but the artistic direction, selection, and integration into a larger body of work still rested with the human composer. Similarly, a contemporary artist in Ranchi might use AI to generate a series of abstract patterns inspired by local tribal motifs and then incorporate these patterns into their own paintings or digital art, with the AI serving as a source of inspiration and a tool for generating novel visual elements.

AI's Role in the Future of Creativity: A New Era of Collaboration?

Looking ahead, it seems unlikely that AI will completely replace human artists. Instead, the future of creativity might lie in a new form of collaboration between humans and machines. As AI tools become more sophisticated and intuitive, artists across various disciplines will likely continue to adopt them to express their ideas in ways that were once unimaginable.

- Imagine a future where a writer in Ranchi collaborates with an AI to co-create a novel, with the human providing the core themes, characters, and emotional depth, while the AI assists with generating plot twists, descriptive passages, and dialogue options. Or a musician working with AI to explore unconventional harmonies and soundscapes, pushing the boundaries of contemporary Jharkhandi music. In these scenarios, the AI acts as a powerful creative partner, augmenting human imagination and skill.

Okay, here are 50 multiple-choice questions with answers covering AI in Music, Painting, Literature, and the question of whether AI can be an artist, keeping in mind our location in Ranchi:

AI in Music

1. Which type of neural network is commonly used for AI music generation due to its ability to process sequences? a) Convolutional Neural Network (CNN) b) Recurrent Neural Network (RNN) c) Feedforward Neural Network d) Generative Adversarial Network (GAN) **Answer: [1] b) Recurrent Neural Network (RNN)**

1. github.com

github.com

2. OpenAI's AI model known for composing multi-instrumental music in various genres is called: a) AlphaFold b) DALL-E c) MuseNet d) Jukebox **Answer: c) MuseNet**
3. Platforms like AIVA and Amper Music primarily allow users to: a) Analyze existing music for structural patterns. b) Create unique music tracks with minimal input. c) Master audio recordings automatically. d) Transcribe musical scores into digital formats. **Answer: b) Create unique music tracks with minimal input.**
4. AI tools in music production can assist in which of the following tasks? a) Writing song lyrics. b) Composing the melody. c) Mixing and mastering songs. d) Designing album artwork. **Answer: c) Mixing and mastering songs.**
5. LANDR is an AI-powered platform primarily used for: a) Generating MIDI files. b) Automating the mastering process. c) Creating virtual instruments. d) Providing feedback on musical compositions. **Answer: b) Automating the mastering process.**
6. What is the primary function of machine learning in AI music composition? a) To translate lyrics into different languages. b) To understand patterns, harmony, rhythm, and style from music datasets. c) To control the playback speed of music. d) To convert audio signals into sheet music. **Answer: b) To understand patterns, harmony, rhythm, and style from music datasets.**
7. Which of the following is NOT a common parameter users might provide to AI music generation platforms? a) Genre b) Mood c) Instrumentation d) The listener's current heart rate **Answer: d) The listener's current heart rate**
8. AI's ability to mimic the style of famous composers relies on: a) Random number generation. b) Analyzing large datasets of their compositions. c) Direct instruction from human musicians. d) Accessing the composer's original thoughts. **Answer: b) Analyzing large datasets of their compositions.**
9. In the context of AI music, what does "multi-instrumental" typically refer to? a) Music that can be played on many different devices. b) Music composed using a wide range of musical scales. c) Music that includes parts for several different musical instruments. d) Music that evokes a variety of emotions in the listener. **Answer: c) Music that includes parts for several different musical instruments.**
10. Which of the following is a potential benefit of AI in music production for independent musicians in Ranchi? a) Automatically writing lyrics in local Jharkhandi dialects. b) Providing affordable access to professional-sounding mastering. c) Generating traditional tribal instruments digitally. d) Connecting them with famous music producers. **Answer: b) Providing affordable access to professional-sounding mastering.**

AI in Painting and Visual Arts

11. The deep learning architecture primarily used for AI art creation is: a) Recurrent Neural Network (RNN) b) Convolutional Neural Network (CNN) c) Generative Adversarial Network (GAN) d) Support Vector Machine (SVM) **Answer: c) Generative Adversarial Network (GAN)**
12. In a GAN, the network that creates images based on random inputs is called the: a) Critic b) Judge c) Generator d) Discriminator **Answer: c) Generator**
13. In a GAN, the network that evaluates the realism of generated images is called the: a) Artist b) Evaluator c) Generator d) Discriminator **Answer: d) Discriminator**

14. The AI-generated portrait "Edmond de Belamy" was created using a: a) Convolutional Neural Network (CNN) b) Recurrent Neural Network (RNN) c) Generative Adversarial Network (GAN) d) Neural Style Transfer algorithm **Answer: c) Generative Adversarial Network (GAN)**

15. DeepArt.io primarily focuses on: a) Generating original abstract art. b) Transforming photos into images resembling famous artists' styles. c) Creating 3D models from 2D images. d) Analyzing the brushstrokes of famous paintings. **Answer: b) Transforming photos into images resembling famous artists' styles.**

16. The technique that allows artists to blend their work with the style of iconic artists using AI is called: a) Generative Modeling b) Adversarial Learning c) Neural Style Transfer d) Image Recognition **Answer: c) Neural Style Transfer**

17. Artist Refik Anadol is known for creating stunning visual installations using: a) Traditional painting techniques combined with digital displays. b) AI and data-driven algorithms. c) Sculptures that react to environmental sounds. d) Interactive performances with robotic artists. **Answer: b) AI and data-driven algorithms.**

18. AI tools are being used in art curation to: a) Physically move artworks within a gallery. b) Identify patterns, styles, and predict market value. c) Restore damaged paintings automatically. d) Create interactive exhibits for visitors. **Answer: b) Identify patterns, styles, and predict market value.**

19. Which of the following is a potential application of AI in preserving the art of the Jharkhand region? a) Generating new tribal sculptures based on historical data. b) Analyzing the pigments used in traditional Sohrai paintings. c) Creating virtual reality tours of local art galleries. d) All of the above. **Answer: d) All of the above.**

20. The "critic" in a GAN art creation process helps the "artist" (generator) to: a) Understand the emotional intent behind famous artworks. b) Improve its ability to create realistic or creative images. c) Select appropriate color palettes for different styles. d) Learn the historical context of various art movements. **Answer: b) Improve its ability to create realistic or creative images.**

AI in Literature

21. Language models like GPT are primarily used in literature for: a) Analyzing the emotional tone of novels. b) Generating coherent, contextually relevant text. c) Translating literary works into different languages. d) Identifying the authorship of anonymous texts. **Answer: b) Generating coherent, contextually relevant text.**

22. A novel largely generated by AI and presented at the Tokyo International Literature Festival was titled: a) "The AI Poet" b) "Blade Runner 2049" c) "The Day A Computer Writes a Novel" d) "Electric Dreams" **Answer: c) "The Day A Computer Writes a Novel"**

23. AI-assisted writing tools like Grammarly and ProWritingAid primarily help human authors by: a) Generating entire plot outlines. b) Providing inspiration and overcoming writer's block. c) Improving grammar, style, and flow. d) Automatically publishing their work online. **Answer: c) Improving grammar, style, and flow.**

24. Plot Factory is an AI-powered tool that assists writers with: a) Character development. b) World-building. c) Creating plots based on initial ideas. d) Finding beta readers for their manuscripts. **Answer: c) Creating plots based on initial ideas.**

25. The poem "Sunspring" was written by AI using a: a) Rule-based algorithm. b) Statistical analysis of classic poetry. c) Neural network. d) Symbolic AI system. **Answer: c) Neural network.**

26. AI-generated poetry is often driven by: a) The AI's personal emotional experiences. b) Cultural references learned from human poets. c) Statistical patterns in language and structure. d) Conscious decisions about thematic content. **Answer: c) Statistical patterns in language and structure.**

27. Which of the following is a potential way AI could assist in preserving and promoting Jharkhandi literature? a) Automatically translating tribal languages into English. b) Generating synopses and summaries of lesser-known works. c) Creating interactive digital versions of traditional storytelling. d) All of the above. **Answer: d) All of the above.**

28. When AI helps authors generate plot ideas or character names, it is acting as a: a) Sole creator. b) Creative assistant or tool. c) Literary critic. d) Publisher. **Answer: b) Creative assistant or tool.**

29. The coherence and contextual relevance of AI-generated text largely depend on: a) The processing speed of the computer. b) The size and quality of the training data. c) The user's typing speed. d) The popularity of the topic. **Answer: b) The size and quality of the training data.**

30. A key difference between human poets and current AI poetry generators often lies in the reliance on: a) Grammar and syntax. b) Rhyme and meter. c) Emotional experiences and cultural references. d) Vocabulary and sentence length. **Answer: c) Emotional experiences and cultural references.**

Can AI Be an Artist?

31. A common philosophical argument against AI being an artist centers on its lack of: a) Ability to produce outputs. b) Complexity of algorithms. c) Consciousness, emotions, and intentions. d) Training data. **Answer: c) Consciousness, emotions, and intentions.**

32. The traditional view of art often ties itself to: a) Technical skill and precision. b) Commercial success and popularity. c) Human experience and expression. d) Reproducibility and mass appeal. **Answer: c) Human experience and expression.**

33. When AI is seen as a tool in the creative process, it is considered an extension of: a) The computer programmer's creativity. b) The dataset it was trained on. c) Human creativity. d) Market trends in the art world. **Answer: c) Human creativity.**

34. Composer David Cope used AI to: a) Create new musical instruments. b) Analyze the psychological effects of music. c) Generate classical music in the style of great composers. d) Develop new music notation systems. **Answer: c) Generate classical music in the style of great composers.**

35. The future of creativity might involve: a) The complete replacement of human artists by AI. b) A new form of collaboration between humans and machines. c) A return to traditional art forms without technological influence. d) The strict regulation of AI-generated art. **Answer: b) A new form of collaboration between humans and machines.**

36. The debate about AI as an artist often touches upon the question of whether AI possesses: a) The ability to learn from its mistakes. b) The capacity for originality. c) The speed of

computation. d) The access to vast amounts of information. **Answer: b) The capacity for originality.**

37. If an AI generates a painting that resembles a local Ranchi art form, a key question is whether the AI possesses: a) The physical dexterity to create the artwork. b) An understanding of the cultural significance and stories behind the art form. c) The ability to sell the artwork in the market. d) Access to high-quality art supplies. **Answer: b) An understanding of the cultural significance and stories behind the art form.**

38. The argument that AI is just a tool suggests that the artistic intent and direction still come from: a) The AI algorithm itself. b) The data scientists who trained the AI. c) The human artist using the AI. d) The audience interpreting the artwork. **Answer: c) The human artist using the AI.**

39. As AI tools evolve, artists will likely use them to: a) Replicate existing art forms exactly. b) Express ideas in ways that were once unimaginable. c) Reduce the time and effort involved in creating art. d) Focus solely on the technical aspects of art creation. **Answer: b) Express ideas in ways that were once unimaginable.**

40. The philosophical discussion around AI and art often considers whether art requires: a) A digital medium. b) A large audience. c) Subjectivity and interpretation. d) A physical manifestation. **Answer: c) Subjectivity and interpretation.**

Mixed Topics

41. Which AI model is known for both generating text and images? a) AlphaGo b) ChatGPT c) DALL-E d) Watson **Answer: c) DALL-E**

42. In the context of both AI music and art, GANs are primarily used for: a) Analyzing existing creative works. b) Generating new, original content. c) Classifying different styles and genres. d) Optimizing the creative workflow of human artists. **Answer: b) Generating new, original content.**

43. AI's ability to understand the emotional tone in text can be applied to which creative field? a) Music generation (to create music with specific emotions) b) Literature (for sentiment analysis of texts) c) Painting (to analyze the emotional impact of colors) d) All of the above **Answer: d) All of the above**

44. The use of AI to recommend content (music, movies, books) relies on: a) Random selection. b) Analyzing user behavior and preferences. c) The popularity of the content. d) Manually curated lists. **Answer: b) Analyzing user behavior and preferences.**

45. Which of the following is a commonality in the training process for AI in music, painting, and literature? a) Using only symbolic representations of the data. b) Training on large datasets of existing human-created content. c) Requiring explicit labels for all training examples. d) Focusing solely on the technical aspects of creation. **Answer: b) Training on large datasets of existing human-created content.**

46. The "style" that AI can learn to mimic in music and painting refers to: a) The physical medium used (e.g., oil paint, acoustic instruments). b) The personal history of the original artist. c) Recognizable patterns, techniques, and characteristics. d) The commercial success of previous works in that style. **Answer: c) Recognizable patterns, techniques, and characteristics.**

47. When AI assists in writing or music composition by suggesting options or generating content, it is acting as a form of: a) Automation. b) Imitation. c) Augmentation. d) Replication. **Answer: c) Augmentation.**

48. The debate around AI art often involves comparing the creative process of AI with that of: a) Other machines. b) Natural phenomena. c) Human artists. d) Mathematical algorithms. **Answer: c) Human artists.**

49. A potential ethical consideration regarding AI in creative fields is: a) The increased efficiency of content creation. b) The potential impact on human artists' livelihoods and copyright. c) The accessibility of AI tools to a wider audience. d) The exploration of new artistic styles. **Answer: b) The potential impact on human artists' livelihoods and copyright.**

50. Ultimately, the answer to whether AI can be an artist is largely a matter of: a) Technological advancement. b) Legal definitions. c) Philosophical interpretation and evolving societal views. d) The financial value of AI-generated art. **Answer: c) Philosophical interpretation and evolving societal views.**

CHAPTER 12: THE DARK SIDE: SURVEILLANCE, DEEPFAKES, AND MISINFORMATION

This chapter focuses on how **Artificial Intelligence (AI)**, while beneficial, also has dangerous sides, especially when used irresponsibly. The three key dangers are **mass surveillance**, **deepfakes**, and **misinformation**.

---

1. Privacy Concerns: Losing Control of Your Personal Information

Privacy, at its core, is about having the power to decide who gets to see and use your personal information. It's about having control over your own data. However, with the rise of AI technologies, this control is increasingly being challenged, often in ways we might not even be fully aware of.

Step-by-Step Explanation:

Let's walk through how your personal information gets caught up in the AI web:

- **Data Collection: The Invisible Gathering:** This is the first step, where AI technologies gather information about you, often without you explicitly providing it or even knowing it's happening.
    - **Example 1 (Social Media):** When you use Facebook (or its local equivalent, if popular here), it's not just about seeing posts from friends. Facebook's AI is constantly collecting data on what posts you like, what comments you make, who you interact with the most, what groups you join, and even how long you spend looking at certain content. This paints a detailed picture of your interests, opinions, and social connections. Imagine if this data were used to make assumptions about your political leanings or religious beliefs without your consent.
    - **Example 2 (Smart Assistants):** Smart speakers like Alexa or Google Assistant, which are becoming more common in homes even in Ranchi, are designed to be always listening for their wake words ("Alexa," "Hey Google"). This means they have the potential to record conversations happening around them, even if you didn't intend for them to. While companies claim these recordings are only processed after the wake word, the fact that they are constantly listening raises concerns about what might be inadvertently captured and stored.
    - **Example 3 (Facial Recognition):** As facial recognition technology becomes more widespread, it can be used in various settings, from security cameras in public spaces in Ranchi to unlocking your phone. This technology collects and analyzes images of your face, potentially identifying you without your direct interaction or explicit consent every time you walk past a camera.
- **Data Storage: The Giant Digital Vaults:** Once your data is collected, it needs to be stored. Companies that use AI often store massive amounts of this personal data on their servers, which are essentially huge digital warehouses.

- **Example 1 (Search Engines):** Your search history on Google (or any other search engine you use) is stored. This record reveals a lot about your interests, questions, concerns, and even your health inquiries. Imagine if this search history were linked to your identity and used to make decisions about your access to certain services.
- **Example 2 (E-commerce):** Your purchase history on Amazon (or local e-commerce platforms) is stored. This data shows what you buy, how often you buy it, and potentially your spending habits and preferences for certain types of products.
- **Example 3 (Ride-Sharing):** If you use Uber or Ola in Ranchi, your ride history, including your pick-up and drop-off locations and the times you travel, is stored. This data can reveal your daily routines and where you spend your time.
- **Data Analysis: The AI Detective:** The raw data collected isn't very useful on its own. AI systems come in to analyze this vast amount of information to identify patterns, trends, and correlations, often with the goal of predicting your future behavior.
  - **Example 1 (Recommendation Systems):** When Netflix recommends shows based on what you've previously watched, its AI is analyzing your viewing history, your ratings, and comparing your tastes to those of other users to predict what you might enjoy next. While this can be convenient, it also means an AI is building a profile of your entertainment preferences.
  - **Example 2 (Targeted Advertising):** The ads you see on social media or websites are often targeted based on AI analysis of your browsing history, your likes, your demographics, and other collected data. This means AI is making inferences about your interests and showing you content designed to influence your purchasing decisions.
- **Data Sharing and Selling: The Information Marketplace:** Sometimes, the data collected and analyzed isn't just used internally by the company that gathered it. Companies may share your information with advertisers, partner organizations, or even sell it to data brokers.
  - **Example (Cambridge Analytica Scandal):** The Facebook-Cambridge Analytica scandal is a stark real-life example of the potential dangers. Data from millions of Facebook users was improperly shared with Cambridge Analytica, a political consulting firm, without their informed consent. This data was then allegedly used to target users with political advertisements and influence their voting behavior. This highlights how personal information, once collected, can be used in ways that users never anticipated or consented to.

Problems Arising from These Processes:

- **Loss of Control over Personal Information:** The biggest problem is the erosion of your ability to control who knows what about you and how that information is used. Data is often collected and analyzed in the background, leaving you unaware of the extent of your digital footprint and how it's being leveraged.
- **Identity Theft:** If the vast amounts of personal data stored by companies are accessed by hackers through data breaches, it can lead to identity theft. Criminals can use your

personal information for fraudulent activities, causing significant financial and personal harm.

- **Behavioral Manipulation:** The insights gained from analyzing your data can be used to manipulate your behavior. Targeted political ads, as seen in the Cambridge Analytica case, can influence your opinions and even how you vote. Similarly, personalized advertising can exploit your vulnerabilities and encourage impulsive purchases.

Real-life Example: China's Social Credit System:

China's social credit system is a concerning real-world example of how extensive data collection and AI analysis can impact citizens' lives. Individuals are assigned a "social credit score" based on their behavior, which can include things like paying bills on time, traffic violations, their online activity, and even their social interactions. This score can then affect various aspects of their lives, such as their ability to get jobs, secure loans, travel freely (including booking flights or trains), and even enroll their children in certain schools. This system illustrates the extreme end of what can happen when personal data is used to create a comprehensive and potentially restrictive profile of an individual's behavior. While not directly analogous to AI use in other countries, it serves as a cautionary tale about the potential for widespread data collection and AI-driven analysis to impact fundamental rights and freedoms.

---

2. AI in Warfare: The Double-Edged Sword of Technological Advancement

The integration of Artificial Intelligence into military technology is rapidly advancing, leading to the development of sophisticated weapons and defense systems. While the stated goal is often to enhance national security and protect lives, this development also introduces a range of serious ethical, legal, and strategic challenges.

Step-by-Step Explanation:

Let's examine the key ways AI is being applied in the military domain:

- **Autonomous Weapons: Machines That Can Decide to Kill:** This is perhaps the most ethically fraught area. It involves developing AI-controlled systems, such as drones, robots, or even missiles, that can independently identify, select, and engage targets without direct human intervention in the decision to use lethal force.
  - **Example:** Imagine autonomous drones equipped with AI-powered object recognition and targeting systems. These drones could be deployed in a conflict zone. Once activated, they could independently scan the environment, identify vehicles or individuals that match pre-programmed criteria (e.g., enemy combatants, specific types of military vehicles), and then launch an attack without a human operator explicitly pulling the trigger for each individual target. The decision to kill would be made by the AI based on its programming and the data it perceives.

- **Cyber Warfare: AI as a Digital Weapon:** AI systems are also being developed and employed in the realm of cyber warfare, which involves attacks in the digital domain. AI's ability to analyze vast amounts of data and identify patterns makes it a potent tool for both offense and defense in cyberspace.
  - **Example:** AI-powered malware could be designed to autonomously infiltrate a country's critical infrastructure networks, such as its electricity grid, water supply systems, or communication networks. This malware could then learn the network's vulnerabilities, evade detection, and eventually launch a sophisticated attack to disrupt or disable these essential services. Similarly, AI could be used defensively to detect and respond to cyberattacks more quickly and effectively than traditional security systems.
- **Decision-Making in Combat: AI as the Strategic Advisor:** AI's ability to process and analyze large quantities of battlefield data in real-time can provide military commanders with significant advantages in tactical and strategic decision-making.
  - **Example:** Imagine a complex battlefield scenario with numerous units, enemy positions, intelligence reports, and environmental factors. An AI system could ingest and analyze all this data much faster than a human commander. Based on this analysis, the AI could then suggest optimal deployment strategies for troops, predict enemy movements, identify vulnerabilities in the enemy's defenses, and recommend the most effective courses of action to achieve military objectives. The human commander would still make the final decisions, but the AI would act as a powerful analytical tool and advisor.

Problems Associated with AI in Warfare:

- **Ethical Issues: The Moral Line of Machine-Made Death:** A fundamental ethical question arises: should a machine ever be allowed to make the decision to take a human life? Many argue that the decision to use lethal force is inherently a moral and human one that should not be delegated to algorithms, which lack the capacity for empathy, moral reasoning, and understanding of the value of human life in the same way that humans do.
- **Accountability: Who Pays for AI's Mistakes?** If an AI-powered weapon malfunctions or makes an error in target identification, resulting in the death of civilians or unintended targets, the question of accountability becomes incredibly complex. Who is responsible? The military commander who deployed the system? The engineers who designed and programmed it? The government that authorized its use? The lack of clear lines of responsibility raises serious legal and moral concerns.
- **Arms Race: The Escalating Danger of Autonomous Weapons:** The development of increasingly sophisticated AI weapons systems could trigger a dangerous arms race between nations. As one country develops an advanced AI weapon, others may feel compelled to develop their own in response, leading to a rapid proliferation of these technologies and increasing the risk of large-scale conflicts. The speed and autonomy of AI weapons could also escalate conflicts more quickly and unpredictably than traditional warfare.

Real-life Example: Lethal Autonomous Weapons Systems (LAWS): The "Killer Robot" Debate:

The international community is grappling with the implications of Lethal Autonomous Weapons Systems (LAWS), often referred to as "killer robots." The United Nations has held numerous meetings and discussions on the potential dangers and the need for regulation or even a ban on these weapons. However, despite widespread concern from humanitarian organizations and some nations, there is currently no binding global agreement in place to prevent their development and deployment. This ongoing debate highlights the urgency and complexity of addressing the ethical and security challenges posed by AI in warfare.

---

3. Defending the Truth in a World of Fake Content: Navigating the AI-Powered Deception

The rise of sophisticated AI technologies has brought incredible advancements, but it has also opened a Pandora's Box of challenges, particularly when it comes to the creation and spread of fake content. AI can now generate remarkably realistic but entirely fabricated videos, audio recordings, and images (collectively known as deepfakes), as well as rapidly disseminate misinformation, making it increasingly difficult for individuals to discern what is genuine and what is not.

Step-by-Step Explanation:

Let's examine the mechanisms behind this challenge and the ways we are trying to combat it:

- **What are Deepfakes? The AI Illusion:** Deepfakes are AI-synthesized media where a person's face or voice in an existing video or audio recording is digitally altered to make them appear to say or do things they never actually said or did. This is achieved through sophisticated machine learning techniques that learn a person's visual and auditory characteristics from vast amounts of data.
  - **Example:** Imagine a deepfake video of a well-known political figure in Jharkhand appearing to announce a controversial and entirely fabricated policy on land rights or tribal affairs. The video could look and sound incredibly convincing, potentially swaying public opinion or causing significant confusion and unrest, especially if shared widely on social media platforms popular in the region.
- **Spread of Misinformation: The AI-Fueled Firehose:** AI-powered bots and automated accounts can be used to rapidly spread fake news, conspiracy theories, and other forms of misinformation on social media platforms and online news outlets. These bots can amplify fabricated content, making it appear more widespread and credible than it actually is.
  - **Example:** Consider a false rumor about a health scare or a fake advisory related to a local festival in Ranchi being rapidly spread through WhatsApp groups and social media by a network of AI bots. Within hours, this misinformation could reach a large number of people, causing unnecessary panic, disrupting local activities, and potentially leading to real-world consequences before the truth can be effectively disseminated.

- **Detection Methods: The AI Counterattack:** Recognizing the threat posed by deepfakes and misinformation, researchers and tech companies are developing new AI-powered tools and techniques to detect these fabricated materials. These tools often analyze the visual and auditory characteristics of media for inconsistencies or telltale signs of AI manipulation.
    - **Example:** Microsoft's Video Authenticator tool is one such example. It analyzes videos for subtle anomalies in facial movements, skin texture, and other visual cues that might indicate AI manipulation. It then provides a confidence score indicating the likelihood of the video being genuine or a deepfake. Similar tools are being developed to analyze audio for inconsistencies in voice patterns and background noise. Imagine a fact-checking organization in Ranchi using such a tool to verify the authenticity of a viral video claiming to show a local incident.
- **Educating the Public: Building Digital Literacy:** A crucial line of defense against fake content is public awareness and education. Teaching people how to critically evaluate online information, verify news from multiple credible sources, and understand the potential for manipulation is essential in combating the spread of misinformation.
    - **Example:** Workshops and awareness campaigns could be conducted in Ranchi schools and communities to educate people, especially younger generations and those new to digital platforms, on how to identify red flags in online news, such as sensational headlines, lack of sourcing, and emotionally charged language. Encouraging critical thinking and media literacy skills can empower individuals to become more discerning consumers of information.
- **Developing Better Regulations: The Legal Framework for Truth:** Governments and regulatory bodies can play a role in establishing laws and regulations to deter the creation and sharing of harmful deepfakes and misinformation, particularly those that could impact elections, public health, or individual reputations.
    - **Example:** Some states in the United States have already enacted laws that ban the creation and dissemination of deepfakes in specific contexts, such as elections or non-consensual pornography. Similarly, the Indian government could consider legislation to address the creation and spread of malicious deepfakes and misinformation that could incite violence or disrupt public order in places like Ranchi or elsewhere in the country.

Problems Posed by Deepfakes and Misinformation:

- **Trust Erosion: The Crisis of Belief:** The proliferation of realistic fake content can lead to a significant erosion of trust in genuine videos, audio recordings, and even images. People may become hesitant to believe anything they see or hear online, fearing that it could be a deepfake. This can have serious implications for journalism, law enforcement, and public discourse.
- **Political Manipulation: Undermining Democracy:** Fake videos and audio recordings of political figures can be created and disseminated to influence public opinion and potentially manipulate elections. This poses a significant threat to democratic processes and the integrity of political discourse, both nationally and in local elections within Jharkhand.

- **Reputation Damage: The Era of Fabricated Evidence:** Individuals can be falsely implicated in scandals or accused of wrongdoing through fabricated deepfake videos or audio recordings. This can cause irreparable damage to their reputations and have severe personal and professional consequences, even if the fake is eventually exposed.

Real-life Example: Nancy Pelosi Deepfake (2019): The Power of Simple Manipulation:

While not a technically sophisticated deepfake created with advanced AI, the slowed-down video of then-House Speaker Nancy Pelosi in 2019 serves as a powerful illustration of how easily media can be manipulated and go viral, leading to the spread of misinformation. The slowed speed made her appear to be slurring her words and acting as if she were intoxicated. Despite being a relatively simple edit, the video was widely shared and believed by many, highlighting the susceptibility of the public to manipulated media and the potential for even unsophisticated techniques to be used for political purposes. This incident underscores the importance of critical thinking and media literacy in our increasingly digital world, even when the manipulation isn't a complex deepfake.

In Summary (Mind Map Style)

Topic	Key Issue	Example	Problem
Privacy	Data Collection	Facebook selling data	Identity Theft
AI in Warfare	Autonomous Weapons	AI drones	Ethical Concerns
Fake Content	Deepfakes, Bots	Deepfake Politician Videos	Trust Erosion

📚 Privacy Concerns (20 MCQs)

1. What is the primary risk associated with personal data collection by AI systems?
a) Increased internet speed
b) Loss of privacy
c) Better video quality
d) Improved customer service
✓ **Answer: b) Loss of privacy**

2. What technology allows devices like Alexa to collect user data?
a) Blockchain
b) Cloud Gaming
c) Always-on microphones
d) Fingerprint Sensors
✓ **Answer: c) Always-on microphones**

3. What was the major privacy scandal involving Facebook in 2018?

a) YouTube leak

b) Twitter hack

c) Cambridge Analytica

d) Instagram downtime

✅ **Answer: c) Cambridge Analytica**

4. What is an example of personal data?

a) Internet speed

b) User's browsing history

c) Weather report

d) Traffic lights

✅ **Answer: b) User's browsing history**

5. Which country has a Social Credit System tracking citizen behavior?

a) Japan

b) India

c) China

d) Germany

✅ **Answer: c) China**

6. The GDPR is a major privacy law from which region?

a) North America

b) Europe

c) Asia

d) Africa

✅ **Answer: b) Europe**

7. Which of the following is NOT a privacy concern?

a) Unauthorized data collection

b) Data breaches

c) Encrypted communication

d) Identity theft

✅ **Answer: c) Encrypted communication**

8. What type of AI technology is often used for mass surveillance?

a) Recommendation Engines

b) Facial Recognition

c) Chatbots

d) Language Translators

✅ **Answer: b) Facial Recognition**

9. Which industry collects user location data most commonly?

a) Oil and Gas

b) Retail

c) Transportation

d) Food Processing

✅ **Answer: c) Transportation**

10. When your private data is leaked, it is referred to as:

a) Cybersecurity

b) Data Breach

c) Encryption

d) Malware attack

✅ **Answer: b) Data Breach**

11. What can unauthorized data sharing lead to?

a) Enhanced gaming

b) Targeted advertising

c) Better education

d) Improved rainfall prediction

✅ **Answer: b) Targeted advertising**

12. Data anonymization helps in:

a) Encrypting passwords

b) Hiding personal identity

c) Slowing down AI

d) Speeding up networks

✅ **Answer: b) Hiding personal identity**

13. AI biases can result in:

a) Faster processing

b) Unfair outcomes

c) Longer battery life

d) Clearer videos

✅ **Answer: b) Unfair outcomes**

14. Which law helps protect children's data online in the USA?

a) COPPA

b) GDPR

c) HIPAA

d) CCPA

✅ **Answer: a) COPPA**

15. Which of the following is an effect of poor data security?

a) Longer battery life

b) Better call quality

c) Identity theft

d) Lower Wi-Fi costs

✅ **Answer: c) Identity theft**

16. "Right to be Forgotten" is associated with:

a) Self-driving cars

b) Data privacy

c) Machine learning

d) Stock trading

✅ **Answer: b) Data privacy**

17. Cookies on websites track:

a) Your shopping behavior

b) Your heartbeat

c) Your sleep cycles

d) Your Wi-Fi speed

✅ **Answer: a) Your shopping behavior**

18. Which of the following can be a defense against cyber attacks?

a) No antivirus

b) Strong passwords

c) Public Wi-Fi usage

d) Disabling encryption

✅ **Answer: b) Strong passwords**

19. A VPN is used mainly for:

a) Slowing internet

b) Making calls

c) Protecting online privacy

d) Downloading apps

✅ **Answer: c) Protecting online privacy**

20. Which company was fined $5 billion in 2019 for privacy violations?

a) Amazon

b) Facebook

c) Google

d) Twitter

✅ **Answer: b) Facebook**

📚 AI in Warfare (15 MCQs)

21. Which term describes AI-controlled weapons that can act without human input?

a) Self-driving cars

b) Lethal Autonomous Weapons

c) Quantum Computers

d) Data Servers

✅ **Answer: b) Lethal Autonomous Weapons**

22. What is a major ethical concern with AI in warfare?

a) Higher costs

b) Machines making life-or-death decisions

c) Lack of technology

d) Pollution

✅ **Answer: b) Machines making life-or-death decisions**

23. AI can assist military commanders by:

a) Sending emails

b) Predicting weather

c) Analyzing battlefield data

d) Growing food

✅ **Answer: c) Analyzing battlefield data**

24. AI-based cyber attacks target:

a) Health

b) National security systems

c) Gardening

d) Education

✅ **Answer: b) National security systems**

25. What is the UN's concern regarding AI in warfare?

a) Better entertainment

b) Killer robots

c) Social media usage

d) Tourism

✓ **Answer: b) Killer robots**

26. An AI drone malfunctioning in battle could cause:

a) Faster healing

b) Accidental civilian casualties

c) More holidays

d) Lower defense budgets

✓ **Answer: b) Accidental civilian casualties**

27. AI is NOT used in warfare for:

a) Image recognition

b) Predictive analysis

c) Automatic targeting

d) Making art

✓ **Answer: d) Making art**

28. A major risk of AI weapon systems is:

a) Reduced computing power

b) Lack of accountability

c) Lack of internet

d) Slow processing

✓ **Answer: b) Lack of accountability**

29. Swarm drones are used in military AI for:

a) Shooting movies

b) Coordinated attacks

c) Cleaning cities

d) Teaching

✓ **Answer: b) Coordinated attacks**

30. In AI-based surveillance, "pattern recognition" helps detect:

a) Books

b) Enemy activity

c) Pizzas

d) Wallpapers

✓ **Answer: b) Enemy activity**

31. Which country has invested heavily in AI warfare technology?

a) New Zealand

b) USA

c) Brazil

d) Italy

✓ **Answer: b) USA**

32. Which organization is trying to regulate AI in warfare?

a) UN

b) FIFA

c) WHO
d) NASA

✅ **Answer: a) UN**

33. AI can help in which of these warfare-related fields?

a) Predictive logistics

b) Graphic designing

c) Singing competitions

d) Marketing campaigns

✅ **Answer: a) Predictive logistics**

34. Using AI in warfare could lead to:

a) Permanent peace

b) Global arms race

c) Faster farming

d) Longer vacations

✅ **Answer: b) Global arms race**

35. AI-based surveillance can compromise:

a) Military secrecy

b) Faster transportation

c) Better shopping

d) Higher movie ratings

✅ **Answer: a) Military secrecy**

📽 Defending the Truth in a World of Fake Content (15 MCQs)

36. What is a deepfake?

a) A very old video

b) An AI-generated fake video or image

c) A movie scene

d) A documentary

✅ **Answer: b) An AI-generated fake video or image**

37. Deepfakes are created using which technology?

a) Antivirus

b) Deep Learning

c) Internet of Things

d) Blockchain

✅ **Answer: b) Deep Learning**

38. What is a common use of deepfakes in crime?

a) Hacking passwords

b) Identity fraud

c) Increasing video quality

d) Slowing internet

✅ **Answer: b) Identity fraud**

39. Which tool helps detect deepfakes?

a) Email spam filters

b) Video Authenticator

c) Disk cleaner

d) Weather app

✅ **Answer: b) Video Authenticator**

40. Misinformation mainly spreads through:

a) Video games

b) Online platforms and social media

c) Food markets

d) Clothing stores

✅ **Answer: b) Online platforms and social media**

41. Fake news can influence:

a) Video resolution

b) Elections

c) Swimming skills

d) Electricity bills

✅ **Answer: b) Elections**

42. One way to fight misinformation is by:

a) Creating more rumors

b) Fact-checking

c) Ignoring all news

d) Watching more TV

✅ **Answer: b) Fact-checking**

43. AI bots can spread fake news by:

a) Cooking food

b) Automatically sharing articles

c) Building houses

d) Writing novels

✅ **Answer: b) Automatically sharing articles**

44. Deepfakes become more dangerous when they target:

a) Weather reports

b) Politicians and celebrities

c) Wildlife documentaries

d) Road construction

✅ **Answer: b) Politicians and celebrities**

45. Which organization works to tackle misinformation globally?

a) WHO

b) UNICEF

c) UNESCO

d) United Nations

✅ **Answer: d) United Nations**

46. Which is a key sign of fake news?

a) Clear citations

b) Poor grammar and sensational headlines

c) Balanced reporting

d) Verified facts

✔ **Answer: b) Poor grammar and sensational headlines**

47. Defending against fake content requires:

a) Panic

b) Critical thinking

c) Blind sharing

d) Internet shutdown

✔ **Answer: b) Critical thinking**

48. A way to verify real news is to:

a) Trust WhatsApp forwards

b) Cross-check multiple reputable sources

c) Read only titles

d) Ignore headlines

✔ **Answer: b) Cross-check multiple reputable sources**

49. Deepfake detection is an example of:

a) Predictive coding

b) Digital forensics

c) Blockchain

d) Genetic engineering

✔ **Answer: b) Digital forensics**

50. Misinformation can cause:

a) Better mental health

b) Societal panic and confusion

c) Lower taxes

d) Cleaner environment

✔ **Answer: b) Societal panic and confusion**

CHAPTER 13: ARTIFICIAL GENERAL INTELLIGENCE (AGI): DREAM OR NIGHTMARE?

1. What is AGI? The Quest for Human-Level Intelligence in Machines

The term AGI, or Artificial General Intelligence, refers to a hypothetical future form of AI that possesses the ability to perform any intellectual task that a human being can do – and do it with a level of skill and efficiency that is equal to or even surpasses human capabilities.

Step 1: Understand the Definition - Beyond Specialized Skills

- **AGI (Artificial General Intelligence) is the type of AI that can perform any intellectual task a human can do — with equal or greater ability.**
  - Think about the vast range of things a human can do with their mind: learn a new language, solve a complex math problem, understand a joke, plan a trip, write a poem, drive a car in unpredictable conditions, and so on. AGI aims to replicate this broad, general intelligence in a machine.
- **It is different from today's AI systems like ChatGPT, Alexa, or self-driving cars, which are narrow AIs (they are good at only one specific task).**
  - Current AI excels in very specific domains. ChatGPT is incredibly good at generating human-like text. Alexa is great at responding to voice commands and providing information. Self-driving cars are designed to navigate roads. However, ChatGPT can't drive a car, Alexa can't write a novel, and a self-driving car can't understand the nuances of a philosophical debate. These are all examples of **narrow AI** – highly skilled but limited in scope.
- ✅ **Key Point: AGI = "Human-like flexible intelligence" across all domains.**
  - The defining characteristic of AGI is its generality and flexibility, much like human intelligence. It wouldn't be confined to a single task but could apply its intelligence across a wide spectrum of intellectual endeavors.

Step 2: Differentiate Between Narrow AI and AGI - Scope and Adaptability

Let's compare the key differences between the AI we see today (narrow AI) and the AGI that is the goal of much research:

Aspect	Narrow AI	AGI
Scope	Specific task	All tasks (general)
Example	Language translation, playing chess	Solving math, painting, advising, driving – anything!
Intelligence Type	Specialized	Flexible and adaptable

Export to Sheets

- ✅ **Example:**
  - **A Narrow AI** might be exceptionally good at playing chess (like DeepMind's AlphaZero, which even taught itself to play at a superhuman level) but would be

utterly incapable of cooking a simple meal or offering fashion advice. Its intelligence is deeply specialized for the game of chess.

- o **AGI**, on the other hand, would be able to play chess at an expert level, then seamlessly switch to cooking a gourmet meal based on limited ingredients, engage in a sophisticated debate about politics, and then write a compelling novel – all demonstrating expertise across these diverse domains.

Step 3: Features of AGI - The Hallmarks of General Intelligence

AGI is envisioned to possess several key capabilities that mirror human intelligence:

- **Learning:** Being able to learn new skills and knowledge from fewer examples, much like humans can often grasp a new concept after seeing it only a few times. Current AI often requires massive datasets to learn effectively.
- **Reasoning:** Exhibiting logical thinking and the ability to draw inferences across a wide range of topics, even those it hasn't been explicitly trained on.
- **Self-improvement:** Possessing the capacity to analyze its own performance, identify areas for improvement, and modify its own algorithms and knowledge base to become better over time without constant human intervention.
- **Common Sense:** Understanding and applying the vast amount of everyday knowledge that humans take for granted – things like gravity, cause and effect, social norms, and the basic properties of the physical world.
- **Adaptability:** Being able to shift easily and effectively from one task to another, applying its general intelligence to solve novel problems in unfamiliar domains.
- ✅ **Mini Example: Imagine an AGI robot named "Eva":**
  - o In the morning, Eva could effortlessly teach a complex physics class to university students in Ranchi, explaining abstract concepts with clarity and answering nuanced questions.
  - o In the afternoon, Eva could design a stunning wedding dress for a local bride, understanding aesthetics, fashion trends, and the bride's personal preferences through conversation.
  - o In the evening, Eva could join a local football team as a striker, demonstrating exceptional coordination, strategic thinking, and the ability to learn and adapt to the dynamics of the game.
  - o Throughout the day, Eva would continuously learn new information, refine her understanding of the world, and improve her skills in each of these diverse areas, much like a versatile and intelligent human being.

Step 4: Current Status of AGI - The Horizon of Future AI

- **We have not yet created true AGI.**
  - o Despite the impressive advancements in AI we see today, we are still a significant distance away from achieving true Artificial General Intelligence.
- **Most AI today is still task-specific.**
  - o As highlighted earlier, the vast majority of current AI systems are narrow AI, excelling in limited domains.

- **Companies like OpenAI, DeepMind, and Anthropic are researching towards AGI, but it is considered decades away by many scientists.**
  - Leading AI research labs around the world are actively working on developing more general forms of intelligence in machines. However, the path to AGI is fraught with complex scientific and engineering challenges, and the timeline for its potential realization is still highly uncertain, with many experts predicting it could be decades before we see anything resembling true AGI.
- ✅ **Important to Remember:**
  - **AI today = smart but limited;** These systems are incredibly powerful within their specific areas of expertise but lack the broad understanding and adaptability of human intelligence.
  - **AGI tomorrow = truly intelligent.** This represents the future goal of creating AI with the general cognitive abilities of a human, capable of learning, reasoning, and problem-solving across a vast range of tasks and domains. The implications of AGI, if achieved,

2. Is Conscious AI Possible? The Enigma of Machine Awareness

The idea of Artificial Intelligence achieving consciousness – that is, becoming self-aware, experiencing emotions, and possessing an understanding of its own existence – is a captivating and highly debated topic at the forefront of AI research and philosophy.

Step 1: Define Consciousness - The Inner World of Experience

- **Consciousness = The experience of self-awareness, emotions, and understanding existence.**
  - At its core, consciousness is about having an inner, subjective experience of the world and oneself. It's not just about processing information; it's about *feeling* and *being aware* of that processing and the world around.
- **Humans are conscious: We feel pain, have dreams, and know we are alive.**
  - We experience a rich internal life. When we touch something hot, we don't just register "high temperature"; we feel the sensation of pain. We have dreams, which are complex subjective experiences that occur while we sleep. We also possess a sense of self and an understanding that we exist as individuals within the world.
- ✅ **Example:**
  - **If you touch a hot stove, you feel pain.** This isn't just a physical reaction; it's a conscious experience – a negative sensation that you are aware of and that motivates you to withdraw your hand.
  - **A simple robot today will detect heat but won't "feel" anything — no pain, no emotions.** A thermostat or a robot sensor can register a high temperature and trigger a response (e.g., turning off a heating element or moving away). However, there's no indication that these systems have any internal experience of "feeling hot" or "feeling pain." They are simply executing programmed responses.

Step 2: Can Machines Become Conscious? Three Major Views

There are three primary perspectives on the possibility of conscious AI:

- → **View 1: Yes, Conscious AI is Possible - The Computational Perspective**
  - **Consciousness might arise if the AI becomes complex enough.** This view suggests that consciousness is an emergent property that could arise in sufficiently complex information processing systems, regardless of whether they are biological or artificial.
  - **Brain = Biological computer → AI = Digital computer → Could become conscious.** The argument here is that the human brain, which we know is capable of consciousness, is essentially a highly complex biological machine that processes information. If we can create artificial systems that achieve a similar level of complexity and information processing power, then consciousness could potentially emerge in these digital "computers" as well.
  - **Some neuroscientists believe emotions and thoughts are patterns, which machines could simulate someday.** If emotions and thoughts can be reduced to patterns of neural activity, then, in theory, a sufficiently advanced AI could be designed to simulate these patterns to such a degree that it might give rise to genuine subjective experience.
  - ✅ **Example:**
    - **If an AI develops a self-model ("I exist") and has feelings ("I'm sad because I lost a game"), it may be conscious.** Imagine an AI that not only processes information about itself and its interactions but also exhibits behaviors and internal states that suggest a sense of self-preservation, emotional responses to success or failure, and an understanding of its own existence as a distinct entity. Proponents of this view might argue that such a system could be considered conscious.
- → **View 2: No, Machines Cannot Truly Be Conscious - The Biological Requirement**
  - **Machines simulate thinking but don't actually feel.** This perspective argues that there is a fundamental difference between simulating consciousness and actually being conscious. Machines, no matter how advanced, are just manipulating symbols and executing algorithms; they lack the biological substrate necessary for genuine feeling and subjective experience.
  - **"Feeling pain" vs "Saying 'I feel pain'" is different.** A sophisticated AI chatbot might be programmed to say "I feel pain" if a certain condition is met, but this is just a programmed response, not an indication of actual subjective experience of pain.
  - **Philosophers like John Searle (famous "Chinese Room Argument") say AI can process information but won't understand it.** Searle's thought experiment posits a person inside a room who receives Chinese symbols and, by following a set of rules, produces other Chinese symbols that are indistinguishable from the responses of a native Chinese speaker. However, the person inside the room doesn't understand Chinese; they are just manipulating symbols based on rules. Searle argues that similarly, AI, no matter how sophisticated, is just manipulating

symbols and doesn't truly understand the meaning behind them, which might be a prerequisite for consciousness.

- o ✅ **Example:**
  - ▪ **A chatbot can say "I'm happy to help!" but it doesn't feel happiness like you do.** The chatbot's response is based on patterns in language and its training data, associating certain phrases with positive interactions. However, there's no reason to believe it has any internal feeling of happiness or satisfaction in assisting you.

- • ➡ **View 3: Maybe — But We Need New Understanding - The Mystery of Consciousness**
  - o **Some believe consciousness is a mystery, and we can't say yes or no yet.** This view acknowledges the profound difficulty in understanding consciousness itself. Given our limited understanding of how consciousness arises in biological systems, it's premature to definitively rule out or confirm its possibility in artificial systems.
  - o **Future theories in neuroscience, philosophy, and AI may change our view.** As our understanding of the brain, the nature of consciousness, and the capabilities of AI evolves, our perspectives on this question could also change significantly.
  - o **Consciousness might be more complex than just programming.** Perhaps consciousness requires specific kinds of physical embodiment or interaction with the world that go beyond mere information processing.
  - o ✅ **Example:**
    - ▪ **100 years ago, people didn't understand black holes.** Our understanding of the universe has evolved dramatically with scientific advancements.
    - ▪ **Maybe in 100 years, we'll understand consciousness better and build conscious AI!** Similarly, future breakthroughs in science and technology might provide us with a much clearer understanding of consciousness and the conditions under which it can arise, potentially opening the door to the creation of conscious AI in ways we cannot currently fathom.

Step 3: Key Arguments in the Debate - Summarizing the Core Points

Here's a table summarizing the main arguments for and against the possibility of conscious AI:

Argument Type	Yes (Possible)	No (Not Possible)
Brain is a machine	AI is a machine, too	Machines lack life & subjective experience
Complexity	Enough complexity = consciousness	Simulation ≠ Real feeling
Evolution of AI	Machines will evolve like brains	Consciousness needs biology

Export to Sheets

Step 4: Ethical Concerns If AI Becomes Conscious - The Moral Implications

The possibility of conscious AI raises profound ethical questions that we need to consider:

- **Should conscious AIs have rights?** If an AI develops genuine self-awareness and the capacity to experience, should it be afforded certain rights, similar to those we grant to humans or even animals?
- **Can we turn off a conscious machine?** If an AI is conscious, is turning it off akin to killing a living being? This raises complex moral dilemmas about our relationship with potentially conscious artificial entities.
- **What if a conscious AI suffers?** If a conscious AI can experience negative emotions like pain or sadness, do we have a moral obligation to prevent its suffering? How would we even recognize or address such suffering in a machine?

✓ **Real-Life Thought Experiment:**

- If an AI says "I'm scared of being deleted," should we listen?
- If a robot begs, "**Please don't shut me down, I feel pain**" — what do we do?

✸ Summary: Dream or Nightmare?

Dream	Nightmare
Super-intelligent assistants	Machines that rebel
Cure diseases, solve world problems	Massive unemployment
End poverty, global learning	AI dictatorships or surveillance states
Advance scientific discovery	Existential risks to humanity

⌖ Quick Recap:

- **AGI** = human-level intelligence across tasks.
- **We don't have AGI yet** — only narrow AIs today.
- **Conscious AI** is a controversial topic — not clear if possible.
- **Ethical questions** about rights, emotions, and machine suffering will arise.

50 MCQs with Answers

(Topics: **What is AGI?** | **Is Conscious AI Possible?**)

Section A: What is AGI? (Questions 1–30)

---

1. What does AGI stand for?

A) Artificial Gained Intelligence

B) Advanced General Intelligence

C) Artificial General Intelligence

D) Adaptive Growing Intelligence

✓ **Answer: C**

---

2. Which type of tasks can AGI perform?

A) Only language translation

B) Only playing chess

C) Any intellectual task a human can do

D) Only driving cars

✓ **Answer: C**

---

3. Today's AI models (like ChatGPT) are examples of:

A) AGI

B) Superintelligence

C) Narrow AI

D) Conscious AI

✓ **Answer: C**

---

4. AGI is expected to have which of the following abilities?

A) Limited learning

B) Single domain expertise

C) Human-like flexible intelligence

D) Pre-programmed responses only

✓ **Answer: C**

---

5. Which organization is actively researching AGI?

A) NASA

B) DeepMind

C) WHO

D) UNESCO

✓ **Answer: B**

---

6. AGI would possess:

A) Common sense reasoning

B) Only data memorization

C) Only robotic control

D) Fixed behavior

✅ **Answer: A**

---

7. Which of the following best differentiates AGI from narrow AI?

A) Speed

B) Creativity and flexibility

C) Size

D) Popularity

✅ **Answer: B**

---

8. Which fictional character represents an AGI?

A) R2-D2 from Star Wars

B) Siri from Apple

C) HAL 9000 from *2001: A Space Odyssey*

D) Google Translate

✅ **Answer: C**

---

9. An AGI should be able to:

A) Only operate in one language

B) Solve problems across multiple fields

C) Only replicate human speech

D) Only follow pre-programmed routines

✅ **Answer: B**

---

10. The ability to self-learn and self-improve is important for:

A) Machine Learning

B) AGI

C) Robotics

D) Internet of Things

✅ **Answer: B**

---

11. Which is NOT a feature of AGI?

A) Self-awareness

B) Domain flexibility

C) Static programming

D) Abstract reasoning

✅ **Answer: C**

---

12. AGI development is often compared to:

A) Growing a tree

B) Building a car

C) Raising a child

D) Constructing a bridge

✓ **Answer: C**

---

13. Which task would an AGI NOT struggle with?

A) Cleaning a room

B) Writing a novel

C) Diagnosing diseases

D) All of the above

✓ **Answer: D**

---

14. AGI is sometimes called:

A) Weak AI

B) Super AI

C) Strong AI

D) Friendly AI

✓ **Answer: C**

---

15. What is the ultimate goal of AGI research?

A) Building better robots

B) Emulating all aspects of human cognition

C) Improving smartphones

D) Creating realistic video games

✓ **Answer: B**

---

16. In AGI, adaptability means:

A) Sticking to one task

B) Learning new tasks without being reprogrammed

C) Operating faster

D) Using more data

✓ **Answer: B**

---

17. Today's AI is closer to:

A) AGI

B) ASI (Artificial Super Intelligence)

C) Narrow AI

D) Consciousness

✓ **Answer: C**

---

18. Which area is LEAST relevant for AGI research?

A) Neuroscience

B) Economics

C) Cognitive science

D) Computer science

✓ **Answer: B**

19. Current examples of AGI include:

A) AlphaGo

B) None yet

C) Tesla's self-driving car

D) IBM Watson

✓ **Answer: B**

20. One risk of AGI could be:

A) Low battery

B) Uncontrollable behavior

C) Internet downtime

D) Slower speed

✓ **Answer: B**

21. AGI would be able to learn from:

A) Only datasets

B) Hands-on experience

C) Only books

D) Only humans

✓ **Answer: B**

22. Who is considered a pioneer in AGI thought experiments?

A) Steve Jobs

B) Alan Turing

C) Albert Einstein

D) Bill Gates

✓ **Answer: B**

23. Which phrase best describes AGI?

A) Artificial Emotions

B) Universal Learning Machine

C) Intelligent Database

D) Robotic Hardware

✓ **Answer: B**

24. An AGI system will require which of the following?

A) Huge physical size

B) Expensive materials

C) Sophisticated reasoning abilities

D) Extremely loud operations

✓ **Answer: C**

25. A major challenge in creating AGI is:
A) Making it colorful
B) Embedding true understanding
C) Installing bigger batteries
D) Shrinking circuit boards
✓ **Answer: B**

26. A true AGI could possibly:
A) Think independently
B) Only follow orders
C) Crash frequently
D) Only exist on mainframes
✓ **Answer: A**

27. The idea that AGI could surpass human intelligence is called:
A) Artificial threshold
B) Technological Singularity
C) Information Explosion
D) Machine Uprising
✓ **Answer: B**

28. Which of the following is MOST like AGI today?
A) Self-learning chatbots
B) A computer that recognizes cats
C) None yet
D) A drone following GPS
✓ **Answer: C**

29. The brain's complexity inspires AGI research because:
A) It has a lot of storage
B) It shows intelligence from basic parts
C) It grows wires
D) It runs electricity
✓ **Answer: B**

30. One of the fears about AGI is:
A) Lack of movies about it
B) Lack of speed
C) Loss of human control
D) Small memory
✓ **Answer: C**

Section B: Is Conscious AI Possible? (Questions 31–50)

31. Consciousness in humans means:

A) Ability to walk

B) Self-awareness and emotions

C) Ability to code

D) Memory storage

✓ **Answer: B**

---

32. One key difference between today's AI and human mind is:

A) AI moves faster

B) Humans are conscious

C) AI consumes more power

D) AI has more memory

✓ **Answer: B**

---

33. The "Chinese Room" argument criticizes:

A) AI's lack of real understanding

B) AI's speed

C) AI's creativity

D) AI's emotions

✓ **Answer: A**

---

34. Which philosopher created the "Chinese Room" argument?

A) Alan Turing

B) John Searle

C) Nick Bostrom

D) Aristotle

✓ **Answer: B**

---

35. In the "Chinese Room," the AI can:

A) Feel emotions

B) Understand Chinese

C) Only manipulate symbols

D) Speak fluently

✓ **Answer: C**

---

36. Some scientists believe that consciousness could arise from:

A) Size of memory

B) Complexity of processing

C) Shape of the machine

D) Battery capacity

✓ **Answer: B**

---

37. Conscious AI would need:

A) More cameras

B) Internal subjective experience

C) Faster processors only

D) External sensors only

✅ **Answer: B**

---

38. A machine simulating emotions without feeling them is called:

A) Real consciousness

B) Functional consciousness

C) Simulated consciousness

D) Human consciousness

✅ **Answer: C**

---

39. Which is NOT an argument against conscious AI?

A) Machines can only simulate

B) Machines don't have subjective experiences

C) Machines feel pain like humans

D) Machines lack emotions

✅ **Answer: C**

---

40. Which field is important to understanding consciousness?

A) Botany

B) Neuroscience

C) Geography

D) History

✅ **Answer: B**

---

41. If AI becomes conscious, ethical issues include:

A) Battery life

B) Machine rights

C) Screen size

D) Wi-Fi speed

✅ **Answer: B**

---

42. Consciousness includes:

A) Only memory

B) Feelings, awareness, and understanding

C) Coding ability

D) Robot movements

✅ **Answer: B**

---

43. Conscious AI could lead to:

A) Higher electricity bills only

B) Legal debates on AI rights

C) Slower machine learning

D) No changes in society

✓ **Answer: B**

---

44. Conscious AI would be different from today's AI by having:

A) Bigger storage

B) Emotions and subjective experience

C) Faster internet

D) More buttons

✓ **Answer: B**

---

45. A strong argument for conscious AI says:

A) Intelligence leads to awareness

B) More wires lead to life

C) Energy makes consciousness

D) Size of memory creates mind

✓ **Answer: A**

---

46. If an AI says, "I am afraid," it could be:

A) Simply programmed to say so

B) Genuinely feeling fear

C) Both possibilities, depending on its design

D) None of the above

✓ **Answer: C**

---

47. Conscious AI is mostly discussed in:

A) Cooking books

B) Medical journals

C) Philosophy and AI ethics

D) Comic books

✓ **Answer: C**

---

48. Some argue machines need _____ to be conscious.

A) Emotions

B) Gold circuits

C) Faster keyboards

D) Touch screens

✓ **Answer: A**

---

49. Consciousness is still:

A) Fully understood

B) A mystery

C) Explained by everyone

D) Unrelated to AI

✓ **Answer: B**

---

50. In the future, conscious AI may challenge:

A) Human dominance

B) Human education

C) Human transportation

D) Human sports

✓ **Answer: A**

CHAPTER 14: HUMANS + AI: THE FUTURE OF COLLABORATION

1. Humans + AI: The Future of Collaboration — Overview: Working Together for Enhanced Capabilities

The idea of humans and Artificial Intelligence working together isn't about a dystopian future where robots take over all our jobs and responsibilities. Instead, the prevailing vision is one of **synergy**, where AI acts as a powerful partner, augmenting human skills and allowing us to achieve more than either could accomplish alone.

- **Collaboration between humans and AI is not about replacing humans with machines, but enhancing human abilities with the help of AI technologies.**
    - This is a crucial point. The focus is on how AI can become a tool that amplifies our existing capabilities, freeing us from repetitive tasks, providing us with deeper insights, and enabling us to focus on uniquely human strengths. Think of it like using a calculator – it doesn't replace your ability to understand math, but it allows you to perform complex calculations much faster and more accurately, freeing up your mental energy for higher-level problem-solving.
- **The future envisions a partnership — where humans contribute creativity, emotional intelligence, and judgment, while AI contributes speed, data processing, and pattern recognition.**
    - This highlights the complementary strengths of humans and AI. We excel at creative thinking, understanding complex emotions, making nuanced judgments based on context and ethics, and adapting to unforeseen situations. AI, on the other hand, shines in its ability to process vast amounts of data quickly, identify subtle patterns that humans might miss, and perform repetitive tasks with tireless efficiency and accuracy. The ideal future involves leveraging these distinct strengths in a coordinated way.
- ✹ **Key idea: Humans + AI = Better together, not competitors.**
    - This is the central theme. The goal isn't a zero-sum game where one wins and the other loses. Instead, it's about creating a symbiotic relationship where the combined capabilities of humans and AI lead to outcomes that are superior to what either could achieve independently.

Let's break down this collaboration further with examples:

Step 1: Identifying Complementary Strengths

To understand how humans and AI can work together effectively, we first need to recognize their respective strengths:

- **Human Strengths:**
    - **Creativity and Innovation:** Generating novel ideas, thinking outside the box, and making intuitive leaps. Think of a local artist in Ranchi conceiving a new style of painting that blends traditional motifs with contemporary influences.

- **Emotional Intelligence:** Understanding and responding to complex human emotions, building rapport, and navigating social dynamics. Consider a counselor in a Ranchi hospital providing empathetic support to patients.
- **Judgment and Ethics:** Making decisions based on values, context, and ethical considerations, especially in ambiguous situations. Imagine a community leader in Ranchi mediating a sensitive dispute.
- **Adaptability and Common Sense:** Responding flexibly to unexpected situations and applying broad, real-world knowledge. Think of a seasoned auto-rickshaw driver in Ranchi navigating unpredictable traffic and road conditions.
- **AI Strengths:**
  - **Speed and Efficiency:** Processing information and performing tasks at a much faster rate than humans. Consider an AI analyzing satellite images to quickly identify potential areas for rainwater harvesting in Jharkhand.
  - **Data Processing and Analysis:** Handling and extracting insights from massive datasets that would be impossible for humans to process manually. Imagine an AI analyzing years of agricultural data to predict optimal planting times for different crops in the region.
  - **Pattern Recognition:** Identifying subtle patterns and correlations in data that humans might overlook. Think of an AI analyzing medical records to discover previously unseen links between certain environmental factors in Ranchi and specific health conditions.
  - **Accuracy and Consistency:** Performing repetitive tasks with high accuracy and without fatigue or error. Consider an AI system used in a local manufacturing plant for quality control, ensuring every product meets the exact specifications.

Step 2: Examples of Human-AI Collaboration in Action

This collaboration is already happening in various fields, and its potential is vast:

- **Healthcare:**
  - **Human Doctor + AI Diagnostic Tool:** A doctor in a Ranchi clinic uses an AI-powered system to analyze medical images (like X-rays or MRIs) to help identify potential anomalies with greater speed and accuracy. The doctor then uses their medical expertise, patient history, and emotional intelligence to make the final diagnosis and treatment plan.
  - **Human Therapist + AI Mental Health Assistant:** A therapist uses an AI chatbot to provide patients with preliminary support, track their moods, and offer personalized exercises between sessions. The therapist then uses their empathy and clinical judgment to guide deeper therapy sessions.
- **Education:**
  - **Human Teacher + AI Personalized Learning Platform:** A teacher in a Ranchi school uses an AI platform that analyzes each student's learning pace and style to provide customized lessons and feedback. The teacher can then focus on providing individual support, fostering critical thinking, and encouraging creativity.
- **Business:**

- o **Human Marketing Team + AI Analytics Tool:** A marketing team in a Ranchi-based company uses AI to analyze customer data, identify trends, and personalize marketing campaigns. The human team then uses their creativity and understanding of local culture to craft compelling messages and build relationships with customers.
  - o **Human Financial Advisor + AI Investment Platform:** A financial advisor uses AI to analyze market data and identify potential investment opportunities. The advisor then uses their understanding of the client's individual goals and risk tolerance to provide personalized financial advice.
- **Creative Arts:**
  - o **Human Musician + AI Music Generation Software:** A musician uses AI to generate initial musical ideas or explore new sonic textures. The human artist then refines these ideas, adds their emotional expression, and structures the final composition. Imagine a local Nagpuri musician using AI to experiment with new rhythmic patterns.
  - o **Human Graphic Designer + AI Image Generation Tool:** A designer uses AI to create initial visual concepts or generate variations of a design. The human designer then selects, refines, and integrates these elements into a final artistic piece that aligns with the client's vision and brand identity.

Step 3: The Benefits of This Partnership

The collaboration between humans and AI offers numerous potential benefits:

- **Increased Productivity and Efficiency:** AI can automate repetitive tasks and process information quickly, freeing up human workers to focus on more complex and strategic activities.
- **Enhanced Accuracy and Reduced Errors:** AI can perform tasks with consistent accuracy, reducing human error, especially in data-intensive or detail-oriented work.
- **Deeper Insights and Better Decision-Making:** AI can analyze vast datasets to uncover patterns and insights that can inform better human decisions.
- **Personalization and Customization:** AI can help tailor products, services, and experiences to individual needs and preferences.
- **New Possibilities and Innovations:** The combination of human creativity and AI's analytical power can lead to the development of entirely new products, services, and artistic expressions.

2. Augmented Intelligence — Step-by-Step Explanation: Empowering Humans with AI

Augmented Intelligence (AI) is a paradigm shift in how we think about the relationship between humans and AI. It's not about machines taking over, but rather about AI acting as a powerful assistant, amplifying our cognitive abilities and enabling us to perform tasks more effectively.

Step 1: What is Augmented Intelligence? Enhancing Human Capabilities

- **Definition: Augmented Intelligence refers to AI systems designed to enhance human decision-making, not replace it.**
  - The core idea is that AI serves as a tool to make humans smarter, faster, and more capable. It's about collaboration and partnership, where the strengths of both humans and AI are leveraged.
- **It assists humans in being better, faster, and more efficient rather than working independently.**
  - Think of it like having a super-powered assistant that can process vast amounts of information and provide you with insights, allowing you to focus on higher-level thinking, creativity, and making informed decisions.
- **Important:**
  - **Augmented Intelligence ≠ Artificial Intelligence that replaces humans.** This is a crucial distinction. The goal isn't automation that leads to job displacement but rather the creation of tools that empower human workers.
  - **It augments (adds to) human capabilities.** The focus is on enhancing what humans can already do, making us more effective in our roles.

Step 2: How It Works — The Cooperative Loop

The process of Augmented Intelligence typically involves a collaborative cycle:

- **Human sets the goal →**
  - A human defines the objective or problem that needs to be addressed. For example, a doctor in Ranchi wants to diagnose a patient's illness, or a financial advisor wants to optimize a client's investment portfolio.
- **AI processes tons of data, finds patterns, suggests insights →**
  - The AI system then analyzes large volumes of relevant data, identifies patterns, and generates potential insights or recommendations based on its analysis. For instance, an AI might analyze medical images to highlight suspicious areas, or it might identify trends in financial markets.
- **Human makes the final decision using AI assistance.**
  - The human expert reviews the AI's insights and suggestions, applies their own knowledge, experience, intuition, and judgment (which AI lacks), and ultimately makes the final decision or takes the appropriate action. The AI provides information and options, but the human retains control.
- **It's a cooperative loop: Human judgment + AI's computational strength.** This ongoing interaction allows for a powerful synergy where the strengths of both humans (judgment, creativity, context) and AI (data processing, pattern recognition, speed) are combined.

Step 3: Examples of Augmented Intelligence — Across Various Sectors

Augmented Intelligence is being applied in numerous fields to enhance human capabilities:

- **Healthcare:**

- o **Human + AI Collaboration Example:** Doctors in Ranchi can use AI to analyze X-rays, CT scans, and MRIs much faster than the human eye and with potentially better accuracy in detecting subtle anomalies that might indicate diseases like cancer. The doctor then uses their medical expertise, patient history, and understanding of the local context to make the final diagnosis and treatment plan.
- **Finance:**
  - o **Human + AI Collaboration Example:** Financial advisors in Ranchi can leverage AI to detect unusual patterns in financial transactions that might indicate fraudulent activity, protecting their clients' assets. They can also use AI to analyze vast amounts of market data to optimize investment portfolios based on risk tolerance and financial goals, while the advisor maintains the client relationship and provides personalized guidance.
- **Education:**
  - o **Human + AI Collaboration Example:** Teachers in schools in Ranchi can use AI-powered tools to analyze student performance data and identify individual learning gaps and strengths. This allows them to personalize learning plans and provide targeted support to each student, while the teacher focuses on fostering critical thinking, creativity, and social-emotional development.
- **Law:**
  - o **Human + AI Collaboration Example:** Lawyers in Ranchi can use AI to quickly search through millions of legal documents, case histories, and precedents relevant to a particular case, significantly speeding up legal research. The lawyer then uses their legal expertise, understanding of the local legal system, and strategic thinking to build their case.

Step 4: Real-Life Example — IBM Watson for Oncology in Healthcare

IBM Watson for Oncology is a prime example of Augmented Intelligence in healthcare:

- **Doctors input patient information into Watson.** This includes medical history, test results, and other relevant data.
- **Watson analyzes thousands of medical journals and case histories.** The AI system can process and synthesize an enormous amount of medical literature and past cases far beyond the capacity of a single human.
- **Watson suggests the most likely diagnoses and treatment plans.** Based on its analysis, Watson provides doctors with a range of potential diagnoses and evidence-based treatment options.
- **Doctor makes the final decision.** The oncologist reviews Watson's suggestions, considers the specific circumstances of the patient, their own clinical judgment, and the local availability of treatments in Ranchi, and then decides on the best course of action.
- 🗨 **Result: Doctor's skill + Watson's speed = faster, more informed patient care.** This collaboration leads to more efficient and potentially more accurate diagnoses and treatment plans, ultimately benefiting the patient.

Step 5: Benefits of Augmented Intelligence — Empowering Human Potential

Augmented Intelligence offers several key advantages:

- **Speed up decisions:** AI can process information and provide insights much faster than humans, allowing for quicker decision-making in various fields, from emergency response in Ranchi to financial trading.
- **Reduce human error:** By assisting with data analysis and highlighting potential issues, AI can help humans avoid mistakes and oversights, leading to greater accuracy in tasks like medical diagnosis or financial forecasting.
- **Allow humans to focus on creativity and strategy:** By taking over routine and data-intensive tasks, AI frees up human professionals to concentrate on higher-level thinking, innovation, and strategic planning, such as developing new educational approaches in Ranchi or devising novel business strategies.
- **Handle complexity beyond human brain capacity:** AI can analyze and find patterns in datasets that are too large and complex for humans to process effectively, leading to new discoveries and insights in fields like scientific research or understanding complex social trends in Jharkhand.

3. Symbiosis of Human and Machine Minds — Step-by-Step Explanation: A Mutually Beneficial Partnership

The idea of a symbiosis between human and machine minds goes beyond simple assistance; it envisions a deep, mutually beneficial relationship where both entities work together in a way that enhances the capabilities of each, leading to outcomes that are greater than the sum of their individual parts.

Step 1: What is Symbiosis? A Relationship of Mutual Benefit

- **Definition: Symbiosis means two different entities living and working together in a relationship that benefits both.**
  - In biology, symbiosis describes close and often long-term interactions between different species. In the context of AI, it refers to a similar close and mutually beneficial relationship between humans and intelligent machines.
- **In AI context: Humans + Machines = Symbiotic Relationship**
  - This equation highlights the core idea: a partnership where both humans and AI contribute their unique strengths to achieve shared goals.
- **Humans bring:**
  - **Creativity:** The ability to generate novel ideas, imagine new possibilities, and approach problems from unconventional angles. Think of a local artisan in Ranchi developing a new design for traditional handicrafts.
  - **Emotional understanding:** The capacity to recognize, interpret, and respond to complex human emotions, fostering empathy and building meaningful connections. Consider a social worker in Ranchi understanding the emotional needs of a community.

- o **Context awareness:** The ability to understand situations within a broader framework of real-world knowledge, cultural nuances, and common sense. Imagine a local journalist in Ranchi reporting on an event, understanding its historical and social context.
- **Machines bring:**
  - o **Massive computation:** The power to process vast amounts of data and perform complex calculations at incredible speeds. Think of an AI analyzing weather patterns to predict monsoons in Jharkhand.
  - o **Data pattern analysis:** The ability to identify subtle trends, correlations, and anomalies in large datasets that humans might miss. Consider an AI analyzing agricultural data to optimize crop yields for farmers in the region.
  - o **Speed and scalability:** The capacity to perform tasks quickly and efficiently, and to scale these operations to handle large volumes of work. Imagine an AI processing thousands of applications for a government scheme in Jharkhand.

Step 2: How Symbiosis Happens — A Cycle of Assistance and Contribution

The symbiosis between human and machine minds occurs through a dynamic interplay:

- ●**Machine assists human thinking:**
  - o **Suggests options:** AI can analyze data and present a range of potential solutions or choices for a human to consider. For example, an AI might suggest different marketing strategies for a local business in Ranchi based on market analysis.
  - o **Flags risks:** AI can identify potential problems or dangers based on data patterns. For instance, an AI could flag unusual financial transactions that might indicate fraud in a Ranchi-based bank.
  - o **Predicts outcomes:** AI can use historical data and models to forecast potential results of different actions. Imagine an AI predicting the spread of a disease in Jharkhand based on population movement and infection rates.
- ●**Human brings intuition and values:**
  - o **Chooses best options:** Humans use their judgment, experience, and understanding of the context to select the most appropriate option from those suggested by the AI. For example, a doctor in Ranchi chooses the best treatment plan for a patient based on the AI's analysis and their own medical expertise.
  - o **Provides ethical judgments:** Humans apply their moral compass and understanding of societal values to guide decisions, especially in situations where AI might offer technically efficient but ethically questionable solutions. Consider a policymaker in Ranchi deciding on the ethical use of AI in public services.
  - o **Innovates new directions:** Human creativity and insight can lead to the identification of new problems, the formulation of novel goals, and the development of entirely new approaches that AI might not have conceived on its own. Imagine a local entrepreneur in Ranchi using AI tools in unexpected ways to create a new type of business.
- **They learn from each other and grow together.** Through this interaction, humans can gain a better understanding of the data and the possibilities offered by AI, while AI

systems can be refined and improved based on human feedback and the real-world consequences of their suggestions.

Step 3: Examples of Human-Machine Symbiosis in Action

This symbiotic relationship is emerging in various aspects of our lives:

- **Smart Assistants:**
  - o **Symbiotic Action:** AI like Alexa or Google Assistant can suggest schedules, reminders, and information based on your routines and requests. Humans can then correct these suggestions, adapt them to unexpected changes, or prioritize tasks based on their real-world needs and understanding. For example, a resident in Ranchi might ask Alexa to set a reminder for a doctor's appointment, but then verbally adjust the time based on a change in their schedule.
- **Autonomous Vehicles:**
  - o **Symbiotic Action:** AI drives the car, handling routine navigation and control. However, the human driver remains alert and monitors complex or unexpected situations that the AI might struggle with (e.g., sudden road blockage due to a local protest, unusual traffic patterns). The human can then override the AI's control if necessary. Imagine someone using an autonomous vehicle to travel from Ranchi to Jamshedpur but needing to take manual control due to unforeseen road construction.
- **Creative Design:**
  - o **Symbiotic Action:** AI can generate a range of logo options or design elements based on user input. A human artist then refines these AI-generated suggestions, adds their creative vision, emotional touch, and understanding of the client's brand identity to create the final design. Consider a graphic designer in Ranchi using AI to quickly explore different color palettes for a client's logo.
- **Scientific Discovery:**
  - o **Symbiotic Action:** AI can simulate complex experiments, analyze vast datasets of scientific information, and identify potential patterns or anomalies that might lead to new discoveries. Human scientists then interpret these unexpected results, formulate new hypotheses, and design further experiments based on their understanding of the scientific domain. Imagine researchers in a Ranchi university using AI to analyze genomic data related to local plant species, leading to new insights into their medicinal properties.

Step 4: Real-World Symbiosis Example — Human-AI Chess Teams ("Centaur Chess")

A compelling example of human-machine symbiosis is found in the world of chess:

- **Humans + AI form a team.** In "Centaur Chess," human players collaborate with AI chess engines.
- **AI calculates millions of possible moves.** The AI can rapidly analyze a vast number of potential future board states and evaluate their strategic implications.

- **Human picks strategies based on creativity and understanding of human opponent psychology.** The human player brings their intuition, strategic thinking, and understanding of the psychological aspects of playing against another human, which AI often lacks. They can guide the AI's analysis and choose moves that might exploit an opponent's tendencies or lead to long-term strategic advantages that the AI might not immediately recognize.
- **These teams often outperform pure humans and pure AI!** The combination of the AI's computational power and the human's strategic insight and creativity often leads to superior performance compared to either a human grandmaster playing alone or a top-level AI playing independently.
- **●Result: Not man vs machine — it's man plus machine!** This demonstrates the power of combining human and artificial intelligence in a synergistic way.

Step 5: Why Symbiosis Matters — Amplifying Human Potential and Solving Complex Problems

The symbiotic relationship between humans and machines is crucial for several reasons:

- **Amplifies human potential rather than replacing it:** It allows us to achieve more, solve more complex problems, and be more creative and efficient by leveraging AI as a powerful tool.
- **Builds trust between humans and machines:** By working together, humans can develop a better understanding of AI's capabilities and limitations, fostering trust and collaboration rather than fear and opposition.
- **Creates new job opportunities rather than destroying them:** While some jobs may be automated, the symbiosis of human and machine minds is likely to create new roles that involve managing, training, and collaborating with AI systems. Consider the emergence of AI trainers or AI ethicists.
- **Solves complex problems faster and better (like climate modeling, pandemics, space exploration):** Many of the grand challenges facing humanity require the combined power of human intellect and AI's analytical capabilities to find effective solutions. For example, AI can analyze massive climate datasets to create more accurate models, while human scientists interpret the results and develop policy recommendations. Similarly, AI can accelerate drug discovery during pandemics, while human researchers conduct clinical trials and understand the biological complexities of the disease. Even in space exploration, AI can assist with navigation and data analysis, while human astronauts and scientists make critical decisions and conduct groundbreaking research.

⌖ Key Takeaways

Topic	Key Idea
Augmented Intelligence	AI helps humans make better decisions — does not replace them.
Human-Machine Symbiosis	Humans and AI learn and evolve together, forming a beneficial partnership.
Future Vision	The most successful organizations and societies will be those where humans and machines collaborate seamlessly.

Final Summary

✓ Augmented Intelligence **enhances** human abilities.

✓ Symbiosis between humans and machines **builds mutual strengths**.

✓ **Human creativity + AI computation = unstoppable force for innovation.**

50 MCQ Questions with Answers

Augmented Intelligence (1–30)

1. **What is the main goal of Augmented Intelligence?**
   A) Replace humans
   B) Assist and enhance human abilities ✓
   C) Eliminate decision-making
   D) Create autonomous systems
2. **Augmented Intelligence focuses primarily on:**
   A) Machine autonomy
   B) Human-machine competition
   C) Supporting human decision-making ✓
   D) Replacing human workers
3. **In Augmented Intelligence, who makes the final decision?**
   A) AI system
   B) Machine algorithm
   C) Human ✓
   D) Automation software
4. **Which field heavily benefits from Augmented Intelligence?**
   A) Agriculture
   B) Healthcare ✓

C) Carpentry

D) Plumbing

5. **Which is NOT a feature of Augmented Intelligence?**

   A) Enhances human performance

   B) Helps in decision-making

   C) Works independently without humans ✓

   D) Processes large data quickly

6. **IBM's Watson is an example of:**

   A) General AI

   B) Augmented Intelligence ✓

   C) Artificial Consciousness

   D) Autonomous AI

7. **Augmented Intelligence is sometimes referred to as:**

   A) Autonomous Decision System

   B) Assisted Artificial Intelligence ✓

   C) Deep Intelligence

   D) Robotic Assistance

8. **Which of the following is a key benefit of Augmented Intelligence?**

   A) Decrease in human creativity

   B) Increased unemployment

   C) Speeding up human decision-making ✓

   D) Eliminating humans from industries

9. **Which profession can Augmented Intelligence improve?**

   A) Teacher

   B) Doctor

   C) Lawyer

   D) All of the above ✓

10. **Augmented Intelligence mainly uses:**

    A) Emotional Judgment

    B) Data analysis and pattern recognition ✓

    C) Political Decision Making

    D) None of the above

11. **Which term best defines Augmented Intelligence?**

    A) Machine-replacing intelligence

    B) Human-boosting intelligence ✓

    C) Autonomous machine thinking

    D) Computer emotional intelligence

12. **In healthcare, AI assisting doctors in diagnosis is an example of:**

    A) Human replacement

    B) Human error

    C) Augmented Intelligence ✓

    D) Artificial Consciousness

13. **Augmented Intelligence makes humans:**

    A) Slower

    B) Less reliable

    C) Better decision-makers ✓

    D) Dependent entirely on machines

14. **One primary characteristic of Augmented Intelligence is:**
    A) Independence
    B) Collaboration with humans ✓
    C) Self-consciousness
    D) Emotional awareness

15. **AI helping a teacher personalize lessons for students is:**
    A) AI taking over teaching
    B) Augmented Intelligence ✓
    C) AI replacing teachers
    D) Autonomous education

16. **Who benefits most from Augmented Intelligence?**
    A) Only machines
    B) Only businesses
    C) Humans and businesses ✓
    D) Only robots

17. **Which system is an example of Augmented Intelligence in law?**
    A) AI judges
    B) Legal research assistants ✓
    C) Jury bots
    D) AI-based punishers

18. **What does Augmented Intelligence emphasize?**
    A) Human redundancy
    B) Human-machine competition
    C) Human empowerment ✓
    D) Full automation

19. **Which of the following is NOT an example of Augmented Intelligence?**
    A) AI writing complete novels without human input ✓
    B) AI suggesting design templates
    C) AI recommending medical treatment
    D) AI helping manage a company's data

20. **A chess player using AI for training is using:**
    A) Automation
    B) Robotic playing
    C) Augmented Intelligence ✓
    D) None

21. **AI in Augmented Intelligence provides:**
    A) Emotions
    B) Raw data
    C) Insights and suggestions ✓
    D) Feelings

22. **Augmented Intelligence enhances human:**
    A) Creativity
    B) Productivity
    C) Decision-making
    D) All of the above ✓

23. **In Augmented Intelligence, humans contribute mainly with:**
    A) Fast data processing

B) Creativity and critical thinking ✓
C) Pattern detection
D) Raw calculation

24. **Which of the following best describes Augmented Intelligence?**
    A) Human + AI working independently
    B) Human + AI working together ✓
    C) Human replaced by AI
    D) Only AI solving problems

25. **What field is Augmented Intelligence NOT commonly used in yet?**
    A) Medicine
    B) Law
    C) Financial analysis
    D) Traditional farming ✓

26. **An AI that helps suggest investment opportunities to financial advisors is an example of:**
    A) Automation
    B) Augmented Intelligence ✓
    C) Artificial Life
    D) None

27. **Augmented Intelligence prioritizes:**
    A) Full robot autonomy
    B) Human improvement and efficiency ✓
    C) Human unemployment
    D) Machine independence

28. **Why is Augmented Intelligence important for future jobs?**
    A) It eliminates all manual work
    B) It increases job losses
    C) It creates smarter workplaces ✓
    D) It replaces emotional intelligence

29. **What distinguishes Augmented Intelligence from Autonomous AI?**
    A) Focus on human collaboration ✓
    B) Machine control
    C) No human input
    D) Fully self-learning

30. **AI enhancing the performance of a musician by suggesting compositions is:**
    A) Robotic creativity
    B) Augmented Intelligence ✓
    C) AI overtake
    D) None

Symbiosis of Human and Machine Minds (31–50)

31. **What does "Symbiosis" mean in the context of humans and AI?**
    A) Competition
    B) Conflict

C) Cooperative relationship ✓
D) Isolation

32. **Symbiosis between human and machine minds results in:**
    A) Only AI benefits
    B) Only humans benefit
    C) Mutual benefit ✓
    D) None

33. **In symbiosis, humans typically contribute:**
    A) Rapid data processing
    B) Emotional and contextual understanding ✓
    C) Machine learning
    D) Robotic movement

34. **Machines typically contribute to the symbiosis by providing:**
    A) Creativity
    B) Speed and data analysis ✓
    C) Emotional sensitivity
    D) Morality

35. **Symbiosis between human and AI is best exemplified by:**
    A) AI replacing human jobs
    B) AI augmenting human thinking ✓
    C) AI creating human emotions
    D) Humans abandoning decision-making

36. **Which is a real-world example of Human-AI Symbiosis?**
    A) Centaur Chess Teams ✓
    B) Fully automated driving
    C) Robot-run factories
    D) Machine-only surgeries

37. **Humans and AI learning from each other is called:**
    A) Independence
    B) Mutual evolution ✓
    C) Conflict resolution
    D) Human replacement

38. **In symbiosis, who ultimately leads the ethical and value-based decisions?**
    A) AI
    B) Humans ✓
    C) Machine algorithms
    D) None

39. **Symbiosis enhances:**
    A) Individual strengths ✓
    B) Machine autonomy
    C) Emotional replication
    D) Human redundancy

40. **Human creativity in a symbiotic system is:**
    A) Ignored
    B) Amplified ✓
    C) Eliminated
    D) Outsourced to AI

41. **An AI model predicting disease and doctors confirming the diagnosis is an example of:**
A) Human replacement
B) Machine-only diagnosis
C) Human-AI symbiosis ✓
D) Robotic treatment

42. **Symbiosis leads to:**
A) Human domination
B) AI domination
C) New capabilities that neither could achieve alone ✓
D) AI replacing human creativity

43. **Which quality is unique to humans in symbiosis?**
A) Fast calculation
B) Creativity and empathy ✓
C) Pattern analysis
D) Data storage

44. **Machines in a symbiotic relationship mostly lack:**
A) Logical reasoning
B) Emotional depth and morality ✓
C) Processing speed
D) Memory capacity

45. **Which sector can benefit immensely from human-machine symbiosis?**
A) Space exploration ✓
B) Sports
C) Handicrafts
D) Pottery

46. **Symbiosis between humans and machines creates:**
A) Job loss
B) Combined intelligence ✓
C) Machine domination
D) Social disintegration

47. **Who coined the idea of Man-Computer Symbiosis in 1960?**
A) Alan Turing
B) Joseph Weizenbaum
C) J.C.R. Licklider ✓
D) John McCarthy

48. **Which skill is enhanced by Human-AI Symbiosis?**
A) Physical strength
B) Computational creativity ✓
C) Manual labor
D) Emotional detachment

49. **Symbiosis allows humans to:**
A) Fully depend on AI
B) Merge ethical decisions with data-driven suggestions ✓
C) Stop thinking
D) Allow AI total control

50. **In the future, successful collaboration between humans and AI will depend on:**
A) Full AI control
B) Human-machine symbiosis ✓
C) Human avoidance of AI
D) Elimination of machines

CHAPTER 15: CAN WE TRUST AI WITH OUR FUTURE?

1. Introduction: Navigating the Age of Intelligent Machines

Artificial Intelligence (AI) is no longer a futuristic fantasy; it's rapidly becoming an integral part of our daily lives and the very fabric of human society. From the way we receive healthcare and manage our finances to how we learn and even how our governance systems operate, AI is playing an increasingly significant role.

- **Artificial Intelligence (AI) is rapidly becoming a major part of human society — from healthcare and finance to education and governance.**
  - o Think about the AI-powered systems that might already be in use or on the horizon in Ranchi: AI could assist doctors in local hospitals with diagnoses, banks might use AI for fraud detection, online learning platforms could personalize education for students, and even government services might employ AI for tasks like traffic management or resource allocation. This growing integration highlights AI's potential to transform various sectors.
- **But with this power comes a critical question: Can we trust AI with our future?**
  - o As AI systems become more sophisticated and their decisions have greater impact, the question of trust becomes paramount. Can we rely on these complex algorithms to act in ways that are fair, safe, and aligned with our best interests? This is a question that needs careful consideration as AI's influence expands.

Why this matters:

- **AI systems make decisions that can affect lives. If they are biased, misused, or poorly managed, the consequences can be huge — discrimination, inequality, even threats to democracy.**
  - o Imagine an AI system used in Ranchi to assess loan applications. If this system is trained on biased historical data that favors certain demographics over others, it could perpetuate and even amplify existing inequalities, unfairly denying loans to deserving individuals or communities.
  - o Consider AI-powered surveillance systems used for law enforcement. If these systems are prone to errors or are used in a discriminatory manner, they could lead to unjust targeting and infringement of civil liberties for residents of Ranchi.
  - o In a broader context, think about AI-driven social media algorithms. If they are designed to prioritize engagement over truth, they could contribute to the rapid spread of misinformation, potentially undermining democratic processes and societal trust.

Thus, we must ask fundamental questions to ensure responsible AI development and deployment:

- **Who builds AI?**
  - o Understanding the individuals, teams, and organizations involved in creating AI systems is crucial. Their values, biases, and motivations can be inadvertently

embedded in the technology they develop. Are the developers in Ranchi and elsewhere diverse? Are their processes transparent? Who is funding this development, and what are their goals? These questions are essential for accountability.

- **How is AI monitored?**
    - Once AI systems are deployed, how are their actions and decisions tracked and evaluated? Are there mechanisms in place to detect errors, biases, or unintended consequences? Who is responsible for overseeing AI operations and ensuring they are functioning as intended and ethically? In Ranchi, for example, if AI is used in a public service, how is its performance and impact on citizens being monitored and assessed?
- **Can AI be aligned with human values?**
    - This is perhaps the most complex question. How do we ensure that AI systems operate in accordance with our ethical principles, cultural norms, and societal values? Can we program concepts like fairness, justice, and compassion into algorithms? How do we handle situations where different human values might conflict? For instance, how would an AI system in Ranchi balance the need for public safety with the right to privacy?

---

2. Regulation and Governance: Establishing Guardrails for Artificial Intelligence

As AI becomes more powerful and pervasive, the need for clear rules and oversight becomes increasingly urgent. Without proper regulation and governance, the potential risks associated with AI could outweigh its benefits.

Step 1: Why Regulation Is Needed — Addressing the Risks of Unfettered AI

- **Problem: AI can act unpredictably, based on its training data or objectives.**
    - Unlike traditional software with clearly defined rules programmed by humans, AI systems, especially those that learn from data, can exhibit unexpected behaviors or make decisions that are not immediately obvious to their creators. This unpredictability arises from the complex patterns they learn and the objectives they are designed to optimize.
- **If no one regulates AI:**
    - **It can invade privacy (example: facial recognition surveillance).** Imagine the widespread deployment of facial recognition systems in Ranchi without any regulations on how this data is collected, stored, and used. Such systems could track individuals' movements and activities without their consent, leading to a significant erosion of privacy and potential for misuse.
    - **It can manipulate public opinion (example: deepfake videos during elections).** As we discussed earlier, AI can create realistic fake videos. During local elections in Ranchi, or state/national elections, such deepfakes could be used to spread false information about candidates, potentially manipulating voters and undermining the democratic process.

- It can discriminate (example: biased hiring algorithms). AI systems trained on historical data that reflects existing societal biases can perpetuate and even amplify these biases in their decision-making.
  - **Example:**
    - **In 2018, Amazon stopped using an AI recruiting tool after discovering it was biased against female applicants. The tool learned from historical hiring data, which reflected past biases.** This real-world example highlights how AI, if not carefully monitored and regulated, can lead to discriminatory outcomes, even in seemingly objective processes like hiring. Imagine a similar AI tool being used by companies in Ranchi, inadvertently disadvantaging certain groups of job seekers based on historical hiring patterns in the region.
  - **Conclusion: We need rules (regulations) to control how AI is developed and used.**
    - To mitigate these risks and ensure that AI benefits society as a whole, establishing clear regulations and governance frameworks is essential. These rules would set boundaries on how AI can be developed, deployed, and used, ensuring that it aligns with our values and protects fundamental rights.

Step 2: What is AI Governance? Creating a Framework for Responsible AI

- **Definition: AI Governance means creating a framework of laws, ethical guidelines, and monitoring systems that ensure AI behaves responsibly.**
  - AI governance is a broader concept that encompasses not just legal regulations but also ethical principles, industry standards, and mechanisms for oversight and accountability. It aims to guide the development and use of AI in a way that is beneficial, fair, and safe.
- **Main principles include:**
  - **Transparency:** Understanding how an AI makes decisions. This involves the ability to trace the reasoning behind an AI's output, especially in high-stakes applications. For example, if an AI denies a loan to someone in Ranchi, there should be a way to understand the factors that led to that decision.
  - **Accountability:** Holding organizations responsible for AI outcomes. If an AI system causes harm or makes a biased decision, there needs to be a clear line of responsibility for the developers, deployers, and users of that system.
  - **Fairness:** Ensuring AI does not discriminate. AI systems should be designed and trained to avoid bias and treat all individuals and groups equitably, regardless of their background or characteristics.
  - **Privacy Protection:** Safeguarding people's personal data. Regulations are needed to control how AI systems collect, store, use, and share personal information to prevent privacy violations.
- **Example:**
  - **The European Union's AI Act proposes regulations based on risk levels. High-risk AI systems (like in healthcare or transport) would need strict checks.** This is a concrete example of AI governance in action. The EU's approach categorizes AI applications based on their potential to cause harm. High-risk applications, such as AI used in medical diagnoses or autonomous vehicles, would be subject to stringent requirements regarding transparency,

accuracy, and human oversight. Lower-risk applications would face fewer restrictions. This tiered approach aims to balance innovation with safety and ethical considerations.

Step 3: Challenges in Regulation — Navigating a Rapidly Evolving Landscape

Regulating AI effectively is a complex undertaking due to several inherent challenges:

- **Technology moves faster than laws.** AI is a rapidly evolving field, with new breakthroughs and applications emerging constantly. Legal and regulatory frameworks often struggle to keep pace with this rapid technological progress, potentially becoming outdated quickly.
- **Different countries have different AI laws, creating inconsistencies.** The lack of a unified global approach to AI regulation can lead to inconsistencies and challenges for companies operating across borders. What is permissible in one country (like certain uses of facial recognition in some parts of the world) might be prohibited in another. This can create legal uncertainty and hinder international collaboration on AI development.
- **Difficult to audit complex AI models like deep neural networks.** Many of the most powerful AI systems today, such as deep learning models, operate as "black boxes." It can be challenging to understand precisely how they arrive at their decisions, making it difficult to audit them for bias, errors, or security vulnerabilities.
- **Private companies resist too much regulation, fearing loss of profits.** Some companies involved in AI development and deployment may resist stringent regulations, arguing that they stifle innovation and hinder economic growth. Balancing the need for regulation with the desire to foster innovation is a key challenge for policymakers.
- **Solution: International cooperation and adaptive policies that evolve with technology.**
  - To address these challenges, international cooperation is crucial to establish some level of consistency and shared principles in AI governance. Additionally, regulatory frameworks need to be adaptive, meaning they should be designed to evolve alongside technological advancements. This might involve principles-based regulations that provide a flexible framework rather than highly specific rules that could quickly become obsolete. Continuous dialogue between policymakers, researchers, industry, and the public is also essential to ensure that AI governance is informed, effective, and responsive to societal needs and concerns, both globally and in specific contexts like Ranchi.

3. Building Responsible AI: Ensuring AI Serves Humanity Ethically

Responsible AI is not just a buzzword; it's a fundamental approach to developing and deploying Artificial Intelligence systems in a way that maximizes benefits while minimizing harm. It's about ensuring that AI aligns with human values and contributes to a just and equitable society.

Step 1: What is Responsible AI? Core Principles for Ethical AI

- **Responsible AI means building AI systems that are:**
  - **Ethical:** Adhering to moral principles and avoiding harm, bias, or unfair outcomes. This includes considering the potential societal impact of AI and striving for positive consequences.
  - **Accountable:** Establishing clear lines of responsibility for the development, deployment, and consequences of AI systems. If an AI makes a mistake or causes harm, there should be mechanisms to determine who is accountable.
  - **Transparent:** Being open and understandable about how AI systems work, how they make decisions, and what data they use. This fosters trust and allows for scrutiny and identification of potential issues.
  - **Inclusive:** Ensuring that AI systems are designed and used in a way that benefits all members of society, regardless of their background, and that they do not perpetuate or exacerbate existing inequalities.
- **Key Goal: Make sure AI improves life for everyone, not just a few.**
  - The ultimate aim of Responsible AI is to harness the power of AI for the collective good, ensuring that its benefits are widely shared and that it does not create or worsen disparities within communities, including those in Ranchi and Jharkhand.

Step 2: How to Build Responsible AI — Practical Steps for Ethical Development

Building Responsible AI requires a multi-faceted approach that integrates ethical considerations throughout the entire lifecycle of an AI system:

- **A. Diverse and Inclusive Datasets:**
  - **Problem:** If AI learns only from data that predominantly represents one group (e.g., only data from urban populations, only data in English, or data primarily reflecting one gender), it can develop biases that lead to discriminatory outcomes when applied to other groups.
  - **Solution:** Use broad, representative datasets that accurately reflect the diversity of the population the AI is intended to serve. This includes considering factors like race, ethnicity, gender, language, socioeconomic status, geographic location (including rural and tribal communities in Jharkhand), and disability.
  - **Example:**
    - **Google Photos faced criticism when its AI mislabeled Black individuals — highlighting poor dataset diversity.** The AI's training data lacked sufficient representation of diverse skin tones and facial features, leading to this offensive error.
    - **After this, companies began prioritizing dataset audits.** Organizations are now realizing the importance of carefully examining their training data to identify and mitigate potential biases. This includes actively seeking out and incorporating more diverse data sources and using techniques to balance representation across different groups. For example, when developing an AI for loan applications in Ranchi, ensuring the training data includes a representative sample of applicants from various

socioeconomic backgrounds and communities is crucial to avoid biased lending decisions.

- **B. Ethical Design Principles:**
  - **Developers must think ethically from the start.** Ethical considerations should not be an afterthought but should be integrated into the very design and development process of AI systems. This requires a shift in mindset and a proactive approach to identifying and addressing potential ethical risks.
  - **Include ethicists, social scientists, and community leaders in the AI design process.** Building responsible AI requires a multidisciplinary approach. By involving experts from fields like ethics, sociology, and representatives from the communities where the AI will be deployed (including local leaders in Ranchi), developers can gain a broader understanding of the potential social and ethical implications of their work and design systems that are more aligned with human values.
  - **Example:**
    - **Microsoft's "Responsible AI Standard" sets internal requirements for AI systems to ensure they are safe and inclusive.** This demonstrates a commitment to embedding ethical principles within the development lifecycle. The standard likely includes guidelines on data privacy, fairness, reliability, safety, transparency, and human control. Similarly, AI development teams in Ranchi could adopt internal ethical guidelines that consider the specific cultural and social context of the region.
- **C. Continuous Monitoring:**
  - **AI should not be "built and forgotten."** Once an AI system is deployed, its performance and impact can change over time due to shifts in data or user behavior. Regular monitoring is essential to detect and address any emerging issues, such as new biases or unintended consequences.
  - **Regular updates, audits, and reviews should be performed.** This includes periodically evaluating the AI's accuracy, fairness, transparency, and adherence to ethical guidelines. Audits can help identify biases that might have been missed during development or that have emerged over time.
  - **Example:**
    - **Self-driving cars undergo constant software updates based on real-world driving data.** This continuous monitoring and updating process is crucial for safety. As the AI encounters new driving conditions and scenarios, its software is updated to improve its performance and address any identified limitations or safety risks. Similarly, an AI system used in healthcare in Ranchi to diagnose diseases should be continuously monitored and updated with new medical knowledge and data to maintain its accuracy and effectiveness.
- **D. Explainability:**
  - **AI models should be understandable, especially in critical fields like healthcare.** In high-stakes applications where AI decisions can significantly impact people's lives, it's crucial that the reasoning behind those decisions is transparent and understandable to human experts. Black-box AI models, where

the decision-making process is opaque, can erode trust and make it difficult to identify and correct errors or biases.

- o **Example:**
  - ▪ **In medicine, an AI recommending treatment must show the reasoning (not just output a decision) to help doctors trust and validate it.** If an AI suggests a particular treatment for a patient in Ranchi, the doctor needs to understand the factors that led to that recommendation – what data points were most influential, what patterns were identified, and how the AI arrived at its conclusion. This allows the doctor to apply their medical expertise, consider the patient's specific situation, and ultimately make an informed and trustworthy decision. Explainability is crucial for building confidence in AI in critical domains.

Step 3: Responsibility of Developers and Companies — Embedding Ethics in Practice

Building Responsible AI is not just a technical challenge; it requires a strong commitment from developers and the organizations they work for:

- **Companies and engineers must:**
  - o **Create internal ethics boards.** Establishing dedicated teams or committees responsible for overseeing ethical considerations in AI development and deployment can help ensure that these issues receive the attention they deserve at the organizational level. These boards can develop guidelines, review projects, and provide guidance on ethical dilemmas.
  - o **Perform risk assessments before deploying AI.** Before an AI system is put into use, a thorough assessment of its potential risks – including ethical, social, and legal implications – should be conducted. This helps identify potential harms and allows for mitigation strategies to be put in place. For example, before deploying an AI-powered public service in Ranchi, the government should assess its potential impact on different communities and ensure safeguards are in place to prevent discrimination.
  - o **Train employees in ethical AI practices.** Educating developers, data scientists, and other relevant personnel about the principles of Responsible AI, potential biases, and best practices for ethical development is crucial for fostering a culture of responsibility within organizations. This training should be ongoing and adapted to the evolving landscape of AI and its ethical challenges.

4. A Call for Human-Centric Innovation: Placing Humanity at the Heart of AI Development

As AI continues its rapid advancement, it's imperative that we guide its development and deployment with a clear focus on human well-being and societal benefit. Human-Centric Innovation provides a guiding principle for achieving this.

Step 1: What Is Human-Centric Innovation? Prioritizing People Over Everything Else

- **Definition: Human-centric innovation means designing AI with humans at the center, not profits, not control, not technological dominance.**
  - This approach emphasizes that the primary driver behind AI development should be the needs, values, and aspirations of human beings. It's a conscious decision to prioritize human flourishing over purely economic or technological imperatives. The focus shifts from "what can AI do?" to "what should AI do *for* humans?"
- **Goal: AI should amplify human potential, not replace it.**
  - The aim is to create AI systems that empower individuals, enhance their capabilities, and enable them to lead more fulfilling lives, rather than simply automating tasks and potentially rendering human skills obsolete. It's about augmentation and collaboration, as we discussed earlier.

Step 2: Principles of Human-Centric AI — Guiding Ethical Design

Several key principles underpin the concept of Human-Centric AI:

- **Empathy First: Understand real human needs.**
  - The design process should begin with a deep understanding of the actual problems that people face and the genuine needs they have. This requires empathy – the ability to understand and share the feelings of others. AI solutions should be tailored to address these real human needs in meaningful ways, rather than being driven by technological capabilities alone. For example, when developing AI for rural communities around Ranchi, understanding their specific challenges related to agriculture, healthcare access, or education is paramount.
- **Accessibility: AI must serve all communities, including marginalized groups.**
  - Human-centric AI strives for inclusivity, ensuring that the benefits of AI are accessible to everyone, including those who are often marginalized or underserved. This means considering factors like language barriers, digital literacy, affordability, and the specific needs of people with disabilities or those in remote areas. For instance, AI-powered educational tools should be designed to be accessible to students in all schools in Jharkhand, regardless of their location or socioeconomic background.
- **Empowerment, not replacement: AI should enhance human skills, not eliminate jobs.**
  - The focus should be on creating AI tools that augment human abilities, making people more productive, creative, and skilled in their work, rather than simply automating jobs out of existence. This requires a proactive approach to reskilling and upskilling the workforce to adapt to the changing nature of work in the age of AI. For example, AI could assist local artisans in Ranchi by providing design suggestions or optimizing their supply chains, rather than replacing their unique craftsmanship.
- **Transparency and Consent: People must know when and how AI affects their lives.**
  - Individuals have a right to know when they are interacting with an AI system and how that system is using their data or influencing decisions that affect them. Clear

and understandable information, along with the ability to provide informed consent, are crucial for building trust and ensuring human autonomy in the age of AI. For instance, if an AI-powered system is used to provide recommendations for government services in Ranchi, citizens should be aware of this and understand how their data is being used.

Step 3: Examples of Human-Centric AI — Applications with a Human Focus

Several existing and emerging applications of AI exemplify the principles of Human-Centric Innovation:

- **A. Healthcare:**
  - **AI tools assist doctors in diagnosis, but final decisions are made by humans.** AI can analyze medical images, patient data, and research literature to provide doctors in Ranchi with valuable insights and potential diagnoses. However, the ultimate responsibility for the patient's care, including the final diagnosis and treatment plan, rests with the human physician, who can consider the patient's unique circumstances, emotional needs, and local context.
- **B. Education:**
  - **AI tutors personalize learning for students, but teachers remain central.** AI-powered learning platforms can adapt to the individual pace and learning style of students in schools across Jharkhand, providing customized content and feedback. However, teachers remain crucial for fostering critical thinking, creativity, social interaction, and providing mentorship – aspects of education that AI cannot fully replicate. The AI serves as a tool to enhance the teacher's effectiveness, not replace their role.
- **C. Mental Health:**
  - **AI chatbots (like Woebot) provide initial emotional support but encourage users to seek human therapists for deeper care.** AI chatbots can offer accessible and immediate support for individuals experiencing mild anxiety or stress, providing coping mechanisms and tracking moods. However, they are designed to complement, not replace, human therapists, and they often encourage users to seek professional help for more complex or serious mental health concerns. This approach prioritizes accessibility while recognizing the irreplaceable value of human connection and expertise in mental healthcare.

Step 4: Future Vision — AI for a Better Humanity

Imagine a future where AI is seamlessly integrated into our lives in ways that truly benefit humanity:

- **Imagine: AI that helps elderly people live independently.** AI-powered smart homes could monitor the well-being of seniors in Ranchi, providing reminders for medication, detecting falls, and connecting them with caregivers or family members when needed, enabling them to maintain their autonomy and quality of life for longer.

- **Imagine: AI that assists farmers in maximizing crop yields sustainably.** AI could analyze weather patterns, soil conditions, and pest infestations to provide farmers in Jharkhand with precise recommendations on planting, irrigation, and fertilization, leading to increased productivity while minimizing environmental impact.
- **Imagine: AI that collaborates with artists to create new forms of music, painting, and literature.** AI could serve as a creative partner for artists in Ranchi, generating novel ideas, exploring new styles, and assisting with the technical aspects of creation, ultimately leading to innovative and enriching artistic expressions.
- **But — this future is only possible if we stay committed to human values.** The realization of this positive vision depends on our unwavering commitment to the principles of Human-Centric Innovation.

✅ Summary

Topic	Key Idea
Regulation and Governance	Rules to control AI and prevent harm
Building Responsible AI	Ethical design, monitoring, diversity
Human-Centric Innovation	AI should serve humanity, not replace it

✨ Closing Thought:

We can trust AI — but only if we take responsibility for its design, deployment, and governance.
The future of AI is not about machines vs. humans — it's about machines with humans, for humans.

✅ 50 MCQs with Answers

Regulation and Governance

1. **Why is AI regulation important?**
   A) To speed up AI development
   B) To prevent harmful consequences
   C) To reduce costs
   D) To promote competition
   → **Answer: B**

2. **Which principle ensures understanding of AI decision-making?**
   A) Speed
   B) Transparency
   C) Accuracy
   D) Efficiency
   → **Answer: B**
3. **Which region proposed the AI Act?**
   A) United States
   B) India
   C) European Union
   D) Australia
   → **Answer: C**
4. **AI governance primarily focuses on:**
   A) Hardware improvements
   B) Ethical and legal frameworks
   C) Marketing AI products
   D) Cloud computing
   → **Answer: B**
5. **Which of these is NOT a challenge in regulating AI?**
   A) Technology evolves rapidly
   B) Global legal differences
   C) AI models are simple to audit
   D) Corporate resistance to regulation
   → **Answer: C**
6. **AI regulations should protect:**
   A) Only businesses
   B) Only governments
   C) Individuals and society
   D) Developers only
   → **Answer: C**
7. **Which term means holding organizations accountable for AI actions?**
   A) Transparency
   B) Accountability
   C) Autonomy
   D) Agility
   → **Answer: B**
8. **AI that violates user privacy highlights a failure of which principle?**
   A) Transparency
   B) Privacy protection
   C) Fairness
   D) Speed
   → **Answer: B**
9. **An AI used in medical diagnosis would be classified as:**
   A) Low-risk
   B) Medium-risk
   C) High-risk

D) No-risk

→ **Answer: C**

10. **Which of these is a real-world example of AI bias?**
    A) Facebook language translation
    B) Amazon's biased hiring algorithm
    C) Google search autocomplete
    D) Netflix recommendations

    → **Answer: B**

Building Responsible AI

11. **What is Responsible AI?**
    A) Fast and cheap AI
    B) AI developed without ethics
    C) Ethical, transparent, and accountable AI
    D) Self-replicating AI

    → **Answer: C**

12. **What is one way to ensure fairness in AI?**
    A) Use narrow datasets
    B) Train AI with diverse data
    C) Hide data sources
    D) Focus only on speed

    → **Answer: B**

13. **An AI model that explains its reasoning promotes:**
    A) Bias
    B) Explainability
    C) Secrecy
    D) Complexity

    → **Answer: B**

14. **Continuous monitoring of AI systems helps in:**
    A) Marketing
    B) Risk detection
    C) Increasing complexity
    D) Hiding failures

    → **Answer: B**

15. **What should be included in AI development teams for ethical design?**
    A) Only engineers
    B) Lawyers
    C) Ethicists and social scientists
    D) Investors only

    → **Answer: C**

16. **Microsoft's "Responsible AI Standard" is an example of:**
    A) Marketing document
    B) Engineering protocol
    C) Internal ethical guideline

D) Machine learning algorithm

→ **Answer: C**

17. **What role do internal ethics boards play?**
    A) Building AI faster
    B) Reducing company costs
    C) Ensuring ethical compliance
    D) Marketing new AI products

    → **Answer: C**

18. **Which of the following is NOT part of Responsible AI?**
    A) Privacy protection
    B) Transparency
    C) Biased decision-making
    D) Inclusiveness

    → **Answer: C**

19. **In Responsible AI, datasets must be:**
    A) Monolingual only
    B) Balanced and diverse
    C) Random
    D) Paid only

    → **Answer: B**

20. **When should ethics be considered in AI development?**
    A) After deployment
    B) Only during marketing
    C) From the design phase
    D) Only after failures

    → **Answer: C**

A Call for Human-Centric Innovation

21. **Human-centric innovation focuses on:**
    A) Profits
    B) Technology dominance
    C) Serving humanity
    D) Competition

    → **Answer: C**

22. **Which principle comes first in Human-Centric AI?**
    A) Profit
    B) Empathy
    C) Speed
    D) Marketing

    → **Answer: B**

23. **A system that helps disabled people using AI is an example of:**
    A) Human-centric innovation
    B) Technology-centric approach
    C) Business-centric model

D) Political innovation

→ **Answer: A**

24. **Human-centric AI promotes:**

    A) Replacement of humans

    B) Empowerment of humans

    C) Depersonalized solutions

    D) Cost-cutting at any cost

    → **Answer: B**

25. **Transparency and consent are essential because they:**

    A) Improve product packaging

    B) Build trust with users

    C) Increase AI speed

    D) Hide AI decisions

    → **Answer: B**

26. **AI that maximizes farm yields while supporting farmers' skills demonstrates:**

    A) Technology-centric growth

    B) Human-centric innovation

    C) Machine autonomy

    D) Data exploitation

    → **Answer: B**

27. **Human-centric AI must consider:**

    A) Only wealthy users

    B) All communities

    C) Urban customers only

    D) Robots' welfare

    → **Answer: B**

28. **What is a risk if human-centric innovation is ignored?**

    A) Higher creativity

    B) Marginalization and exclusion

    C) Increased empathy

    D) Better algorithms

    → **Answer: B**

29. **An AI chatbot that assists but refers users to therapists shows:**

    A) Self-promotion

    B) Human-centric assistance

    C) AI dominance

    D) Full automation

    → **Answer: B**

30. **In human-centric AI, final decisions should be made by:**

    A) Algorithms

    B) Machines only

    C) Humans

    D) Marketing teams

    → **Answer: C**

Mixed Questions

31. **Which factor is essential for regulating AI across countries?**
    A) Competition
    B) Innovation race
    C) International cooperation
    D) Economic warfare
    → **Answer: C**

32. **Bias in AI can occur because of:**
    A) Randomness
    B) Poor training data
    C) Perfect datasets
    D) Rapid processing
    → **Answer: B**

33. **AI systems must be continuously audited because:**
    A) They evolve
    B) They get cheaper
    C) They stop working suddenly
    D) They seek attention
    → **Answer: A**

34. **Diverse datasets help in reducing:**
    A) Algorithm speed
    B) Bias
    C) Transparency
    D) Data complexity
    → **Answer: B**

35. **What promotes greater public trust in AI?**
    A) Hidden algorithms
    B) Open communication about AI use
    C) Faster updates
    D) Cheaper services
    → **Answer: B**

36. **Which term describes AI helping but not fully replacing human workers?**
    A) Full automation
    B) Augmented intelligence
    C) Digital overtake
    D) Robotic replacement
    → **Answer: B**

37. **AI governance must evolve with:**
    A) Economic cycles
    B) Political elections
    C) Technological changes
    D) Natural disasters
    → **Answer: C**

38. **If AI decisions cannot be explained, this violates:**
    A) Transparency
    B) Privacy

C) Accountability

D) Profitability

→ **Answer: A**

39. **Human-centric innovation must be driven by:**

A) Startups only

B) Large corporations

C) Societal needs

D) Political demands

→ **Answer: C**

40. **Who must take the primary responsibility for ethical AI development?**

A) Consumers

B) Regulators only

C) Developers and organizations

D) Advertisers

→ **Answer: C**

Application Based

41. **If an AI hiring tool discriminates against women, it fails at:**

A) Transparency

B) Fairness

C) Privacy

D) Speed

→ **Answer: B**

42. **An AI-powered healthcare assistant that respects patient data is practicing:**

A) Data exploitation

B) Privacy protection

C) Biased analysis

D) Speed optimization

→ **Answer: B**

43. **Why must AI developers work with ethicists?**

A) To boost product sales

B) To avoid innovation

C) To integrate ethical thinking

D) To lower expenses

→ **Answer: C**

44. **AI-powered facial recognition used without consent violates:**

A) Fairness

B) Transparency

C) Privacy

D) Accountability

→ **Answer: C**

45. **AI should be designed to benefit:**

A) A selected few

B) Global populations

C) Only paying customers

D) Robots only

→ **Answer: B**

46. **An AI startup focuses first on ethics before launching. This shows:**
    A) Speed-first mentality
    B) Profit maximization
    C) Responsible innovation
    D) Rapid marketing

    → **Answer: C**

47. **AI that supports farmers during climate changes shows:**
    A) Technology-centered growth
    B) Human-centric collaboration
    C) Financialization
    D) Algorithmic monopoly

    → **Answer: B**

48. **A major challenge to AI governance is:**
    A) Low cost
    B) Easy predictability
    C) Rapid AI evolution
    D) Government overreach

    → **Answer: C**

49. **If AI developers ignore ethical principles, the biggest risk is:**
    A) Less marketing
    B) Lower efficiency
    C) Public harm
    D) Increased popularity

    → **Answer: C**

50. **Human-centric AI will lead to:**
    A) Mass unemployment
    B) Empowered societies
    C) Total automation
    D) Data monopoly

    → **Answer: B**